*'One can resist
the invasion of an army;
but one cannot resist
the invasion of ideas.'*

Victor Hugo

Waterstone's Guide to

IDEAS

Edited by Nick Rennison

CONTENTS

INTRODUCTION

As a new millennium begins, the time is right to look back at the greatest ideas that the previous thousand years have produced. When the last millennium began Europe was dominated by the Church and men speculated on the nature of God; as it ended the West was dominated by science and the technology the scientific revolution of the last two centuries has produced. The last millennium has seen greater change than any other period in human history. The books and authors in this guide have, in one sense, been chosen to reflect that change. Using the guide one can trace an evolution, say, from the earth-centred universe of the early middle ages through the heliocentric theories of Copernicus and Kepler to the classical mechanics enshrined in the work of Newton and then on to the relativistic universe described by Einstein and quantum physicists like Heisenberg. In another sense, the books chosen reflect not change but continuity. Not one of the books in this guide is a historical curiosity. Every single one has a continuing relevance today. Machiavelli may have written *The Prince* in Renaissance Italy but many of his thoughts on politics and the nature of leadership still illuminate contemporary business and politics. Mary Wollstonecraft's *A Vindication of the Rights of Women* is not just a document of historical feminism but sets an agenda for women's rights that remains relevant.

Philosophers like Schopenhauer, Kierkegaard and Nietzsche, it could be argued, speak more directly to the beginning of the twenty first century than they did to the nineteenth century in which they lived.

When one is looking at the thought of a thousand years, how does one choose what to include and what not to include? In choosing the ideas and the books in this Guide I have followed a few simple criteria. In the broadest sense all the books deal with our relationship to the world. This relationship has been expressed in religious, philosophical, political, sociological, psychological or scientific terms and books of all these categories are included in the guide. The books are all, as I have said, works of continuing relevance and this is reflected in the fact that they are all, whatever their original date of publication, in print in readily available editions. The Guide is arranged in chronological order and travels from St. Anselm in the 1090s to Stephen Hawking in the 1990s. I hope this is a journey that readers find stimulating and thought-provoking.

St
ANSELM
c.1095
Proslogion

Anselm was born in Aosta, Piedmont in 1033 and became a pupil of the great Norman churchman Lanfranc at the abbey of Bec in Northern France. Succeeding Lanfranc as prior and abbot at Bec, Anselm was also chosen by William Rufus to replace his mentor as Archbishop of Canterbury in 1093. Anselm was reluctant to accept what he saw as an appointment that would lead inevitably to conflict with the king. He was right. The rest of Anselm's life was much distracted by argument between the church and the state as represented first by William Rufus and then by Henry I. Anselm was the author of many philosophical and theological works and was one of the most sophisticated of those medieval intellectuals who wanted to use reason and argument to buttress rather than undermine faith. His ontological argument, as expounded in the *Proslogion,* is a classic formulation of an intellectual justification for the existence of God which has continued to engage philosophers to the present day. In its simplest form Anselm's argument follows three stages. It is possible, he says, for a being, greater than which is inconceivable, to exist in the intellect. However, if this being exists in the intellect only, it would be possible to imagine a greater being which existed in reality. Therefore, if God is defined as a being, greater than which is inconceivable can exist, He must exist in reality.

WRITINGS BY ST. ANSELM

The Major Works
Oxford UP pbk £7.99
0192825259

St Anselm
Basic Writings
Open Court P. pbk £9.95
0875481094

The Prayers and Meditations of St Anselm
Penguin pbk £8.99
0140442782

WRITINGS ON ST. ANSELM

Southern, Richard (Ed)
St Anselm: A Portrait in a Landscape
Cambridge UP pbk £17.95
0521438187

A scholarly but accessible work which brings together much material from diverse sources on Anselm's life and thought.

Peter
ABELARD
c.1115

Nosce Teipsum

Born into a noble family from the region around Nantes, Peter Abelard was originally intended for a military career but chose instead the life of a student and scholar. His brilliance was soon recognised and, by 1108, his lecturing and teaching in the Paris schools were beginning to attract pupils from all over Europe. For the next ten years he was at the height of his academic career, much admired (not least by himself) as an original and provocative thinker. It was then that the events took place described in his *Historia Calamitatum Mearum* (History of My Calamities) and revealed in the correspondence between Abelard and Heloise, events which have made Abelard's love affair far more widely known than his ideas. Heloise was the niece of Canon Fulbert of Notre Dame and twenty years younger than Abelard, but the two fell in love. Heloise bore a son and the lovers were secretly married. Unfortunately Canon Fulbert found out about the relationship and took a brutal vengeance. Abelard was castrated by the Canon's men, obliged to relinquish his academic and ecclesiastical career and enter the abbey of St. Denis as a monk. Heloise was sent to a convent at Argenteuil.

The rest of Abelard's life was marked by a succession of religious and doctrinal disputes. He quarrelled with the authorities at St. Denis and, in 1121, a synod at Soissons condemned his teachings as heretical. Although he was

eventually to become an abbot and even to resume his teaching career in Paris in the 1130s, he continued to make powerful enemies, most notably the monastic reformer, theologian and future saint Bernard of Clairvaux. Under the influence of Bernard, who considered Abelard guilty of alarming heterodoxy in his writings and teachings, the Council of Sens condemned him in 1141 and the sentence was confirmed by the Pope. Although much of the severity of the sentence was mitigated and some kind of reconciliation with Bernard was effected, Abelard was by now a worn-out man and he died the following year at a priory near Chalôn-sur-Saône. Nearly seven hundred years later his remains and those of Heloise were re-interred in the cemetery of Pére La Chaise in Paris.

Abelard's writings were wide-ranging, from commentaries on ancient authors to speculations about the nature of the Trinity, but his most important contribution to philosophy and theology probably lay in the method of dialectical reasoning elaborated in his work *Sic et Non*. Although some of his predecessors had occasionally used a similar method of intellectual debate, it was Abelard, by placing before his pupils a sequence of pro and contra arguments, who formalised it. To Abelard, truth would emerge through confronting and discussing seemingly contradictory statements and arguments from the Church Fathers and

'The master-key of knowledge is, indeed, a persistent and frequent questioning.'

other authorities. The method was to be brought to its greatest medieval complexity by Aquinas a century and a half later. In his other works Abelard contends with most of the philosophical and theological issues of his time, from the debate about the nature of universals (a philosophical term describing the supposed referents of general words like 'green' or 'tree', assumed to be entities quite distinct from specific objects to which those words were applied) to the vexed question of the relationship between human free will and divine providence. (On the nature of universals Abelard was of the opinion that they were mental terms only with no existence in the real world; on the question of free will he was adamant that God's omniscience in no way invalidated our freedom to act.) His influence on his contemporaries (both supporters and antagonists) was considerable and he remained a force in medieval thought throughout the next two centuries. As much through his extraordinary personal story as his ideas he remains today one of the most familiar names in medieval philosophy.

WRITINGS BY ABELARD

Ethical Writings
Hackett pbk £8.50
0872203220

This is the only readily available edition of Abelard's philosophical writings in paperback. It includes the text *Nosce Teipsum*. Oxford University Press publish a hardback edition of *Ethics* (£42.50 01982222173) in their series of Oxford Medieval Texts.

The Letters of Abelard and Heloise
Penguin pbk £8.99
0140442979

WRITINGS ON ABELARD

Clanchy, M.T.
Abelard: A Life
Blackwell pbk £15.95
0631214445

The noted historian Clanchy uses Abelard's varied and turbulent life as a means of examining broader issues of medieval life and thought.

Moses

MAIMONIDES 1190

A Guide for the Perplexed

Generally considered to be the greatest of medieval Jewish philosophers, Moshe ben Maimon (usually known in the West as Maimonides) was born in Cordoba in Spain. When he was in his teens the Almohads, warlike tribesmen from North Africa, conquered the city, demanding non-Muslims should convert on pain of death. Maimonides and his family fled, beginning a period of insecurity and uprootedness in his life which only ended when he settled permanently in Egypt in the 1160s. He spent the rest of his life in Egypt, becoming physician to Saladin's vizier in 1185 and rising to be head of the Jewish community in the country. He died in 1204 and was buried near the Sea of Galilee where his tomb can still be seen.

A Guide for the Perplexed, his greatest work and one which, through its influence on Thomas Aquinas, was to have a major effect on the development of western thought, aims to reconcile Judaism and the Aristotelian philosophical tradition. The book was intended for readers who have some theological and philosophical sophistication. ('The object of this treatise is to enlighten a religious man who has been trained to believe in the truth of our holy law, who conscientiously fulfils his moral and religious duties, and at the same time has been successful in his philosophical studies.') Any reader answering this description would be aware of fundamental differences between Aristotle's views of God and the universe and the account given in Jewish Law. To Aristotle the world, being a necessary consequence of God's existence, has always existed. Jewish scriptures, on the other hand, describe a moment of creation in which God chooses to bring the world into existence. While agreeing with Aristotle that God is, essentially, pure intellect and that human intellect reflects, however dimly, that divine intellect, Maimonides is clear that the account of creation given by Jewish Law and prophets must be the valid one. Yet the prophets themselves were not privy to some non-rational, superior power of insight. They were themselves men of high intellectual power and it was this that gave them their knowledge. Reason and faith are allies, not enemies. In his enquiries into the relationship between the knowledge provided by reason and the knowledge provided by revelation, Maimonides foreshadowed many of the debates of the medieval church. Inasmuch as the competing claims of reason and faith are still cited today, he remains of relevance nearly eight hundred years after his death.

'*Truth does not become more true by virtue of the fact that the entire world agrees with it, nor less so even if the whole world disagrees with it.*'

WRITINGS BY MAIMONIDES

Ethical Writings of Maimonides
Dover pbk £7.95
0486245225

A Guide for the Perplexed
Dover pbk £9.95
0486203514

Essential Maimonides
Kuperard pbk £19.99
1568214642

Maimonides's monumental fourteen-volume Code to Jewish Law is also available in hardback editions published by Yale UP.

WRITINGS ON MAIMONIDES

Leaman, Oliver Moses
Maimonides
Curzon pbk £14.99
0700706763

Cohn-Sherbok, Dan
Fifty Key Jewish Thinkers
Routledge pbk £10.99
0415126282

A collection of brief introductions to the ideas of Jewish thinkers from medieval figures like Maimonides to twentieth century writers like Martin Buber.

Sirat, Colette
A History of Jewish Philosophy in the Middle Ages
Cambridge UP pbk £22.95
0521397278

The most extensive study of the subject readily available.

ST FRANCIS OF ASSISI | c.1220

Selected Works

Born in the Umbrian town of Assisi in either 1181 or 1182, Giovanni Bernardone was the son of a rich merchant and in his teens took full advantage of his privileged position in life. A legend exists that, at this time he was given the nickname Il Francesco, because of his love of the French songs of the troubadours, but it is more probable that his father had changed Giovanni to Francesco when his son was still a small child. Held captive for a period during a war between Assisi and Perugia, Francis began the process of self-examination which led him, in 1206, to renounce his father's wealth and to live as a hermit. This dramatic renunciation, publicly made, and the ascetic life he now led, rapidly brought him followers. In 1210 the Pope Innocent III gave his official blessing to Francis's gospel-inspired rules for the living of a simple life and allowed him and his followers to preach on moral topics. By 1219 the Franciscan movement had more than 5,000 members and Francis, together with St. Clare of Assisi, had founded a branch of his new order for women, called the Poor Clares.

In 1219, during the Fifth Crusade, Francis and a small band of disciples travelled to the Holy Land and he was present at the siege of Damietta. After preaching to the Christian forces Francis attempted to do the same to the enemy. He was captured and taken before the sultan Melek al-Kamil at his court in Egypt. Francis's efforts to convert the sultan were fruitless but he was received courteously and sent on his way. He returned to Italy in 1220 to find himself embroiled in developing political and religious differences within his movement, which he strove to reconcile by recasting the original rules of the Order. In 1224, during a forty day fast, Francis became the first well-documented person to receive the stigmata (the wounds of Christ) on his own body. Much of the rest of his life he was racked by sufferings brought on by the rigours of his asceticism and he died on October 3rd 1226. Two years later he was canonised by Pope Gregory IX.

Francis was not, in any sense of the word, a philosopher but his ideas, it can be argued, had as much influence on the medieval world as those more sophisticated arguments of thinkers like Aquinas and William of Ockham. It was, indeed, Francis's simplicity that affected his contemporaries the most and his insistence on a direct and uncomplicated interpretation of the message of the Gospels has been a recurring motif in Christian history and thought. Whenever, in the centuries since his death, there has been a religious movement that has castigated the worldliness of the established church and called for a return to the uncorrupted values of Christ, the figure of Francis has been, to a greater or lesser extent, invoked. Many of his works (letters, sermons, hymns) have survived to bear witness to the purity of his vision of a life devoted uncomplicatedly to God.

'It is in giving that we receive; it is in pardoning that we are pardoned; and it is in dying that we are born to eternal life.'

WRITINGS BY ST FRANCIS	**WRITINGS ON ST FRANCIS**

WRITINGS BY ST FRANCIS

The Works
Hodder pbk £2.99
0340608080

The Little Flowers of St. Francis
Vintage pbk £5.99
037570020X

WRITINGS ON ST FRANCIS

Byrne, Lavinia
The Life and Wisdom of St. Francis
Hodder pbk £3.99
0340709685

God's Pauper
Faber pbk £9.99
0571115098

Novel by Nikos Kazantzakis about Francis.

St Thomas

AQUINAS   1267-73

Summa Theologica

Thomas Aquinas is arguably the most important figure in medieval philosophy and one of the most influential figures in the whole of western thought. His achievement was to show that the faculties of reason were not incompatible with the Christian faith and that the great works of classical philosophy, notably those of Aristotle, could be reconciled with the word of God revealed in the Bible. His two great works, *Summa Contra Gentiles* (c.1260) and *Summa Theologica* (1267-73) contain his mature thought. In addition to these massive works Aquinas wrote voluminously on Christian doctrine, Aristotle and the Arab doctors, in addition to writing polemics to order for the Church.

Thomas Aquinas was born around 1225 in the castle of Roccasecca near Naples. After being schooled at the Benedictine abbey of Monte Cassino, he was sent to the University of Naples, founded by the Emperor Frederick II as an alternative to the papal University of Bologna. In 1244, to the consternation of his family, Aquinas became a Dominican friar. As a member of a noble family, he would have been expected to take the more socially befitting role of monk (and, one day, abbot) rather than adopt the peripatetic life of a friar. He was kidnapped by his elder brothers and held hostage for a year at Roccasecca, where he composed two short works on logic, which are thought to be his earliest works. At Roccasecca,

a famous incident occurred. One night his brothers, perhaps to test his devotion to his calling, perhaps out of pity that their hopelessly overweight younger brother had yet to experience the pleasures of the flesh, sent a naked girl into his cell. Aquinas grabbed a red-hot poker and chased her away, and from then on 'avoided women as if they were snakes.'

Unable to deter Thomas from life as a friar, his family released him and he went to study with the great scholar Albertus Magnus in Cologne. Albertus was one of the founding fathers of the Dominicans and he realised at once that his new pupil possessed extraordinary gifts. Aquinas's fellow pupils mocked him because of his size, calling him 'the Dumb Ox.' Albertus retorted that 'this dumb ox will fill the world with his bellowing.'

In 1252 Albertus sent Aquinas to Paris to continue his studies. Although he was considered too young to begin advanced studies, Albertus convinced the Master General of the Dominicans that Aquinas was unique and that his age should not deter them from offering him a place. During his time in Paris Aquinas had to lecture on theology, which meant lecturing on the standard theology textbook, the *Sentences* of Peter Lombard. These lectures constitute his first major work. In 1255 Aquinas received the degree of Master and undertook further lectures in theology.

'Therefore it is necessary to arrive at a prime mover, put in motion by no other; and this everyone understands to be God.'

These largely centred on Biblical texts and a number of Biblical commentaries survive from this time. More important, however, is the work begun at the suggestion of the Spanish Dominican missionary Raymond of Peñafort, the *Summa Contra Gentiles*.

The *Summa* was written as a theological manual for missionaries in Spain and North Africa, a fact made explicit by the title under which it is known in an English translation: On the Truth of the Catholic Faith. Unlike most evangelical tracts, however, the *Summa* treats matters of faith and truth from a philosophical perspective, and exhibits a rare degree of sophistication and subtlety. The work is divided into four books. The first deals with the nature of God, the second with God's relationship to His creation, the third with the notion that happiness is only to be found in the knowledge of God, and the last examines specific Christian doctrines such as the Incarnation and the Trinity. Writing for an audience who would not accept the validity of Christianity solely on the basis of its being Christianity, Aquinas makes constant appeal throughout the *Summa* to reason, 'to which all men are forced to assent.' Aquinas makes clear that, although certain truths about God can only be known by faith, others can be posited through reason. Through reason, for instance, we know that we can talk of God only in analogous terms ('God is like light' etc.).

In the *Summa* Aquinas frequently discusses ideas first mooted by Aristotle. There are several reasons for this. Firstly, Aquinas knew that his audience would be familiar with Aristotle from the work of the Arab doctors.

More important, however, was the fact that Aristotle was known to have systematically studied all of nature. He had reasoned that the world is immortal and that the highest good we can experience lies in the contemplation of God. If reason was to be shown to be compatible with Christianity and, indeed, its servant, then Aristotle needed to be given a Christian stamp of approval. Thirdly, the influence of the Arab scholar Averroes needed to be combatted. Averroes, a strictly logical Aristotelian, held that Aristotle's arguments, if carried to a conclusion, imply that each and every human being does not have an individual soul, but partakes of one common collective soul. God remains largely outside the workings of the universe and metaphysics is supplanted by materialism.

Aquinas's study of Aristotle led to improved versions of existing translations, and also to the translation of remaining parts of the corpus. When Aquinas was born, all of Aristotle (except his work on logic) was outlawed. By the time the *Summa Contra Gentiles* was completed, all of Aristotle's known works were set texts in Paris (despite Papal bulls condemning this). The *Summa Contra Gentiles* was completed in Italy after Aquinas's departure from Paris in 1259. He was to remain in Italy, teaching in Rome or at the Papal courts of Orvieto and Viterbo, for ten years. During this time he wrote an attack on the Greek church at the instigation of Pope Urban IV, as well as hymns for the feast of Corpus Christi, newly instituted in 1264.

Towards the end of the 1260s, Aquinas began his most ambitious work, the *Summa Theologica*. Intended as a theological textbook to replace Peter Lombard's *Sentences*, the *Summa* runs to over two million words, somewhat daunting for a work intended merely as an introduction to the subject. Whereas in the *Summa Contra Gentiles*, Aquinas was largely appealing to non-Christians of an Aristotelian persuasion, in the new *Summa*, knowing that his readership is a Catholic one, he goes into much greater detail (not to mention length) on subjects such as the Trinity and the Sacraments. The first part of the *Summa Theologica* expands on the first two books of the *Summa Contra Gentiles*. Appeals to Aristotle are now replaced with his own, more mature thought. For instance, he introduces his celebrated Five Ways of proving God's existence. In the first way he notes that the world is subject to change in which certain things are moved from potentiality to actuality and that there must be a first mover which we call God. In the second way he points out that the world has an order of efficient causality (things now moving are having an effect on other things) and that there must exist something, God, which is the first in this chain of causality. In the third way he notes that some things come into being while others pass away and argues that there must be some entity which is necessary of itself and not subject to generation and destruction. In the fourth way he notes that certain things are more full of goodness and nobility than others and that the ultimate embodiment of this goodness and nobility, which we see around us in varying levels, is God. In the fifth way he argues that certain things in nature act in harmony with other things to maintain a relatively stable system, despite their lack of awareness, and concludes that there must exist some being which directs these things towards an end they cannot themselves recognise.

Part Two of the *Summa Theologica* expands Book III of the earlier *Summa*. It is modelled on Aristotle's *Ethics* (upon which Aquinas was also writing an extensive commentary at the same time) and is itself divided into two parts, the Prima Secundae and the Secunda Secundae. The work could be seen as Aquinas's 'reply' to Aristotle's work. The Prima Secundae, or first part of the second part, begins with an examination of happiness. Like Aristotle, Aquinas believed that the highest happiness for any human being was the contemplation of the Godhead; any happiness based on earthly things such as fame or wealth was passing and corrupt. He then goes on to look at the will and to examine what makes an action good or bad, which in turn leads to his theory of virtue, or what he calls disposition.' The Prima Secundae ends with a commentary on law and the necessity of divine grace for salvation.

The Secunda Secundae, or second part of the second part, is a much more specialised treatise on each individual virtue and its opposing sin. While still adhering to an Aristotelian framework, and often comparing Christian virtues with Aristotelian ones, Aquinas discusses each topic in much greater depth than Aristotle. His discussion of justice, for instance, is virtually a book in itself, covering everything from slander to embezzlement to murder. The Secunda Secundae concludes with a comparison of the active and the contemplative life, favouring, as did Aristotle, the life of contemplation.

The third part of the Summa is concerned with theological topics such as baptism, confirmation and penance, the importance of the Virgin Mary and the Incarnation. Although obviously writing for students of theology, Aquinas nonetheless touches on ideas of lasting philosophical importance.

Aquinas never finished the *Summa Theologica*. After four years of monumental productivity in Paris and finally in Naples – during which he was writing not only the *Summa* but also the commentaries on Aristotle, and was delivering his lecture series – he underwent a mystical experience while saying mass on December 6th 1273. He told his secretaries that, 'all I have written seems to me like so much straw compared with what has been revealed to me.' He halted work on Part Three of the *Summa* and never wrote anything again. In the early part of the new year, he was invited to attend a Church council in Lyons but died on the way on March 7th 1274.

Although today, Aquinas is regarded as doctrinally sound by the Catholic Church, in 1277 portions of his work were condemned in what was known as the Paris Condemnations (which also attacked other prominent thinkers, including Roger Bacon). In 1323 Aquinas was declared a saint. The Condemnations were revoked two years later. Although Aquinas's position as 'church philosopher' has limited his appeal to some, he has had unlikely supporters. Ludwig Wittgenstein, arguably the most important philosopher of the twentieth century, thought that it is not in his religious beliefs nor even in the answers he found, that we find Aquinas's lasting contribution to philosophy, but in the questions he had the courage to ask.

SEAN MARTIN

WRITINGS BY AQUINAS

Selected Philosophical Writings
Oxford UP pbk £7.99
0192835858

Selected Writings
Penguin pbk £12.99
0140436324

St. Thomas Aquinas on Politics and Ethics
Norton pbk £6.95
0393952436

A valuable addition to the Norton Critical Editions but this is only a brief selection from Aquinas's writings. Aquinas's Summa Theologica is published in full by Cambridge UP.

WRITINGS ON AQUINAS

Copleston, F.C.
Aquinas
Penguin pbk £9.99
0140136746

Kenny, Anthony
Aquinas
Oxford UP pbk £5.99
0192875000

Finnis, John
Aquinas
Oxford UP pbk £13.99
0198780850

The first volume in a recently-launched series of Founders of Modern Political and Social Thought.

Cambridge Companion to Aquinas
Cambridge UP pbk £17.95
0521437695

Roger

BACON 1267

Opus Maius

The work of Roger Bacon stands at a meeting place of Medieval and Modern Europe, some of his ideas anticipating both the Renaissance and the Enlightenment. He was lauded as a scientist and thinker yet also branded as a wizard. Although seen as the first champion of the scientific method, he was also rumoured to have performed alchemical transmutations and he remains an enigmatic character, still steeped in mystery and legend. He was rumoured to have a talking head made of brass and to have gained his extraordinary learning from the Devil. He is said to have drawn up plans for flying machines and machines that enabled a man to breathe at the bottom of the ocean, and to have constructed a mirror that enabled him to see far-off events. He is also said to have invented a microscope, a tank and a pontoon bridge, centuries before such things were realised. When he died his books were nailed to the shelves they sat on and left to rot, such was the conviction felt by his fellow Fransiscans that he had been in league with the forces of darkness.

Bacon was born at Ilchester in Somerset around the year 1214 to a wealthy family that later supported Henry III in the war against the Barons, a position that was to drive them to ruin. He was probably sent up to Oxford at the age of ten or twelve and there proved himself to be an exceptional student, being taught by the most learned men of the day, including Robert Grosseteste, Bishop of Lincoln and the leading mathematician of the time. It was perhaps while he was an undergraduate that Bacon became a Franciscan.

After Oxford, Bacon went to Paris which boasted the greatest university of the day. Bacon's tutor at Paris, unlike Grosseteste at Oxford, was an obscure solitary by the name of Master Peter, a shadowy figure who has escaped the historical record almost completely. Whereas in Oxford, Bacon had received the standard university education of the time, in Paris he was instructed in Peter's own unique style. He learnt alchemy and astrology but was also instructed in the empirical observation of nature. Bacon was to refer to Master Peter as the 'Lord of Experimentation'. Bacon had already been introduced to this method by Grosseteste and would later develop the work of both his masters and, in doing so, lay the foundation for modern science.

Bacon came to believe that through studying Nature, Man could come to have knowledge of the Creator. He returned to Oxford a Doctor of Divinity and began to undertake a series of experiments. For most of the 1250s he seems to have been engaged in diverse works, including astronomy (his celebrated observation tower survived well into the eighteenth century), botany, chemistry, medicine, optics

'Et harum scientarum porta et clavis est Mathematica.' (Mathematics is the door and key to the sciences)

and mathematics. He gathered a small group of students around him – including Friar Bungay, a doctor of divinity and supposed sorcerer – and set rumour-mongers to work with his stargazing and strange instruments. Probably this period was the happiest of Bacon's life.

Bacon's belief that the principles of mathematics and number underlay everything in the world led to a belief in the need to reform the calendar. His suggestions were finally accepted in 1592 when the Gregorian system was adopted. He also created one of the earliest maps of the world. (Now rumoured to be in the Vatican library.) But this was not all. Bacon saw ignorance and abuse everywhere and railed against fellow scholars, including Thomas Aquinas and Albertus Magnus. Heretically he judged the world of classical antiquity to be morally superior to that of the Christians and he called for greater stringency in the Universities. He himself learned Hebrew, Chaldean and Greek in an attempt to try and get both the Bible and the classical authors translated properly. Corrupt texts, he reasoned, would lead to corrupt students.

His outbursts, which would continue unabated into old age, together with the popular perception of him as a necromancer, led to his summons to a Franciscan court in Paris in 1257. He was placed under house arrest for ten years. He was given menial tasks to do each day that left him no time for his studies, and his diet was bread and water.

In 1263 the newly appointed Papal legate to England, Guido Fulcode, heard of Bacon through an intermediary, one Rémond de Laon. The monk of Oxford, Fulcode learned, was possessed of wonderful secrets and the legate determined to correspond with him. By the time the two made contact, Fulcode had become Pope Clement IV and, once he deemed it safe to do so, had Bacon released in 1267 on the condition that he wrote down all his discoveries in one book. Bacon did not write one book for the Pope. He was to write five. The *Opus Maius* was the first of these and it is his masterpiece. In it he demonstrated the same ambition as other 13th century intellectuals to try and encapsulate all human knowledge in one book. It is a vast compendium surveying the sciences as they stood in 1267, and as they stood according to Bacon, who believed that all branches of science were connected. In effect, it is a medieval quest for a 'Theory of Everything.'

Bacon hoped that in producing the *Opus Maius*, he could persuade the Pope both to offer him protection from his persecutors and to introduce reforms in both church and society. The plan was ruined in 1269 by Clement's death. Back in Oxford and reunited with his students, Bacon produced three more works, the *Opus Minus*, the *Opus Tertium* and a treatise whose title has been lost, for the new Pope, Gregory X, before falling foul of the Franciscan hierarchies again. Bacon's supporters tried to save him but, in 1278, he was imprisoned for fourteen years. It is said that he was only released when he revealed certain alchemical secrets to the head of the Franciscans, Raymond Gaufredi. If his opponents hoped that jail and old age would mellow Bacon, they hoped in vain. On his release, Bacon immediately set to work on another book, the *Compendium Theologiae*, an attack on what he saw as the theological errors of the time.

The date of Bacon's death is unknown. 1292 is the last year he appears in the historical record, with the completion of the Compendium. His work fell into obscurity, no doubt due to his reputation as a sorcerer. Stories of his magical prowess kept his name alive and, in the late sixteenth century, he featured in a play by Robert Greene, *The History of Friar Bacon and Friar Bungay*, which competed for audiences with Marlowe's *Doctor Faustus*. Like Faustus, Bacon regrets his magic but, unlike Marlowe's protagonist, he recants and is allowed to live. (It is his slapstick servant Miles who is transported to hell.) In a more recent tribute, Umberto Eco makes Bacon William of Baskerville's hero in *The Name of the Rose*.

Bacon remains one of the most remarkable minds of the Middle Ages, both as a man of his time and an almost clairvoyantly sighted figure, centuries ahead of his time. Maybe the last word should be left to Robert Ellis, a great scholar of his namesake Francis Bacon. After reading some of Roger's work, Ellis is reputed to have said, 'I am inclined to think that he may have been a greater man than our Francis.'

SEAN MARTIN

WRITINGS BY BACON

Opus Maius
Kessinger pbk £60.00
0766104214

WRITINGS ON BACON

E.V. Westacott
Roger Bacon in Life and Legend
Banton pbk £12.20
1856521354

Meister

ECKHART | c.1310

And Medieval Mysticism

SEAN MARTIN *worked for a number of years in Waterstone's in Hampstead. He is now a writer and film-maker. He has a long-standing interest in mysticism and the mystical tradition in literature.*

Meister Eckhart, the greatest of all German mystics, was the most important figure in the remarkable flowering of mysticism that took place throughout Europe in the fourteenth century. He became celebrated as the most learned scholar of his day and manuscripts of his sermons were circulated throughout Europe's religious houses and centres of learning. His work was to become familiar to characters as diverse as the illiterate visionary Margery Kempe and the scholarly Jan Van Ruysbroeck.

Meister Eckhart was born in Thuringia about the year 1260. He joined the Dominican order at Erfurt around 1275 and, from there, he was sent to Cologne, where he may have studied under Thomas Aquinas's teacher, Albertus Magnus (d. 1280). By 1293 Eckhart was teaching in Paris and around this time he produced his earliest datable work, the *Talks of Instruction*.

In 1302 Eckhart became a Master of Theology and became known as Meister, rather than Brother, Eckhart. He moved upward through the Dominican hierarchy, becoming the first Provost of Saxony (most of North Germany and Holland) in 1303 and, four years later, became the Vicar General of Bohemia. His brief in

Bohemia was to restore order to Dominican convents and extirpate heresy, an irony since he himself was later charged with the same crime.

Eckhart was to remain busy with administrative posts for the rest of his life. He continued to write and teach while juggling duties in Paris and Strasbourg, before taking up the Studium Generale, the chair in Cologne once held by Albertus Magnus. What should have been the crowning achievement in a lifetime devoted to the Dominicans proved to be Eckhart's undoing. The Dominicans had long been at loggerheads with the Franciscans over numerous points of doctrine and, at the time Eckhart took up the chair in Cologne, the Archbishop there was a particularly stern figure who was deeply opposed to 'mysticism', which he equated with the many heretical groups then flourishing. In 1326 the Archbishop took the unprecedented step of charging Eckhart with heresy, charges related largely to *The Book of Divine Comfort*, a work that dates from about the time he took up the post of Vicar General in Bohemia. Although Eckhart was in no danger of being burnt, he resolved to clear his name. The trial seems to have been politically motivated, another episode in the long battle between the two orders and two former Dominicans (one of whom had been excommunicated) were brought in to testify against Eckhart. By the time Pope John XXII declared in favour of the prosecution, on March 27th

'There is a work which it is right and proper for us to do, and that is the eradication of self. But however great this eradication and reduction of self may be, it remains insufficient if God does not complete it in us.'

1329, Eckhart was dead and so was his reputation. It would take centuries before Eckhart was rescued from the backwaters of theological purgatory.

Yet Eckhart was at the beginning of a remarkable flowering of mystical writing. He was followed by his pupils Tauler and Tuso and by Jan van Ruysbroeck; by Walter Hilton, Julian of Norwich and Richard Rolle; by Catherine of Siena, by the author of *The Cloud of Unknowing*, by Angela de Foligno and Mechtild of Magdeburg; by Bridget of Sweden, Richard Methley, Marguerite Porete, Dorothea of Montau and, in the following century, Thomas à Kempis.

Jan van Ruysbroeck was an Augustinian whose superiors, in 1343, granted him use of the old hermitage at Groenendael in the Forest of Soignes just outside Brussels. Here he settled with two other monks and established what was to become one of the main spiritual centres in the Low Countries. Ruysbroeck's major works all date from the Groenendael period. He is one of the few mystics of the time to combine a sound knowledge of classical authors – Plato, Aristotle, Plotinus and the pseudo-Dionysius among them – with the more traditional lineage of Augustine and the Church Fathers. The idea of a movement upwards (or inwards) is central to Ruysbroeck's thought: *The Adornment of the Spiritual Marriage* and *The Sparkling Stone* describe the growth of the soul towards God and the effort required to achieve such growth. The later *Book of Supreme Truth* is a short summary of his work written, one assumes, for novices or the lay reader.

Ruysbroeck's circle at Groenendael was to have a direct influence on one of the most popular and influential of all devotional works, Thomas à Kempis's *The Imitation of Christ*. Thomas (1380-1471) was a member of the Brethren of the Common Life, a Dutch group founded by Ruysbroeck's disciple Gerard Groote. The group was founded in reaction to what Groote regarded as laxity and corruption amongst the clergy, and devoteed itself to a life of simplicity and prayer. This spirit informs the *Imitation*, written in the 1430s. That admirers of Thomas à Kempis's work range from Ignatius Loyola to John Wesley is a testament both to its author's humility and the tradition that he inherited from Ruysbroeck via the Brethren.

Contemporary with both Ruysbroeck and Eckhart was the first of the great English mystics, Richard Rolle (c.1300-1349). He was widely read in his own time, and wrote many of his works in the vernacular. Unlike Ruysbroeck and Eckhart, however, Rolle was a hermit and not at first attached to any order. (He was later to become the director of a Cistercian nunnery.) As a result, his best-known work, *The Fire of Love* (1343), is a highly individual, first-person account of mystical experience and the hermit's life. The self-educated Rolle writes of thinking that he is actually on fire and his book is essentially a defence of the authenticity and reality of his experiences. As such, it has often been regarded with suspicion but it is worth remembering that feelings of warmth as a result of prayer have, at times, been actively encouraged, particularly in the Orthodox Church. Rolle speaks strongly of the virtues of the solitary life as well as its hardships. He left home to become a hermit and one story has him literally running away to avoid his family dragging him back.

The mystics who followed Rolle were nearly all, like him, solitaries but, apart from a tendency to employ first-person narrative, it is hard to find any other common characteristic across a range of highly individual voices. *The Cloud of Unknowing* (c.1370) was possibly written by an East Midlands country parson and is, in part, a reaction to Rolle. Where Rolle is ecstatic, the Cloud is more sober, exemplifying the *via negativa*. This, the negative way, describes God in terms of what he is not: not human, totally other, indescribably beyond language. This contrasts with the *via positiva* in which God is often described in terms of human characteristics (wrathful, forgiving) or in metaphor (light, love, mystery).

The English mystics of the fourteenth century all wrote independently of each other and, as a result, there is no 'party line' on teaching or in descriptions of the mystical experience. If *The Cloud of Unknowing* can be seen as a 'development' of Rolle (if only in terms of the language used to describe the mystical experience), then Walter Hilton's *The Ladder of Perfection* represents, it can be argued, the apogee of fourteenth century mystical literature. Hilton (1340 – 1396) was a hermit and later a canon at the Augustinian priory in Thurgarton in Nottinghamshire. *The Ladder of Perfection* was written as a practical guide to spiritual development for an anchoress and, judging by the number of manuscripts which survive, it was widely read. The book constantly emphasises prayer and meditation as gifts from God by which we come to know Him, and describes spiritual development in terms of spatial metaphor: we must climb upwards towards perfection. (The use of progresses or ascents would later become widespread in mystical writing.)

The anchoress for whom Hilton wrote would have led a straitened but not necessarily uncomfortable life. An anchoress would usually live in a small house, perhaps with a walled garden, perhaps attached to a monastery or church. She would have servants, would be allowed visitors and, in some cases, would be allowed to move house, if she wished. Julian of Norwich (c.1342 – c.1416) is the most celebrated of all anchoresses, her fame resting on *Revelations of Divine Love*, which describes the visions that she experienced in the course of just one day, May 8th 1373. The book exists in two versions. The shorter of the two was probably written not long after the experiences it describes, the longer some twenty years later, when Julian had become an anchoress, the 'recluse atte Norwyche.' The longer version has proved the more popular, with its vivid descriptions of the visions, and Julian's meditations upon them.

The majority of visionaries were women. Whereas someone like Eckhart or Hilton would belong to an order and would write of the soul's progress towards God through humility and prayer, visionaries such as Julian or Margery Kempe (c.1373 – c1440) were often unattached (at least at first) to a religious order, and would describe conversations with Christ and vistas of heavenly glory. Again unlike an Eckhart or a Ruysbroeck, both Julian and Margery were 'unlettered', with no knowledge of either the classical authors or the Church Fathers. Margery was, in fact, illiterate and dictated her book to priestly scribes. Strictly defined, *The Book of Margery Kempe* (1436) is not mysticism but autobiography (the earliest in English). It describes her life from her marriage at twenty, her illness after childbirth which led to her taking up a life of devotion and her subsequent travels to the Holy Land and Rome. Despite her illiteracy, Margery had books read to her and thus became familiar with both Rolle and Hilton. More important, perhaps, was her discovery of other women visionaries such as St. Bridget of Sweden (1303-1373), Mary of Oignes (d.1213) and Catherine of Siena (d.1380). She also sought counsel from Julian of Norwich (Margery was from King's Lynn). Knowing that other women had trodden the same path before her must have been a great comfort when people were accusing her (as frequently happened) of heresy, madness or fraudulence. It would seem that, if only in mystic circles, women could be seen as equal to men. Christ's words to Margery, which she heard during mass, could equally apply to every woman who followed the calling of the inner life; 'And you will succeed, daughter, in spite of all your enemies.'

WRITINGS BY ECKHART

Selected Writings
Penguin pbk £8.99
0140433430

Sermons and Treatises Volume 1
Element pbk £12.99
1852300051

Sermons and Treatises Volume 2
Element pbk £12.99
185230006X

Sermons and Treatises Volume 3
Element pbk £12.99
1852301821

WRITINGS ON ECKHART

Van de Weyer (ed)
Eckhart in a Nutshell
Hodder pbk £3.99
034069467X

WRITINGS BY OTHER MYSTICS

Ruysbroeck, Jan van
The Adornment of the Spiritual Marriage/The Sparkling Stone
Llanerch pbk £9.95
1897853408

Kempis, Thomas à
The Imitation of Christ
Penguin pbk £6.99
0140440275

The Imitation of Christ
Arrow pbk £5.99
0375700188

Women Mystics
Flanagan, Sabina
Hildegard of Bingen:
A Visionary Life
Routledge pbk £12.99
0415185513

Frances Beer's book *Women and Mystical Experience in the Middle Ages* (Boydell pbk £16.99 0851153437) looks at three female mystics, Hildegard of Bingen, Mechthild of Magdeburg and Julian of Norwich.

English Mystics
Rolle, Richard
The Fire of Love
Penguin pbk £7.99
0140442561

The Cloud of Unknowing
Penguin pbk £7.99
0140443851

Hilton, Walter
The Ladder of Perfection
Penguin pbk £7.99
0140445110

Julian of Norwich
Revelations of Divine Love
(long Version)
Penguin pbk £7.99
0140446737

Kempe, Margery
The Book of Margery Kempe
Penguin pbk £7.99
0140432515

Glasscoe, Marion
English Medieval Mystics
Addison Wesley Longman pbk
£18.99
0582495172

William of

OCKHAM

1320s

Selected Writings

William of Ockham, known for the philosophical principle of Occam's Razor to which he gave his name, was born in the village of Ockham in Surrey and studied at Oxford. It was at Oxford that he joined the Franciscan order. He went on to teach in Paris where his controversial views led to his summons in 1324 to the papal court in Avignon to answer charges of heresy. After a long delay Ockham was found guilty of heresy and, when he refused to retract his views and instead aligned himself with the Spiritual Franciscans (opponents of the Pope), he was excommunicated. He spent the rest of his life in Bavaria, under the protection of the Holy Roman Emperor, and died in Munich in 1349, in all likelihood after contracting the Black Death.

Ockham is one of the most important figures in medieval philosophy. Unlike Aquinas and others who worked in the tradition he established, who argued that statements about the created world could be used as starting points for an intellectual process which eventually told us something about the mind of God, Ockham denied that any knowledge of God was possible from an examination of things in the created world. Knowledge of God was possible but only by means of revelation rather than reason. When reason was turned upon the world knowledge was gained only of individual things. Hence the principle of Occam's Razor with its statement that, when

something can be explained by the assumption of fewer things, it is pointless to look for an explanation which assumes many things. Why assume that a general term such as 'man' or 'cat' is anything but a property of language? Why assume (as both Plato and Aquinas do) that these general terms refer to forms or essences which have an existence other than the existence of individual instances of a man or a cat? The principle demands that these assumed forms and essences be jettisoned. The individual things in the world are all that is real. Ockham's clear distinction between what could be known by reason (individual things in the world) and what could be known only by revelation (God and the divine) has had long term consequences. In a sense, carefully drawing boundaries around what can be known by reason, invites the development of a clearly defined examination of the natural world i.e. of science. And meanwhile God remains beyond those boundaries, forever resistant to that kind of analysis, forever open to knowledge of an entirely different kind.

'Essentia non sunt multiplicanda praeter necessitatem.'
(Entities should not be multiplied unnecessarily)

WRITINGS BY OCKHAM

Philosophical Writings:
A Selection
Hackett pbk £12.95
0872200787

Quodlibetal Questions
Yale UP pbk £22.50
0300075065

A Letter to the Friars Minor
and Other Writings
Cambridge UP pbk £16.95
0521358043

A Short Discourse on Tyrannical
Government
Cambridge UP pbk £13.95
0521358035

WRITINGS ON OCKHAM

Cambridge Companion to Ockham
Cambridge UP pbk £16.95
0521587905

Desiderius

ERASMUS 1511

The Praise of Folly

Desiderius Erasmus was born in Rotterdam, probably in the year 1466. His family origins are obscure, though he is thought to be the result of an illegitimate union – something he sought to conceal all his life. However, it is clear that he grew up as a member of the burgher class and that he received an excellent education. In 1475 Erasmus first attended the academically renowned, though rigid and puritanical, School of the Brothers of Common Life at Deventer, where he learnt Greek and became absorbed in the study of the works of classical literature that were to influence his own writings so profoundly. The death of his parents, a short time later, led to an unhappy period when he was put in charge of three guardians, who cared little for the welfare of their charges and myopically packed Erasmus and his brother off to a much poorer school at Bois–le-Duc.

Eventually, in 1488, Erasmus entered the Augustinian monastery at Steyn near Gouda. There he was free to read and debate and formed a number of friendships, although later writings on the monastic life suggest that it was not to Erasmus's taste. His 'poetic' models at the time were the classical poets Vergil, Horace, Ovid and Juvenal, whereas in prose he mimicked the Latin stylists, Cicero (*De Oratore, Hortensius* and his *Letters to Atticus*) and Quintilian (*Institutio Oratoria*). He was also reading Italian humanists like Valla and Poggio and ecclesiastical literature with equal fervour.

Ordained in 1492, by the Bishop of Utrecht, Erasmus left the cloister and embarked on a restless and peripatetic life that was to bring him to many religious and academic centres (Paris, Louvain, Basle and Oxford) and into contact with most of the great scholars of the new learning. The hard realities (*tumulariae* as he called them) of life outside the cloister forced themselves on Erasmus's attention as did the almost universal corruption of the Church and its grandees. He was particularly unimpressed by his brief stay at the rigidly traditional University of Paris, still dominated by medieval scholasticism.

Frustrated intellectually, and in poor health after his Paris sojourn, Erasmus travelled to England in 1498 and lived in Oxford where he came to know John Colet, with whom he developed a strong intellectual rapport. It was through Colet he first met Thomas More, who was to become such a friend and influence.

Erasmus's best known work, *The Praise of Folly*, was written as he convalesced from an illness in More's home. It was written, Erasmus claimed, in one week, to amuse More, (on whose name its original title, *Moriae Encomium*, is a pun) at a time when Erasmus himself was increasingly disillusioned with the state of the Church under the Pope Julius II. Initially a fantasy imbued with learned frivolity, *The Praise of Folly* metamorphoses into a serious and waspishly subtle indictment of theologians and churchmen, attacking their corruption and ideological barrenness, before finally extolling the virtues of a true Christian way of life. *The Praise of Folly* marks a turning point in religious history. In the past lie the stultifying traditions of the medieval church which Erasmus scorns. Ahead is the new Christianity of the Renaissance, the Reformation of Luther and others and the rise of national consciousness in Northern Europe. *The Praise of Folly* was hugely successful and by 1536 had been translated into French and German. By 1549, Thomas Chaloner had translated it into English. Thanks to the spread of the printing press, it was widely disseminated and became one of the great bestsellers of the 16th century.

Erasmus was a man of vast, if not always profoundly deep, erudition and intellectual powers. His merciless satires on the Church, best exemplified by *The Praise of Folly*, heralded the triumph of the 'new learning', the coming of the Reformation and the rise of Luther. Yet Erasmus, with his abhorrence of violence and his tranquil disposition, was unable to endorse Luther and his Protestant Reformation (indeed, in the 1520s, he entered into controversy with him) and he remained in the fold of the Conservative, Louvain-dominated, Church, seeing it as the safeguard of stability. Huizinga, in his book *Erasmus of Rotterdam,* says that Erasmus's influence was 'extensive' rather than 'intensive' and that he was the only one of the humanists who wrote for the whole of the educated world. Through his many editions and translations of the Bible, of the classics and the Church Fathers, Erasmus transformed that educated world. In essence, Erasmus was an initiator and a introducer of, as Huizinga puts it: 'The creed of education and perfectibility, of warm feeling and faith in human nature, of peaceful kindliness and toleration'. His wide-ranging work was a prelude to, and preparer of, the modern mind.

NIAMH MARNHAM, *Waterstone's*

'In regione caecorum, rex est luscus.'
(In the country of the blind, the one-eyed man is king.)

WRITINGS BY ERASMUS

The Praise of Folly
Penguin pbk £7.99
0140446087

The Praise of Folly and other writings
Norton pbk £7.95
0393957497

The Penguin edition is the most readily available version of Erasmus's famous work but the Norton edition is well annotated and contains a small selection of other essays.

WRITINGS ON ERASMUS

McConica, James
Erasmus
Oxford UP pbk £5.99
019287599X

One of the Past Masters series, this is a concise introduction to Erasmus's life and thought.

Huizinga, Johan
Erasmus of Rotterdam
Phaidon pbk £9.99
0714833665

One of the greatest Dutch scholars of the present century, author of *Homo Ludens* and *The Waning of the Middle Ages*, looked at his Reformation countryman in this incisive study, recently reprinted.

Niccolo

MACHIAVELLI 1513

The Prince

Machiavelli was born on 3rd May 1469 into a well-established Florentine family. His father was not a wealthy man and, at no time in his life, could Machiavelli hope to rival the riches and influence of the great patrician families of the city. However he did enter the Florentine chancery in 1498 and was re-elected annually until 1512. He worked as secretary to the Ten of War and the Nine of the Militia, two of the administrative bodies which ran Florence's domestic and foreign affairs, and was sent abroad on diplomatic missions on several occasions. In 1500 he was sent to the court of the French king Louis XII and in 1502 and 1503 encountered Cesare Borgia, the warlord son of Pope Alexander VI, who was to provide a partial model for Machiavelli's Prince. In 1506 Machiavelli was despatched to Rome to treat with Pope Julius II and, in the following two years, undertook missions to the court of the Holy Roman Emperor, Maximilian. In November 1512 the Medicis returned to power in Florence and ousted Piero Sonderini, Machiavelli's mentor, later executing him. Machiavelli himself was arrested, tortured and obliged to retire to his estates outside Florence where, between 1513 and his death in 1527, he produced most of the works by which he is remembered, including *The Prince, The Art of War, The Discourses* and *The History of Florence*.

Machiavelli's reputation rests primarily on *The Prince*. The book addresses the question of what values and attributes a modern prince needs to be a successful ruler. What made the book controversial, and has made Machiavelli's name a byword for deviousness and expediency ever since, was Machiavelli's clear-eyed acknowledgement that some virtues in private life might be a disadvantage in public life and that some 'vices' might well be essential to a successful ruler's survival.

The Art of War contains ideas that are essential to an understanding of some of the central pillars of Machiavelli's political theory. His interest in military affairs was a practical one – he could see no reason for establishing civil institutions without first guaranteeing their protection. Thus he came to view the relationship between politics and warfare as a fundamental one in both theory and reality. Machiavelli's ideas about the interrelationship, almost the unity, of politics and warfare appealed to many later military thinkers, including Napoleon and Clausewitz.

Although he wielded no great political power himself, Machiavelli's career as a diplomat allowed him to observe the major figures of his day at first-hand and his knowledge of history enabled him to compare them with the heroes and villains of the past. He was able to see how Cesare Borgia dealt with power and relate that to the portraits of the great figures of the classical past in, for example, Plutarch's *Parallel*

'Men never do anything good except out of necessity.'

Lives. Past and present combined to provide the framework in which Machiavelli's theories could evolve.

Machiavelli's idea was that, by creating a government modelled upon the ancients, his contemporaries could enjoy a measure of free will, no longer reliant upon divine providence and blind fortune, the twin gods of the medieval era. Yet, throughout his works Machiavelli shows himself to be a man of his times and familiar with many of the radically new theories of the period and with the humanist arguments of writers and scholars like Pico della Mirandola and Leon Battista Alberti.

In the five centuries since his death Machiavelli has continued to resist easy interpretation. To some he has been the first true political scientist; to others he has been nothing but an advocate of tyranny. In this century, in his own native country, he has been admired by Benito Mussolini for his advice to statesmen and by Antonio Gramsci, the Italian communist leader and major Marxist theorist, who praised Machiavelli's Prince as the perfect model for the political party. Rather than debate Machiavelli's alleged amorality, perhaps one should emphasise his realism. By synthesising his knowledge of classical literature with his own practical experience of Italian politics in a period of great upheaval, he came up with a work unlike any previously published. That it still speaks to, and asks questions of, people caught up in political struggles very different to those of Renaissance Italy is an indication of how far Machiavelli transcended the particular and articulated the general in politics. He will continue to be read by politicians and those endeavouring to understand them well into the new millennium.

STEPHEN GEORGE, *Waterstone's Chichester*

WRITINGS BY MACHIAVELLI

The Discourses
Penguin pbk £8.99
0140444289

The most readily available edition, edited and with an introduction by the political philosopher Bernard Crick.

Discourses on Livy
Oxford UP pbk £8.99
0192829459

The Prince
Penguin pbk £2.99
0140447520

The Prince
Oxford UP pbk £2.99
0192833979

WRITINGS ON MACHIAVELLI

Skinner, Quentin
Machiavelli
Oxford UP £5.99
0192875167

Viroli, Maurizio
Machiavelli
Oxford UP £12.99
0198780893

One in a series Founders of Modern Political and Social Thought.

Curry and Zarate
Introducing Machiavelli
Icon pbk £8.99
1840461160
(Due February 2000)

Sir Thomas

# MORE	1516

Utopia

More was a Londoner, the son of a judge, and was educated at Oxford before himself training as a lawyer at Lincoln's Inn and Furnival's Inn. His worldly career was interrupted by a period when he retired to Charterhouse to spend his time in prayer and devotion but, by 1504, he had entered parliament and taken the path which was to lead him to power and, eventually, to the scaffold. Under the patronage of Wolsey, More held a number of offices of state, including speaker of the House of Commons, and was sent on diplomatic missions abroad. When Wolsey fell from grace in 1529, More succeeded him as Lord Chancellor and held the post for three years. He retired to private life but Henry VIII's divorce and his declaration that he, not the Pope, was the head of the English church brought More inexorably into conflict with the king. More's refusal to recognise any head of the church other than the Pope led to imprisonment and, in 1535, he was executed. Four hundred years later he was canonised.

In addition to his political attainments, More was at the heart of Renaissance humanism in England. He was a friend of men like John Colet and Thomas Linacre who were instrumental in introducing the new learning of the continent to this country. Most importantly he was a friend of the great humanist Erasmus, played host to him when the Dutch scholar visited England and was the instigator of Erasmus's most famous work *The Praise of Folly*

(*Encomium Moriae* in Latin). More wrote and published on a wide variety of topics, from church polemics to a history of Richard III, but *Utopia* (1516), first published in Latin in an edition overseen by Erasmus, remains his most influential literary work. Drawing on the narratives of travels to the New World which were just beginning to appear, More creates a fable in which he is able to examine the possibilities for a government and state radically different from any in existence. In Antwerp More meets Raphael Hythloday, the traveller who has spent time in Utopia ('No-Place'). Hythloday describes a land where property is held in common, where education is available to both men and women and where religious toleration is practised. Implicit in the description of Utopia are criticisms of contemporary England but More is a master of irony and the extent to which he is holding up Utopia's institutions for unquestioning praise is endlessly debatable.

More coined the word 'Utopia' and, although there had been such writings before (Plato's Republic describes an ideal commonwealth), his work can be seen as the impetus behind a long tradition of utopian (and dystopian) writing, which has had a significant impact on the politics of Europe in the last five hundred years. (In some sense, for instance, Marx and Engels's *Communist Manifesto* could be seen as an example of Utopian writing.) The tradition continues to this day. From Bacon's *New*

> *'Utopus that conquered it . . . brought the rude and uncivilized inhabitants into such a good government, and to that measure of politeness, that they now far excel the rest of mankind.'*

Atlantis to Orwell's *Nineteen Eighty Four*, from Edward Bellamy's *Looking Backward* to Samuel Butler's *Erewhon*, this tradition owes its principal debt to Thomas More.

WRITINGS BY MORE

Utopia
Penguin pbk £5.99
0140441654

Utopia
Cambridge UP pbk £6.95
0521347971

One of the Cambridge Texts in the History of Political Thought.

Utopia
W.W. Norton pbk £6.95
0393961451

One of the valuably annotated Norton Critical Editions, this also includes brief extracts from modern utopias/dystopias such as *Brave New World*.

Utopia
Yale UP pbk £8.00
0300002386

This edition is based on the text taken from the standard Yale edition of the Complete Works of Thomas More which is published in a multi-volumed hardback edition by Yale University Press.

WRITINGS ON MORE

Ackroyd, Peter
The Life and Times of Thomas More
Vintage pbk £8.99
0749386401

Kenny, Anthony
Thomas More
Oxford UP pbk £5.99
0192875736

Marius, Richard
Thomas More
Orion pbk £14.99
0753807041

Martin

LUTHER   1520

On the Babylonish Captivity of the Church

Born in 1483, Luther, like many of his contemporaries, entered a monastery as a young man. After several years, and a period at the University of Erfurt, he was ordained as a priest. In 1508 he began lecturing on scripture at the University of Wittenberg. Appointed as Professor of Theology in 1512, Martin Luther came to public attention in 1517 when he nailed his 95 Theses to the door of Wittenberg church.

As a young monk, and as a student at Erfurt, Luther had immersed himself in the teachings of late medieval Catholicism. The Church taught freewill, that the individual achieved salvation through his or her own works; acts of charity, pilgrimage, confession, and dietary observances were all seen as paths to grace. Luther, driven by fear of God, slavishly observed monastic ritual but found no comfort in doing so. His dilemma was the inherent sinfulness of Man. If Man is tainted by original sin, then his works, however well intended, must likewise be tainted and how can such works be pleasing to God? In Luther's mind, the Catholic doctrine presented Man with an unachievable task.

Luther found the answer to his dilemma whilst lecturing on Scripture – 'The just shall live by faith' (Romans 1:17). Salvation is achieved through faith, a gift freely bestowed by God. The individual plays no part in the process and thus is freed from the burden of works. Luther's 95 Theses were a theological attack on the sale

of indulgences by the Dominicans. To Luther, it was obscene to hold that the Church could sell the grace of Christ to the individual Christian.

Rome was slow to react to a doctrinal spat provoked by an obscure provincial academic. Luther was summoned to Rome but after political bargaining between the Pope and the Elector Frederick, it was agreed that the German priest would debate matters with the orthodox theologian Johannes Eck. The two met at Augsburg in 1519. Luther was pushed into sympathising with the heretical ideas of Huss and Wycliff, and into doubting the authority of the Pope. That was a challenge Rome could not ignore and in 1520 a papal bull was issued condemning Luther. He burnt it, publicly.

Initially at least, the humanists lent support to Luther's cause. Some, like Philip Melancthon, actively supported Luther's doctrinal challenge. Others, notably Erasmus, were sympathetic towards his calls for reform. Luther's growing fame helped to secure the support of his patron, the Elector Frederick of Saxony. Wittenberg University was the Elector's and he was keen to protect Saxony's pre-eminent thinker.

In 1520-21 Luther published three tracts, including *On the Babylonish Captivity of the Church*, which set the agenda for the Lutheran Reformation. The Catholic Church was Babylon – Rome had enslaved the true

'I am more afraid of my own heart than of the Pope and all his cardinals. I have within me the great Pope, Self.'

Christian message. Luther proclaimed a priesthood of all believers; there was no longer a hierarchical Church with the layman at the bottom. The life of a blacksmith was holier than that of a monk. Scripture, containing God's promise to man, was to be accessible to all, that is, printed in native tongue rather than Latin. *On Christian Liberty* emphatically spelled out Luther's doctrine of salvation through faith alone. God's grace, freely given, liberates the Christian. That is how the individual achieves salvation. The seven sacraments were reduced to two: baptism and communion. All other observances were meaningless ritual. Pilgrimages, mendicancy, indulgences, confession, prayers for the dead, essentially hundreds of years of religious practice, were suddenly proclaimed redundant.

Wisely, Luther directed his calls for reform to the princes, Germany's ruling elite. They had the power to challenge the worldly might of the papacy and free the Christian faith from its Babylonish captivity. Certainly, the princes had much to gain from so liberating the Church. The Pope was an influential figure in European politics and temporal rulers begrudged Rome's perceived interferences. Perhaps more importantly, the Catholic Church had money and land ripe for the taking.

Concerned by the upheaval in the German principalities, the Emperor Charles V convened the Diet of Worms in 1521. The princes attended and Luther was summoned to appear before the Emperor. It was demanded that he renounce his beliefs. Famously, Luther refused. Condemned by Charles V, Luther was 'kidnapped' on his return from Worms. Those who seized him were agents of Frederick; the Elector had arranged it all for Luther's protection. The reformer was to spend many months hiding under the protection of Frederick while the political controversy raged.

The mutual support between the princes and Luther was furthered by the Peasants' War of 1525-26. German peasants, angered by economic conditions and fuelled by Luther's apparently libertarian message, rose up against their political masters. Luther raged against them and fully supported the savagery with which the uprising was suppressed. His message of freedom was restricted to the spiritual. In the temporal world, the accepted social hierarchy was vital to maintaining good Christian order. In that sense, there was nothing revolutionary about Lutheranism (the Protestants who were to later depose and decapitate kings were followers of Calvin).

1525 also saw Luther publicly savage Erasmus over the issue of predestination. Erasmus too had spent many years railing against the abuses of the Church. Unconcerned with theological differences and viewing tolerance as a prime Christian virtue, Erasmus had earlier called for moderation in Rome's dealings with Luther. However, he recognised that Luther's teachings were the re-emergence of the doctrine of predestination. If God bestows grace on some and not on others, he condemns the latter to Hell. Erasmus could not accept that. In 1524 Erasmus published *On Freewill* to which Luther replied with *On the Bondage of the Will*. Luther began by congratulating Erasmus on having identified the

essence of Luther's ideas. The pleasantries concluded, he proceeded to savage Easmus with the kind of vitriolic polemic of which he was a master. Lutheranism had overtaken Christian Humanism as the leading reforming movement.

The German princes divided between Catholic and Lutheran. The late 1520s saw the Emperor convene several Diets in attempts to solve the increasingly heated split. In 1529 the minority Lutherans protested at the actions of the Catholic princes. Protestantism came into being. The Augsburg Confession, the definitive doctrinal statement of Lutheranism, was drafted in 1530 (largely by Melancthon). There was to be no conciliation. A new faith had emerged and divided the German states.

The political, economic and religious forces of the time would undoubtedly have coalesced to make some kind of anti-papal reformation inevitable, even had Luther not existed to wrestle with his spiritual doubts and concerns. That said, the individual cannot be overlooked. The Reformation would not have taken the particular form it did if it had not been for the force of his character. The man who, at the Diet of Worms in 1521, was challenged by the most powerful man in Western Europe and replied, 'Here I stand, I can do no other', was the man who shaped the Protestant Reformation like no other.

CLAIRE MILBURN, *Waterstone's*

WRITINGS BY LUTHER

Luther and Calvin on Secular Authority
Cambridge UP pbk £9.95
0521349869

One of the Cambridge Texts in the History of Political Thought.

WRITINGS ON LUTHER

Greengrass, Mark
The Longman Companion to the European Reformation
Addison Wesley Longman
pbk £16.50
0582061741

Reardon, Bernard
Religious Thought in the Reformation
Addison Wesley Longman
pbk £18.99
0582259592

Francois

RABELAIS | 1534–53

Gargantua and Pantagruel

Francois Rabelais, whose great five-book satire about two giants, Gargantua and Pantagruel, is awash with wine, private parts and bodily functions, has been known as 'the clowning Homer' ever since his death in 1553. He is the king of buffoons, a kind of literary Falstaff (albeit one with a coarser sense of humour) who was in constant danger of the stake. Voltaire's feeling that Rabelais was 'a drunken philosopher who wrote only when he was intoxicated' has often been the prevailing attitude towards him. Yet Balzac thought that Rabelais was 'the greatest mind in modern humanity', who had almost single-handedly created modern French literature, a view supported, at various times, by Flaubert, Victor Hugo and Anatole France. In the English-speaking world he has had admirers in Laurence Sterne, Jonathan Swift and James Joyce.

Rabelais was born to a middle-class, land-owning family near Chinon in about the year 1494. He was denied any part of the family's wealth after becoming a Franciscan in the 1520s. While in the monastery he got into trouble for stocking the library with classical authors and was granted a dispensation to leave the order for the more liberal Benedictines. Rabelais was keenly aware of the new learning and the development of humanism and, from the start of his career, was an enthusiastic promoter of both.

His spell with the Benedictines was brief and he may have gone on to study law for a time. It was in this period of his life that he produced his first literary work. *An Epistle to Bouchet* was a bad poem in reply to a bad poet. After it Rabelais would reserve his verse-writing skills, such as they were, for the songs and nonsense rhymes of his epic. In the autumn of 1530 Rabelais enrolled as a medical student in Montpellier and it was here that he began to emerge as a great and original writer.

Pantagruel, whose eponymous hero is the demon of thirst from medieval mystery plays, was inspired by the great drought of 1532 and first appeared on bookstands that autumn at the Lyon Fair. In an attempt to protect himself, Rabelais published under the pseudonym of 'the late Alcofribas, Abstractor of Quintessence.' The ploy failed, and Rabelais was to find himself on the run intermittently for the rest of his life, usually from charges of obscenity and sacrilege.

The romance details the birth and upbringing of Pantagruel who journeys to Paris where, in the course of his studies, he meets his foil, Panurge. Panurge is a great trickster figure, able to get out of any jam, adept in causing trouble. His name, from the Greek, means 'good at everything.' Pantagruel and Panurge have a series of adventures in Paris. In what is almost a foreshadowing of Kafka, Pantagruel

'In their rules there was only this one clause: Do what you will.'

has to decide a nonsensical dispute between two lords, Kissarse and Suckpoop; Panurge, after a heavy night, debates with an English philosopher entirely in a kind of semaphore; he devises a (somewhat eyebrow-raising) method of rebuilding the city walls; and, when he is spurned in love, Panurge's revenge is to get every dog in Paris to cock its leg on the unfortunate lady.

Rabelais constantly addresses issues that are both topical and timeless. In the later part of *Pantagruel* (what we now know as *Book Second*) and *Book Fourth* (published 1552), the hero and his companions journey in search of Utopia. These chapters provide Rabelais with a canvas on which to paint a picture of a world opening up, excited by the discoveries of explorers such as Cartier, a world which the New Learning of the Renaissance was ready to master. *Book Third* (published 1546) addresses itself to 'the woman question', in the guise of whether Panurge should marry or not. In dealing with sexual equality, Rabelais mercilessly sends up male fear of female power. Panurge spends almost the entire book worrying about being cuckolded, and seeks counsel from all manner of quacks, experts and dignitaries.

Pantagruel, the demon of thirst, also personifies the thirst for knowledge and serves as a mouthpiece for his creator's humanist leanings and encyclopedic learning. *Gargantua and Pantagruel* as a whole is rich in classical allusions. Rabelais seems to have the whole literature of ancient Greece and Rome in his head. He also shows an acute understanding of the economic factors that drive society. Sir Gaster's attempt to protect his supply of grain

in *Book Fourth* identifies hunger as the root of all human activity; worried that someone else may steal his grain, he invents warfare to protect it. Elsewhere, Rabelais identifies the difference between wars of aggression and wars of defence, such as the war against the cakesellers. Several passages also deal with his views on the ethical treatment of prisoners of war (the cake sellers again and the aftermath of the Dipsodes' attack on Utopia). Rabelais is also an acute social observer. In describing the nuns of Thélème, he shows his precise knowledge of the female toilette and of fashion. His plans for the Abbey itself are architecturally accurate, from which models have been constructed.

It is the *Gargantua*, published in 1534, that most clearly embodies Rabelais the writer and thinker. The book, the opening of the romance (although the second to be written) gives us the biography of Pantagruel's father, Gargantua. After being born from his mother's ear, shouting, 'Give me a drink! Give me a drink!', the young Gargantua's intellectual capacities are soon noticed. He discovers that a goose's neck is ideal for wiping his bottom on and his father is so impressed that he decides to send the boy to be educated. Gargantua is despatched to Paris where he steals the bells from Notre Dame and urinates on the Parisians who have gathered in the street below to watch. His new teacher, Ponocrates, is horrified and turns the belching, farting, drinking young Gargantua into the very model of a Renaissance giant by means of a magical potion. This provides Rabelais with the chance to expand upon Gargantua's letter to his son in *Book Second*, and to deliver his most extensive treatise on education and self-improvement. Mind and body should be equally developed and constantly stimulated. Learning, he implies, never ends.

The turning point in the narrative comes when Gargantua learns that shepherds in his homeland have become involved in a quarrel with some intinerant cake sellers (based on a real incident in Rabelais' hometown). This escalates into a bloody conflict and Gargantua returns home to fight the cake sellers. To his aid comes the fighting (and drinking) friar, John Hackem, who is worried that, if the abbey vineyards are destroyed, they won't be able to drink for a whole year. The cake sellers are defeated and Gargantua, wanting to reward Friar John for his help, offers to make him an abbot. Friar John replies that he would rather found his own abbey and the book ends with one of Rabelais' most celebrated passages, the establishment of the Abbey of Thélème.

The theme of utopia runs throughout the work. Perhaps Rabelais, the curate doctor, so frequently in trouble with the authorities, is trying urgently to communicate his dreams and hopes, or what he has himself experienced in private epiphanies, before his persecutors manage to silence him. The Abbey of Thélème is Rabelais' own utopia where men and women live together in harmony, and a spirit of peace and learning prevail. The abbey's famous motto, 'Do What Thou Wouldst' has been misconstrued as a license for indulgence (most notably by Aleister Crowley who named his temple in Sicily after Rabelais' visionary abbey) but its essential message is that, in the ideal community, individuals' wishes will coincide with what God wishes for them.

SEAN MARTIN

WRITINGS BY RABELAIS

**The Complete Works of
Francois Rabelais**
University of California Press hbk
£65.00
0520064003

**The Histories of Gargantua
and Pantagruel**
Penguin pbk £8.99
014044047X

This is the translation by J.M. Cohen that has been in print since the 1950s. A new Penguin translation by the eminent scholar M.A. Screech is due in autumn 2000.

Nicolaus

COPERNICUS 1543

On the Revolutions of Heavenly Spheres

One of the great revolutions in human thought, in which the perceived centre of the universe was transferred from the earth to the sun, was instituted by the Polish astronomer and mathematician Nicolaus Copernicus. Copernicus was born at Torun in Poland, probably of mixed Slav and German parentage, and, in 1491, went to study at the University of Cracow. Further study took place at prestigious Italian universities such as Bologna and Padua, where Copernicus learned the medical skills he was to use when he returned to his native land. Officially employed as a canon in the cathedral chapter of Frombork (Frauenburg), he was also personal physician to the Bishop, his maternal uncle and found time to devote to the study of the heavens. After the death of his uncle in 1513, Copernicus remained at Frombork where he was deeply involved in both the government of the city and his developing heliocentric theory. A full account of the theory was slow to take shape and *De Revolutionibus Orbium Coelestium (On the Revolutions of Heavenly Spheres)* was not published until the year of his death. Indeed legend has it that he received a finished copy of the book, printed in Nuremberg, only on his deathbed.

The geocentric theory of the universe, to which ancient and medieval astronomers subscribed, traced its roots back to the second century AD and the Alexandrian, Ptolemy. Ptolemy devised an extraordinarily complex system to reconcile anomalies like the temporary retrograde motion of Mars, Jupiter and Saturn (they appear at times to stop and move backwards before resuming a forward motion) with the idea that the earth was the centre around which the planets moved. In a paradigmatic leap forward, Copernicus realised that the system was enormously simplified if the sun were seen as the centre of motion rather than the earth. Retrograde motion could be explained by differences in relative speeds of the planets. It may look as if the stars move around the earth but a spinning earth would produce the same result. Copernicus's own model of the universe (a circular, sun-centred one) was not particularly accurate but his willingness to ignore the geocentric orthodoxy pointed the way for those, such as Kepler, Galileo and, eventually, Newton, who refined the new view of the universe.

'If there should chance to be any mathematicians who, ignorant in mathematics yet pretending to skill in that science, should dare, upon the authority of Scripture wrested to their purpose, to condemn and censure my hypothesis, I value them not and scorn their inconsiderate judgement.'

WRITINGS BY COPERNICUS

**On the Revolutions of
Heavenly Spheres**
Prometheus Books pbk £7.50
1573920355

WRITINGS ON COPERNICUS

Koyre, Alexandre
The Astronomical Revolution
Dover pbk £10.95
0486270955

Michel de

MONTAIGNE 1595

Essays

Born into a wealthy family in Périgord, Montaigne attended the Collège de Guyenne in Bordeaux and then studied law, probably in Toulouse. In his twenties, having spent some time in Paris, he returned to Bordeaux where he was active in the local *parlement* and produced his first literary work, a translation of the *Theologia Naturalis* written by a professor at Toulouse, Raymond of Sebond. (It was this 15th century professor who was to provide the starting point for the longest of Montaigne's essays, often published separately, the *Apologie de Raymond Sebond*.) In 1571 Montaigne's father died and he inherited the family estates where, until his death, he led the life of a cultured country gentleman. Apart from a period as mayor of Bordeaux and travels to Paris, Germany and Italy, he spent his days in study and in the writing of the essays for which he is remembered. An edition was first published in 1580 and subsequent editions included further essays. The posthumous edition of 1595 was the first definitive edition of all the essays.

Montaigne was not, in any sense, a systematic philosopher. Indeed his choice of the form his essays took reflects a distrust of formal philosophy and a belief in the powers of allusion, anecdote and aphorism to illuminate problems and questions which other writers felt obliged to consider more systematically. Montaigne embodies a particular form of Renaissance scepticism ('there is a plague on man, the opinion that he knows something') which emphasised the limitations and pretensions of man in order to maintain more certainly the need for the wisdom of God. He also embodied a burgeoning Renaissance belief in the importance of the individual as the source of knowledge about mankind in general. Montaigne's relentless self-scrutiny, his examination of his own opinions, habits, reading, springs not from self-obsession but from a belief that his own nature will throw light on human nature. As he wrote, 'I have never seen a greater monster or miracle than myself.' Finally Montaigne embodied a Renaissance in which the narrow horizons of earlier periods were broadening under the impact of new learning, new inventions, discoveries of new lands and new peoples. Steeped in the (often re-discovered) classical learning, Montaigne seized upon the new as a means of opening perspectives on the world about him and as further confirmation of the provisional nature of man's knowledge of that world. As the inventor of the modern essay form and as an exemplar of the best of Renaissance humanism, Montaigne will continue to be read.

*'Man is certainly stark mad; he cannot make a worm,
and yet he will be making gods by dozens.'*

WRITINGS BY MONTAIGNE

Montaigne
The Complete Essays
Penguin pbk £14.99
0140446044

Montaigne
The Essays : A Selection
Penguin pbk £7.99
0140446028

The most famous translation of
Montaigne into English is the
seventeenth century version by
John Florio, from which
Shakespeare drew quotations in
several of his plays. However this
is not currently available. The two
editions of the essays published
by Penguin are in a modern
translation by M.A. Screech, a
leading scholar of European
humanism who has also written
widely on Erasmus, Rabelais and
other major figures of the time.

WRITINGS ON MONTAIGNE

Through the centuries many
people have found stimulus in
reading Montaigne. Two creative
writers who have left essays on
Montaigne still worth reading are
Hazlitt (to be found in *Selected
Writings* Penguin pbk £7.99
0140430504) and Ralph Waldo
Emerson (*Selected Essays* Penguin
pbk £7.99 0140390138)

Miguel de
CERVANTES 1605–15
Don Quixote

As Shakespeare is the world's most famous author, so Don Quixote is its most famous character. His legacy in the arts of Western Europe is vast and unfathomable; in Spain the novel occupies a position in the national literature that defies translation into an English equivalent. Its concerns stretch back to the twelfth century and prefigure those of the twentieth century. It is difficult to imagine its influence diminishing while the novel remains the predominant literary form.

The Adventures of Don Quixote was an immediate success on its first appearance in 1604 and several pirate editions swiftly followed. The author, Miguel de Cervantes Saavedra, had struggled to make ends meet for most of his adult life – as a soldier, civil servant and, finally, as a writer. His only previous novel *La Galatea*, together with a number of plays, had been poorly received. His work for the state had led to a temporary excommunication after a dispute over some church-owned corn. His career as a soldier had been cut short after his capture by pirates, an unfortunate event that led to nearly half a decade as a slave in Algiers. Poverty and prison were steadfast companions until the tales of the Knight of the Sad Countenance and his squire, Sancho Panza, brought him fame in his sixth decade. Such was Quixote's appeal that, by 1614, the year the second part of the novel appeared, the first had already been translated into French and

English, and his fellow Spanish writer Avellaneda had tried to cash in with his own sequel. Cervantes's response was his own continuation of the story.

The tremendous success of the first part is easy to understand. There is violent farce in which Sancho frequently receives a pummelling as the price for the service he gives in expectation that he will be rewarded with the governorship of an island. Meanwhile Quixote's own madness, brought about by his obsession with tales of knight errants ('these writings drove the poor knight out of his wits'), provide fantastical comedy. He is transformed into a poor fool who mistakes windmills for giants and flocks of sheep for armies. The heroic stories that had so affected him had already had a long history. In the twelfth century Arthurian legend and French courtly love had combined to produce a potent form – the chivalric tale. From the pens of Beroul, von Eschenbach, von Strassburg and, most famously, Chretien de Troyes, a string of tales centred on knights who fought monsters and wizards, knights who rescued fair maidens, swept through Europe. Chivalric fantasy survives to this day; Cervantes's parody was even more pertinent in his day. A little after the rise of the chivalric myth, another genre that became a major target of Cervantes's satire arrived : the Pastoral Romance. Drawing on the bucolic themes of certain classical authors (particularly

Theocritus and Virgil) a host of idyllic tales of lovelorn shepherds and their rustic pleasures achieved the equivalence of best-seller status. Cervantes targets these tales too.

As entertaining as the humour is, *Don Quixote* owes it greatness to the complexity of its two central characters. Initially the reader laughs cruelly at them, the lunatic and his buffoon, the knight unable to tell reality from fantasy, the credulous squire blindly following his master's lead. And yet gradually, imperceptibly, he or she comes to acknowledge the pair's humanity. Sancho Panza comes to seem less foolish. His loyalty to, and love for, his master has a generosity that dwarfs the petty concerns of the world through which they move. And Quixote's madness becomes a unique and glorious struggle on behalf of the freedom of the imagination and the individual. We laugh at their predicament, assure ourselves of the impossibility of their success and yet we remain committed to their cause.

At the end of the first part the forces of the mundane world have triumphed. The Barber and the Priest, seen at the beginning of the novel burning Quixote's library, have forced his adventure to an end. Yet the fear that the second part might not live up to the standard of the first is swiftly dismissed. If anything the story is richer, fantasy rather than burlesque. Sancho finally gets his governorship but gives it up. There is the episode of the puppet show, the saga of the enchanted head, the battle with the Knight of the Moon and the mysterious descent into the Cave of Montesinos. The humour is subtler, the pace less hectic. We are treated to the extraordinary adventure at the Inn where Quixote overhears a discussion on the relative merits of the first and second parts of *Don Quixote de la Mancha*. It becomes one of the great literary celebrations of life and literature. Inevitably the two return home and the book ends with Quixote's moving death.

Don Quixote transcends the parody and the picaresque tradition which gave birth to it. It is one of the cornerstones of modern European culture. More than a century was to pass before English literature, with *Tom Jones* and the radical playfulness of *Tristram Shandy*, could reach similar heights. In Spanish literature its influence is all-pervasive; it represents the father with which each new literary generation must contend. Borges wrote the tale of Pierre Menard, the man who wrote *Don Quixote* a second time. Its impact on the great Miguel de Unamuno was such that he himself felt compelled to re-write it. In twentieth century media its influence continues. Orson Welles struggled for years to realise a film version of it. It seems likely that what began as parody of a medieval literary genre will continue to inspire writers, artists and film-makers well into another millennium.

MIKE PAINE, *Waterstone's Hampstead*

'I imagine that everything is as I say it is, neither more or less, and I paint her in my imagination the way I want her to be.'

WRITINGS BY CERVANTES

Don Quixote
Norton pbk £13.50
0393315096

Don Quixote de la Mancha
Oxford UP pbk £7.99
0192834835

Johannes

KEPLER   1619

Harmonices Mundi

Kepler was born into a Lutheran family in Württemberg in what was then the Holy Roman Empire and won a scholarship to study at the University of Tübingen. It was while he was there that he was introduced to the helio-centric ideas of Copernicus and, although they remained a matter of deep controversy amongst astronomers, he accepted them almost immediately. Moving to Graz as a teacher of mathematics, he wrote *Mysterium Cosmographicum* (1596), a defence of the Copernican view of the universe in which he also outlined his own ideas about what governed the orbits of the five planets then known. As a Lutheran, Kepler was subject to the ebb and flow of religious antagonisms of the time and, in 1600, it became necessary for him to leave Graz. He moved to Prague to work with the renowned Danish astronomer Tycho Brahe, who was employed by the Emperor Rudolf II. Brahe died the following year and Kepler inherited both his position as Imperial Mathematician and the tables of astronomical data that Brahe had painstakingly compiled over many years.

In 1609 he published *Astronomia Nova* in which he laid out the first two of what came to be known as Kepler's Laws of Planetary Motion. These stated that planets moved in ellipses rather than circles, as Copernicus had believed and that planets move faster as they near the sun. His third law (that the time of each planet's revolution around the sun is propor-tional to its distance from the sun) was published in 1619 in a work called *Harmonices Mundi* (*Harmonies of the World*).

By then the religious upheavals of the time had caught up with Kepler again and he had moved to Linz where he published his most influential work, a kind of survey of contem-porary astronomy from a Copernican and Keplerian perspective. Kepler's last major work was the *Rudolphine Tables*, tables of planetary motion which refined even further the calcula-tions he had used in formulating his laws. He died in 1630. Kepler's importance lies in the way he took the basic insights of Copernicus about a sun-centred universe and gave them a revised but surer foundation in empirical observations. His laws and ideas were the groundwork upon which Newton was eventually to build his model of the universe and have been described as 'the starting point of modern astronomy.'

'The diversity of the phenomena of nature is so great, and the treasures hidden in the heavens so rich, precisely in order that the human mind shall never be lacking in fresh nourishment.'

WRITINGS BY KEPLER

The Epitome of Copernican Astronomy/Harmonies of the World
Prometheus pbk £7.50
1573920363

WRITINGS ON KEPLER

Caspar, Max
Kepler
Dover pbk £11.95
0486676056

The best biography currently available

Koestler, Arthur
The Sleepwalkers
Penguin pbk £11.99
0140192468

Koestler's history of man's changing vision of the universe, from antiquity to Newton, includes a lucid summary of Kepler's life and work as well as interesting material on Copernicus and Galileo.

Francis
BACON   1620

Novum Organum

Bacon was born into the ruling echelon of Elizabethan society. His father was Sir Nicholas Bacon, lord keeper to the Queen and his mother was the sister-in-law of the chief minister Lord Burghley. Bacon himself, after education at Cambridge and Gray's Inn, entered parliament in 1584 and much of his career was spent in the pursuit of worldly power. Appointed solicitor-general in 1607 and attorney-general in 1613, he reached the top of the greasy pole when James I made him Lord Chancellor in 1618. In 1621, having been made Viscount St. Albans earlier in the year, disaster and disgrace struck Bacon. Charged with accepting bribes as a judge, he was sentenced by the House of Lords to a massive fine, imprisonment in the Tower (he spent only a few days there), disqualification from parliament and exclusion from the heart of power, the court. Bacon spent the last five years of his life out of the public eye, at work on his philosophical projects and on his writings.

'I have taken,' Bacon once wrote in a letter, 'all knowledge to be my province.' He was not making some hubristic and ludicrous claim that he was planning to learn everything there was to know but was stating his intention of constructing a method by which knowledge could be organised and used for the benefit of mankind. Although his best known works today are his elegantly constructed essays, the major undertaking of his life was *The Great Instauration*, a never-to-be-completed project intended to embody his aim of taking all knowledge as his province. The first part of this project was published in the first decade of the seventeenth century as *The Advancement of Learning*, a book in which Bacon carefully discriminated between the genuine sciences and the pseudo-learning of charlatans and then created an elaborate overview and classification of those genuine sciences. (In the 1620s Bacon was to produce a much expanded version of this work, written in Latin.) *Novum Organum* was published in 1620 as the second part of the 'great instauration'. In this book Bacon first looks at 'the idols and false notions which are now in possession of the human understanding' before establishing his own method of enquiry. His version of inductive thinking (the procedure by which he felt that general laws and principles could be derived from a large number of particular instances) has been enormously influential. The development of scientific method in the later seventeenth and early eighteenth centuries owed an explicit debt to Bacon and his vision of a carefully systematised knowledge put to the service of mankind is, in various forms, with us still.

'A little philosophy inclineth man's mind to atheism, but depth in philosophy bringeth men's minds about to religion.'

WRITINGS BY BACON

Essays
Penguin pbk £8.99
0140432167

The Essays or Counsels Civil and Moral
Oxford UP pbk £8.99
0192838024

Francis Bacon
Oxford UP pbk £14.95
0192820257

This collection of Bacon's writings, in the Oxford Authors series, includes all his major works in English – The New Atlantis, The Essays and The Advancement of Learning.

Routledge publish a twelve-volume hardback set of Bacon's Collected Works.

WRITINGS ON BACON

Zagorin,Perez
Francis Bacon
Princeton University Press
hbk £19.95
0691059284

GALILEO GALILEI 1632

Dialogue Concerning Two Greatest World Systems

The son of a musician and mathematician, Galileo was born in Pisa and studied medicine at the university in his home town. His real interests, however, lay in mathematics, astronomy and the pioneering scientific experiments for which he is remembered. In 1592 he was appointed professor of mathematics at the University of Padua, a post he held for eighteen years before settling in Florence as mathematician and natural philosopher attached to the court of the Grand Duke of Tuscany. The range of Galileo's intellectual pursuits and achievements is extraordinary. While in his twenties he proved the falseness of Aristotelian ideas about falling bodies (the rate of descent was not, contrary to accepted opinion, proportional to weight), although the story that he did this by dropping objects from the Leaning Tower of Pisa is probably just that – a story. In the first decade of the 17th century Galileo heard about optical instruments that had been built in the Netherlands and, based on the Dutch work, he devised his own series of telescopes. The observations he made through these – mountain ranges on the moon, satellites circling Jupiter – were startling revelations to his contemporaries.

To Galileo they were further proof of the Copernican, heliocentric view of the universe which he had secretly held for some time. As early as 1616 he was warned that Copernican beliefs were deemed by the Church to be anti-Scriptural and therefore heretical but it was not until 1632 and the publication of his *Dialogue Concerning the Two Greatest World Systems* that Galileo openly flouted Church authority on the subject. Summoned to Rome and forced to recant his views Galileo, by this time a sick man, spent the last ten years of his life under a kind of house arrest at his villa near Florence. The story that, after renouncing the Copernican idea of the earth's motion before the Inquisition, Galileo whispered 'Eppur si muove' ('But it does move') is almost certainly apocryphal.

'In questions of science the authority of a thousand is not worth the humble reasoning of a single individual.'

WRITINGS BY GALILEO

Galileo on the World Systems
University of California P. pbk
£15.95
0520206460

WRITINGS ON GALILEO

Cambridge Companion to Galileo
Cambridge UP pbk £14.95
0521588413

Drake, Stillman
Galileo
Oxford UP pbk £5.99
0192875264

Sobel, Dava
Galileo's Daughter
Fourth Estate hbk £16.99
1857028619

Dava Sobel's book traces the extraordinary relationship between Galileo and his illegitimate daughter, Virginia, who entered a convent under the name of Suor Maria Celeste.

René

DESCARTES 1641

Meditations on First Philosophy

René Descartes is one of those people who stand at pivotal points of intellectual history and both reflect and define those pivotal moments. Descartes may not be a household name in this country but his thought and achievements have affected every child who has ever puzzled over a graph and every scientist who has ever puzzled over the existence of the external world. Born at La Haye near Tours in 1596, Descartes was educated by the then newly formed Jesuit order. The first signs of the religious conflagration that was to become the Thirty Years War had appeared in Europe. Descartes remained a devout Catholic throughout his life but it was his search for certainty in a world riven with doubt about the true path that was to shape and drive his intellectual work.

The young Descartes enlisted first in the Dutch and then the Bavarian armies and fought at the Battle of the White Mountain in 1620, a battle which effectively ended the counter-reformation in Bohemia. It was during this time that Descartes began to assemble the elements of his philosophy. The story goes that during the winter of 1620 Descartes took refuge from the cold by sitting in an oven. During the day he spent there, he meditated and emerged with one of the great philosophical systems forming in his mind.

In 1621 Descartes retired from the army and,

after a period of travel in Europe, settled in seclusion in Holland. While Descartes's devotion to the church was firm, its devotion to him, given his sympathy with Galileo, whose heliocentric theories it denounced, was far less certain. Descartes abandoned publication of his work *Le Monde (The World)* because of Galileo's condemnation by the church in 1633. However, Holland at the time was a place where a man of Descartes's intellectual stature could work in relative security and he remained there for twenty years.

Descartes's work during this period was extraordinarily wide-ranging. He was aware of Harvey's work on the circulation of the blood and added many important physiological observations of his own. He believed bodies to be simply complex machines subject to the laws of physics operating within a mechanistic universe, a direct link with Newton's concept of the clockwork universe. The mind is a thing totally distinct from this universe as thought is not extended in space and time. The mind acts as the 'Ghost in the Machine' that interacts with the physical world but is not reducible to it. Descartes made significant contributions in geometry introducing the field of co-ordinate geometry and defining the graph as we now it.

Descartes's greatest contribution to the history of ideas is his radical re-foundation of epistemology (the theory of knowledge). The debate

'The first precept was never to accept a thing as true until I knew it as such without a single doubt.'

that Descartes set in motion has changed in terminology and thrown up many new avenues of inquiry and argument in the three and a half centuries since he first articulated it but in essence the problems keep the character that he ascribed to them. The central text upon which Descartes built his philosophy is the *Meditations on First Philosophy* first published in 1641. The book is astonishing not just for the breadth and implication of its ideas but also for its accessibility. (The book is still a central part of the French high school curriculum.)

The book is divided into six meditations which concern themselves with the general questions- What do I know for certain? How do I know that it is certain? Descartes sets about answering this by calling into question all his beliefs and subjecting them to the test of hyperbolic doubt. As Descartes puts it: 'Reason now leads me to think that I should hold back my assent from opinions which are not completely certain and indubitable just as carefully as I do from those which are patently false. So, for the purpose of rejecting all my opinions, it will be enough if I find in each of them at least some reason for doubt . . . I will go straight for the basic principles on which all of my former beliefs rested.' (First Meditation)

Descartes's system of doubt, he thought, would lead him, in the end, to the most basic foundation upon which knowledge could be built. Can he, at least, be sure that the waking world is any more certain than the dreaming world? Not at all. Perhaps, he conjectures, there is a malicious demon that constantly deceives him as to the nature of the world around him, that the objects he sees and hears and feels are merely apparitions caused by the machinations of this evil demon. In imagining the possibility of such a demon Descartes realises that it is possible that the world revealed to him through his senses is uncertain. If it is uncertain then the senses cannot be a basis for the certainty Descartes is endeavouring to establish. Having discounted the senses he must look elsewhere for certainty and finds it in thought. I think therefore I am (*Cogito ergo sum*) is the fundamental certainty for which he is looking. He cannot doubt that he thinks, therefore he cannot doubt that he exists. Descartes has found a foundation for knowledge based upon reflection alone, a foundation he has deduced from first principles rather than gained from doubtful observation of the sensory world. We can imagine, and indeed witness every day, how our senses can deceive us but we cannot imagine how something deduced from a set of first principles such as a mathematical principle could be false. I may be colour blind so the picture in front of me may not be blue at all, but could I really imagine 2 plus 2 equalling 5? The fact that there must be something which imagines in order for me to hold the sentence in my mind necessitates, for Descartes, a certainty on a par with mathematics.

The course that Descartes takes marks out a schism that has plagued philosophy ever since; the argument between the primacy of knowledge gained by empirical experience and that gained by deduction from first principles. The Britons John Locke, George Berkeley and, particularly, David Hume were to champion Empiricism while the continentals Leibniz and Spinoza continued and developed Descartes's Rationalist scheme. The argument did not stop there. Throughout the subsequent history of philosophy the argument has mutated frequently and strayed into new areas, for instance the philosophy of language and quantum mechanics. In essence the problem is this. Does the world exist if we are not here to perceive it? In a new incarnation this is the problem that has haunted discussions of quantum theory this century by physicists and thinkers like Heisenberg and Schrödinger. Descartes drew the battle lines between those who wanted to ground knowledge outside of human experience and those who felt there could be no other place for human knowledge to originate.

In 1649 Descartes was appointed tutor to Queen Christina of Sweden, who liked to have her lessons at 5 am. The harsh climate and early rising took their toll on Descartes who died in 1650. On its way back to France, Descartes's body suffered from the attentions of relic hunters who believed that it would be little time before this devout Catholic thinker was canonised (Ironically his works were banned by the Papal index). Descartes has not been canonised in the 350 years since his death but his influence on the Western philosophical tradition has been incalculable and he fully deserves the title of 'the Father of Modern Philosophy'.

NOEL MURPHY, *Waterstone's*

WRITINGS BY DESCARTES

Discourse on Method and Meditations on First Philosophy
Yale UP pbk £10.95
0300067739

One of a series called Rethinking the Western Tradition this is a scholarly edition of Descartes' two best known works, intended to provoke students to a reassessment of the nature of his philosophical achievements.

Discourse on Method and Related Writings
Penguin pbk £7.99
0140446990

Meditations and Other Metaphysical Writings
Penguin pbk £7.99
0140447016

WRITINGS ON DESCARTES

Cambridge Companion to Descartes
Cambridge UP pbk £17.95
0521366968

Williams, Bernard
Descartes
Penguin pbk £9.99
0140138404

Sorell, Tom
Descartes
Oxford UP pbk £5.99
019287635X

One of the Past Masters series.

Cottingham, John (ed)
Descartes
Oxford UP pbk £11.99
0198751826

One of the collections of essays published in the series Oxford Readings in Philosophy.

Wilson, Margaret Dauler
Descartes
Routledge pbk £14.99
0415065763

Gaukroger, Stephen
Descartes: An Intellectual Biography
Oxford UP pbk £15.99
0198237243

Cottingham, John
A Descartes Dictionary
Blackwell pbk £13.99
0631185380

Robinson & Garratt
Introducing Descartes
Icon pbk £8.99
1840460636

Thomas

HOBBES   1651

Leviathan

Thomas Hobbes was born in Malmesbury (allegedly, his mother was so shocked by the news of the Spanish Armada heading for England's shores that she gave birth to him prematurely) and entered Magdalen Hall, Oxford when he was 14. While still in his teens he began what was to be a long employment as a tutor with the Cavendish family which introduced him to many of the great men of the day (including Francis Bacon) and enabled him to travel on the Continent. On his second trip abroad in the 1630s he met both Descartes and Galileo. The turmoil of mid-seventeenth century England affected both Hobbes's life and his writings. In 1640 the first stirrings of Parliamentary revolt persuaded Hobbes that he should leave England and six years later he was appointed mathematics tutor to the Prince of Wales, later Charles II, at the English court in exile at Paris. In 1652 he returned to England, made submission to the Council of State and was allowed to settle in London. The rest of his long life was taken up by voluminous and varied writings and by a series of intellectual quarrels and controversies.

Leviathan, which the twentieth century philosopher Michael Oakeshott has described as 'the greatest, perhaps the sole, masterpiece of political philosophy in the English language', was published in 1651. That it was written at a time of civil strife and disputed sovereignty is apparent from even a cursory reading. The first part of the book gives a vivid account of how men lived before the advent of the state. In this state of nature all men are blindly and ruthlessly pursuing their own, selfish ends and the result is the anarchy and warfare described in the book's most famous lines. 'No arts; no letters; no society; and which is worst of all, continual fear and danger of violent death; and the life of man, solitary, poor, nasty, brutish, and short.' In the second part of *Leviathan*, Hobbes outlines the means by which men can escape this fate, by entering into a contract 'to confer all their power and strength upon one man, or upon one assembly of men.' Thus is sovereign power created and, once created, it is indivisible. It cannot be shared (and here the influence of contemporary events is clear) between a king and a parliament. Nor can religious claims take precedence. In Hobbes's commonwealth church is clearly subordinate to state. (Much of the last two parts of his book is given over to a discussion of religion and to attacks on the Catholic church.) The sovereign power has its own responsibilities and can be defied if it fails to protect the individual from that state of warring anarchy which provided the stimulus for its original creation. At the time of its first publication *Leviathan* managed to offend both royalist and parliamentary sensibilities but it has long been recognised as an extraordinarily bold and imaginative attempt to establish the study of politics as a method of enquiry analogous to the newly emerging sciences of the seventeenth century.

'I put for a general inclination of mankind, a perpetual and restless desire of power after power, that ceaseth only in death.'

WRITINGS BY HOBBES

Leviathan
Penguin pbk £6.99
0140431950

Leviathan
Oxford UP pbk £6.99
0192834983

Leviathan
Norton pbk £6.95
0393967980

Leviathan
Cambridge UP pbk £7.95
0521567971

Cambridge Texts in the History of Political Thought

On the Citizen
Cambridge UP pbk £12.95
0521437806

Cambridge Texts in the History of Political Thought

Oxford publish a two-volume edition of Hobbes's correspondence in paperback at £19.95 per volume (0198237472 and 0198237480).

Routledge publish a twelve-volume Collected English Works by Hobbes in hardback.

WRITINGS ON HOBBES

Cambridge Companion to Hobbes
Cambridge UP pbk £14.95
0521422442

Tuck, Richard
Hobbes
Oxford UP pbk £5.99
0192876686

One of the Oxford Past Masters series.

Martinich, A.
A Hobbes Dictionary
Blackwell pbk £18.99
063119262X

Blaise

PASCAL 1669

Pensées

Blaise Pascal's reputation was initially founded upon his precocious ability as a mathematician. Taught by his father – an enthusiast for the subject – he first appeared in print at the age of sixteen in 1640 with an essay on conic sections. By 1654 he was producing groundbreaking work on probability theory, ideas that surfaced in his correspondence with Fermat and in his *Traité du triangle arithmetique*. His genius, however, was such that no one subject could contain it. In the period between those two publications he also invented one of the earliest calculating machines and, as a physicist, was conducting experiments into the nature of a vacuum.

Pascal's scientific fame spread beyond his own country (Wren was another correspondent) yet his posthumous success is almost entirely due to his work in another field altogether. His family's strong religious involvement with Jansenism – an Augustinian movement proclaiming the all-importance of grace as the way to salvation – dates from the 1640s. Pascal's faith wavered at times until the event of the night of the 23rd November 1654 – an occasion that was literally to stay with him for the rest of his life. For some hours, Pascal experienced an epiphanic revelation of God, an understanding that established his faculties of reason, his previous discoveries, as knowledge of a lesser order. His aphoristic description of what happened, 'The Memorial', was found on parchment sewn into his clothing after his death.

The first fruits of this conversion appeared in response to the threats to the Jansenist cause from the Jesuits. The *Lettres Provinciales* were the first works to gain recognition for his literary and polemical gifts and were later to be admired for their skill even by enlightenment figures like Voltaire who had no time for the cause they supported. They met with much success and popularity at the time as well as attracting the attentions of the Catholic Church which placed them on the Index of Prohibited Books and decreed that they should be publicly burned.

Pascal's achievements from now on were overshadowed by increasing and ultimately terminal ill-health. His last years were occupied by what was to be a grand apologia for the version of Christianity in which he believed, a systematic defence and encouragement of faith. It was never fully realised. Instead the fragments, the notes towards this work were published after his death as the *Pensées* to immediate and enduring acclaim. In a series of 'digressions upon each point which relates to the end' Pascal describes what is, in effect, an existential universe but for the presence of God – 'the blind and wretched state of man.' Mankind seeks to fill the long days of boredom with empty diversions: 'we prefer the hunt to the capture.' Creatures of profound contradiction, humans are simultaneously wretched and great, partaking of both an animal

'We know the truth, not only by the reason, but also by the heart.'

existence and a heavenly potential. This is the condition of both beggar and king alike. God is infinite and thus we can only know him through faith, the order of the heart, rather than reason, the order of the mind. Reason does have a minor role, alongside the prophecies and proofs of the Bible and the traditions of the Church which lead us towards His presence. In Pascal's famous Wager, it is reason that tells us that to bet on the existence of God is a gamble that can lose us nothing and may yet win us everything. Pascal uses biblical exegesis, political and sacred history, moral and economic conditions; he relies on our desire for a true understanding of our circumstances and our need for happiness.

The fragmentary nature of the *Pensées* contributes to its pleasures and problems. Its gnomic quality resists easy interpretation in places. The arrangement of the manuscripts led to controversies over its organisation which were not resolved to even general agreement among scholars until the 1950s. Yet its structure is perhaps more beguiling in our century, which gave birth to the oblique works of, for example, Wittgenstein and Edmond Jabès. The increasing secularisation of society in the course of the century may have robbed the *Pensées* of much of the intense religious meaning Pascal originally invested them but they will continue to be read for their insights into the human condition, their elegance of thought and expression and their considerable rhetorical power.

MIKE PAINE, *Waterstone's Hampstead*

WRITINGS BY PASCAL

Pensées
Penguin pbk £7.99
0140446451

Baruch
SPINOZA   1677
Ethics

Spinoza's family were, in origin, Portuguese Marranos (Jews who had pretended conversion to Christianity but secretly maintained their Jewish faith) and his father had emigrated to Amsterdam. It was there that Spinoza was born and it was there that he grew up, his father now a successful merchant. After the death of his parents, he continued to run the family business but his position in the synagogue was undermined by his heterodox opinions and his interest in the more advanced speculations of contemporary astronomers and philosophers. In 1656 he was formally expelled from the synagogue and, long interested in optics, began to earn his living by grinding and polishing lenses. After some years spent associated with a religious and philosophical sect near Leiden, Spinoza moved to The Hague where he worked on both *Tractatus Theologico-Politicus*, which made his name when it was published in 1670 and *Ethica*, published posthumously and now his best known work. He died in Amsterdam at the age of 44 from pulmonary consumption brought on by the glass dust he had inhaled in his work as a lens grinder.

Spinoza, like Descartes before him, was a rationalist who believed that reason alone, rather than the potential delusions of experience, would lead to the truth. (The truths to which reason led Spinoza may often seem fantastic to the modern mind but he remains a rationalist.) Like Descartes again Spinoza put his trust in a mathematical method of reasoning and even his *Ethics* uses forms (axioms, theorems etc.) drawn from mathematics. *Ethics* is divided into five parts: 'On God', 'On the Nature and Origin of the Mind', 'On the Nature and Origin of the Emotions', 'On Human Bondage' and 'On Human Liberty.' Spinoza defines God as the one necessary being and the unique substance outside of which no other substance can be given or even conceived. God or Nature (*deus sive natura*) is the one reality and everything in the world is a part of that Divine Reality however much it may seem to be a separate substance. (Clearly this is a long way from orthodox belief and Spinoza's ideas were thought by many contemporaries to be next door to atheism.) Man's passage from bondage to liberty depends on the recognition that everything is a necessary mode of a divine attribute. Man's bondage is an enslavement to emotions and desires and the only recourse is to transform these into actions. Finally, when it is recognised that 'all bodily affections are referred to God', emotion and desire are transformed into an action that is 'the intellectual love of God.'

'I have taken great care not to laugh at human actions, not to weep at them, nor to hate them, but to understand them.'

WRITINGS BY SPINOZA

Ethics
Penguin pbk £6.99
0140435719

Ethics
Everyman pbk £5.99
0460873474

Two paperback editions of Spinoza's best-known work, each equipped with notes and introduction.

A Theologico-Political Treatise
Dover pbk £9.95
0486202496

On the Improvement of the Understanding
Dover pbk £8.95
048620250X

The publishers Dover perform a useful service by keeping in print two of Spinoza's other treatises. *The Theologico-Political Treatise*, one of only two books Spinoza published in his lifetime, is, with its controversial advocacy of religious tolerance, a particularly significant work.

The Spinoza Reader
Princeton UP pbk £13.75
0691000670

This selection from Spinoza's writings includes the Ethics in full and excerpts from other treatises.

WRITINGS ON SPINOZA

Nadler, Steven
Spinoza: A Life
Cambridge UP hbk £22.95
0521552109

Gullan-Whur, E.
Within Reason: A Life of Spinoza
Pimlico pbk £12.50
0712666524

The last couple of years has seen two biographies of Spinoza published. The book by Steven Nadler is much more at home with the intricacies of Spinoza's thought but Elizabeth Gullan-Whur's *Within Reason* presents a livelier portrait of the man, more accessible to the general reader.

Cambridge Companion to Spinoza
Cambridge UP pbk £15.95
0521398657

Roger Scruton has published two short introductions to Spinoza. *Spinoza* (Oxford UP pbk £5.99 0192876309) is one of the excellent Past Masters series and has been in print for many years. *Spinoza* (Phoenix pbk £2.00 0753802139) is one of a newer series called *The Great Philosophers* which are very inexpensive but also very brief indeed (80 pages).

Gottfried

LEIBNIZ | 1686

Discourse on Metaphysics

Leibniz was born, the son of a university professor, in Leipzig and grew up to be one of the most wide-ranging intellectuals of his, or indeed any, age. He spent much of his adult life working as councillor, diplomat and librarian attached to the court at Hanover but he found time to undertake work in fields as diverse as geology and historiography, mathematics and engineeering, as well as his philosophical writings. In addition he entered into lengthy correspondence with all the leading intellectuals of his day. Much of his writing was unpublished in his lifetime. Indeed some of it remains unpublished. During his lifetime he was best known as a mathematician and was embroiled in an infamous quarrel with Newton over who first developed the calculus. (It seems likely that Newton discovered the foundations of calculus first but that Leibniz did so independently and was the first to publish his findings.)

Like Spinoza and Descartes, Leibniz was a rationalist who believed that reason rather than experience provided the road to truth. Throughout his life he believed that the principles of reasoning could be formulated as a symbolic system, a kind of logical calculus which would mean that controversies could be resolved by means of calculation. Leibniz thought deeply about all the fundamental questions of philosophy and constructed an elaborate, often bizarre, philosophical system based on a small number of general principles. The basis of the system is the monad, the extensionless, mental entities which, Leibniz thought, were the true substances of the world, combinations of which create the material objects in it. The collections of monads called men are knowable in their entirety only to God. For each individual there is a complete notion, to which only God has access and from which the history of that individual, in all its moments, can be deduced. God necessarily creates the individual that fulfils that notion. Leibniz's system is complex and notoriously opaque and subject to the kind of ridicule that Voltaire heaped on his idea of 'the best of all possible worlds' but his, alongside those of Descartes and Spinoza, is the third great system of seventeenth century rationalism.

'The knowledge of eternal and necessary truths is that which distinguishes us from mere animals and gives us reason and the sciences, thus raising us to a knowledge of ourselves and of God.'

WRITINGS BY LEIBNIZ

Philosophical Writings
Everyman pbk £5.99
0460875469

A selection of Leibniz's writings intended for student use which also includes an introduction, notes and selected criticism.

Philosophical Texts
Oxford UP pbk £7.99
0198751532

Another useful selection for students, this includes major works by Leibniz, from the *Discourse on Metaphysics* from 1686 to *Monadology* of 1714.

New Essays on Human Understanding
Cambridge UP pbk £15.95
0521576601

This is a study of John Locke's *Essay Concerning Human Understanding* in which Leibniz analyses and argues with Locke's views on such topics as knowledge and personal identity. Leibniz refrained from publishing it when he heard of Locke's death in 1704.

Political Writings
Cambridge UP pbk £14.95
052135899X

The Leibniz-Clarke Correspondence
Manchester UP pbk £11.99
0719006694

In this correspondence, published here with brief excerpts from Newton's writings, Leibniz criticised many of Newton's ideas and what he saw as their implications. Newtonian ideas were defended by Samuel Clarke, the English rationalist philosopher and theologian.

WRITINGS ON LEIBNIZ

Cambridge Companion to Leibniz
Cambridge UP pbk £16.95
0521367697

Ross, George MacDonald
Leibniz
Oxford UP pbk £5.99
0192876201

One of the Past Masters series of brief introductions to great philosophers and thinkers.

Rutherford, D.
Leibniz and the Rational Order of Nature
Cambridge UP pbk £15.95
0521597374

Russell, Bertrand
The Philosophy of Leibniz
Routledge pbk £16.99
041508296X

Sir Isaac

NEWTON 1687

The Principia

Isaac Newton was born near Grantham in Lincolnshire, studied at Trinity College, Cambridge, and went on to make discoveries in the natural sciences and develop ideas in mathematics that mark a turning point in Western thought. Most famously (and, according to legend, following a train of thought initiated by observing an apple fall from a tree) Newton discovered that all material objects in the universe are affected by the force of gravity. As early as 1666 Newton had elaborated the form of mathematics known as calculus but did not publish his work. (This led to the argument over precedence between Newton and the German mathematician and polymath Gottfried Leibniz who had arrived independently at the same mathematical ideas.) Newton was also interested in optics and the theory of colours and, surprising to us if not his contemporaries, devoted a great deal of energy to researches into alchemy and mystical exegeses of the Bible. Particularly later in his life Newton was public figure as well as private scientist. He was elected one of the MPs for Cambridge University in the aftermath of the Glorious Revolution, was made Master of the Royal Mint and was President of the Royal Society from 1703 until his death.

It is almost impossible to overestimate the impact of Newton's work. To contemporaries and to the generations which immediately followed him, he seemed to have elucidated, finally and comprehensively, the laws which governed the universe. To David Hume he was 'the greatest and rarest genius that ever arose for the ornament and instruction of the species.' Soon after his death Pope wrote:

Nature and Nature's Laws lay hid in Night
God said, Let Newton be! And all was Light!

Newton completed the revolution begun by Copernicus and developed by Kepler and Galileo, and he provided the mathematical and theoretical support for Descartes' dualistic view of mind and matter. By doing so he ushered in the modern era. The mechanistic model of the universe, which the law of gravitation and his three laws of motion unveiled, was to underpin all thinking about the physical world until Einstein.

Despite the work of Kepler and Galileo and others who followed, the riddle of planetary motion still confronted scientists in the second half of the seventeenth century. Other scientists, such as Robert Hooke, had sensed the possibility that there was an attractive force acting between all material bodies, whether celestial or terrestrial, but it was Newton who was able to give mathematical form to this. He was able to establish gravitation as a universal force which worked both to cause the fall of an apple to earth from a tree and to explain the

'Whence is it that Nature does nothing in vain: and whence arises all that order and beauty which we see in the world?'

orbits of the planets around the sun. Newton also proposed three laws of motion:

1) *Everything preserves its motion in a straight line unless it is deflected from that course by a force.*

2) *The rate at which a body travels is in proportion to the force applied to it.*

3) *To every action there is an equal and opposite reaction.*

He appeared to have formulated a few, fundamental laws which were able to explain all known phenomena in terrestrial and celestial mechanics. Reality and the means by which God, the Great Watchmaker, had created it, had been revealed through human intelligence and reason.

WRITINGS BY NEWTON

The Principia
University of California P. pbk
£24.95
0520088174

Writings
Norton pbk £7.95
0393959023

The Norton Critical Edition of a selection of Newton's writings.

WRITINGS ON NEWTON

Hall, Rupert
Isaac Newton: Adventurer in Thought
Cambridge UP pbk £14.95
052156669X

White, Michael
Isaac Newton: The Last Sorcerer
Fourth Estate pbk £8.99
185702706X

Maury, Jean-Pierre
Newton
Thames & Hudson pbk £6.95
0500300232

Rankin, W.
Newton for Beginners
Icon pbk £8.99
1874166072

Speyer, Edward
Six Roads from Newton
Wiley pbk £17.99
0471305030

This accessible science title outlines Newton's ideas and then shows how six discoveries in physics have their roots in those ideas.

John

LOCKE   1690

An Essay Concerning Human Understanding

The work of John Locke is both an important contribution to the history of ideas and a major influence on the political history of the world in the last three centuries. His work has been vastly influential on two fronts: firstly in forming the Empiricist vanguard against the ideas of the Rationalist Descartes and thereby setting in train the dominant strain of philosophy in the English speaking world. Secondly, his political writings established Liberalism as a political credo and were the foundations on which later, for example, the United States and its Constitution were to be established.

Born in 1632, the son of a parliamentarian lawyer, Locke's early life was dominated by the tumultuous politics of his day as the country he knew as a child descended first into the Civil War and then passed through Cromwell's dictatorship into the Restoration of the monarchy. All through his education at Westminster and Oxford he could not help but be affected by the polarised political society around him as it swung from monarchy to military dictatorship and back again. Locke's powerful sense of reason must have driven him to seek a more stable form of government and to actively work towards it. In 1667 he joined the household of the Earl of Shaftesbury, a parliamentary opponent of Charles II, as his personal physician. His wider role as adviser to the Earl on political issues led to his voluntary exile when his patron was tried for treason in

1681. Locke followed Shaftesbury with many other English dissidents to the tolerant atmosphere of the Netherlands in 1683.

It was while in Holland that the nascent threads of his empiricist epistemology came together to form his magnum opus, *An Essay Concerning Human Understanding* which was published in 1690. The main thesis of Locke's Essay is diametrically opposed to that of Descartes. Locke does not seek to deduce knowledge from first principles but considers what ways it is possible for human beings to know anything about the world around them. In this way he tries to ascertain the limits as to what can reasonably be understood about the external world by taking an observational, empirical approach.

Locke's methodology is wonderfully straightforward. He asks himself the question: How do I experience the world? At its simplest Locke's project is to look into his own mind and see what's there. As he puts it: 'I shall not at present meddle with the physical consideration of the mind; or trouble myself to examine wherein its essence consists. It shall suffice to my present purpose to consider the discerning faculties of a man as they are employed about the objects which they have to do with. And I shall imagine I have not wholly mis-employed myself in the thoughts I shall have on this occasion, if in this historical, plain method, I can give any account of the ways whereby our understanding come to attain those notions of the things we have and can set down any measures of the certainty of our knowledge'. *(Essay, Book One-Of Innate Notions.)*

Locke conducts an audit of the contents of his own consciousness and terms those contents Ideas (a slightly misleading terminology). By this he means both internal phenomena (feelings, memories etc.) and external ones (colours, textures, temperatures). Locke gives a primacy to the latter such that these external ideas are considered the building blocks of consciousness. As we grow our minds learn first to register the ideas of texture and colour and slowly formulate these by association into more complex forms or collections of ideas that make up things. We might see a brown colour, feel a hard texture and by association and experience we will develop the complex idea of a table. For Locke such Ideas are the only interface between the external world and the human mind. Of course, as Descartes pointed out, our mind, in the shape of dreams or delusions can deceive us but without trusting in knowledge through experience we can never break out of the shell of our minds. Unlike Descartes, Locke's project did not take as its starting point a desire for certainty but rather he sought to build a picture of the functionality of the mind.

Locke believed that the mind was a *tabula rasa*, a blank sheet of paper upon which experience impressed itself. This idea permeates not only his epistemology but also his ideas on education and, importantly, his political philosophy. The idea clearly lends itself to the liberal notion of equality. Man was created

into a state of nature, a notion he shared with Hobbes. Yet, whereas for Hobbes, humans left to the state of nature will live nasty, brutish and short lives, Locke believed in the essentially noble nature of human reason. Men in the state of nature will band together voluntarily for support, helping each other for common purposes but retaining control over their own destinies and, most importantly, over their natural rights. Government should exist only by consent of the individuals governed and should seek only to defend the rights of those governed to life, liberty and property.

Locke formulated a theory of property in his *Two Treatises of Government* (1690), which was one the most controversial and original pieces of political writing ever produced and still retains its relevance today. Locke's belief was that labour invested in land, assuming there is enough land of similar quality around for others, constituted a right to that land. Having a right to land also gives one the right to dispose of it in whatever way the owner sees fit. The 'labour theory of value' provided a basis for the rise of liberal capitalism and began a debate over who has rights over what. This debate, at the core of political philosophy, is what connects Locke with Marx, with historical events like the Scramble for Africa and with contemporary debates about subjects as diverse as multi-national conglomerates and the rights of the aboriginal peoples of Australia.

French Enlightenment thinkers like Voltaire adopted and adapted Locke's ideas so that they had a major influence in the French Revolution. The framers of the American Constitution were even more impressed by Locke's conception of the liberal 'small

'No man's knowledge here can go beyond his experience.'

government' state, something which has become part of the American national psyche. In his own country Locke's influence has been no less great. His attack on the divine right of kings in the *First Treatise* led to his active involvement in the Glorious Revolution of 1688 and the formulation of a more 'constitutional' monarchy and parliamentary process. Locke died a distinguished man, but the impact of his work was only just beginning. Locke's position as one of the founders of the Enlightenment gives him an unassailable place in European cultural history and in the wider history of the global body politic his thought helped to create.

NOEL MURPHY, *Waterstone's*

WRITINGS BY LOCKE

Essay Concerning Human Understanding
Oxford UP pbk £15.99
0198245955

A paperback edition of one of the volumes in the Clarendon Edition of the Works of John Locke. The other volumes, which include all Locke's known writings in a scholarly edition, are only available in hardback at £55.00 and £70.00 per volume.

Essay Concerning Human Understanding
Penguin pbk £9.99
0140434828

An edition for students, complete with notes and an introduction by Roger Woolhouse.

Two Treatises on Government
Cambridge UP pbk £7.95
0521357306

One of the invaluable Cambridge Texts in the History of Political Thought.

Political Writings
Penguin pbk £8.99
0140433104

WRITINGS ON LOCKE

Cambridge Companion to Locke
Cambridge UP pbk £16.95
0521387728

Dunn, John
Locke
Oxford UP pbk £5.99
0192875604

This volume is one of the
Past Masters series of brief introductions to great philosophers
and thinkers.

Chappell, Vere
Locke
Oxford UP pbk £11.99
0198751974

This volume in the series Oxford
Readings in Philosophy brings
together fifteen articles by
contemporary scholars on topics
and problems in Locke's philosophical writings, particularly *An
Essay Concerning Human
Understanding.*

Jolley, Nicholas
Locke: His Philosophical Thought
Oxford UP pbk £12.99
0198752008

A general introduction to
Locke's thought.

Ayers, Michael
Locke
Routledge pbk £17.99
0415100305

One of Routledge's wide-ranging
and illuminating Arguments of
the Philosophers series. Ayers has
also written the brief introduction to Locke in the Phoenix
Great Philosophers series (pbk
£2.00 0753801957).

George

BERKELEY | 1710

A Treatise Concerning the Principles of Human Knowledge

Berkeley was born in Kilkenny and attended Trinity College, Dublin of which he became a fellow in 1707. His philosophy, much of it formulated in opposition to the prevailing ideas of Locke, was expounded in three works all published while he was still in his twenties. *An Essay Towards a New Theory of Vision* was published in 1709 and was followed in 1710 by *A Treatise Concerning the Principles of Human Knowledge*. In 1713 Berkeley moved to England where he came to know leading literary and intellectual figures like Pope, Addison and Steele and published *Three Dialogues Betweeen Hylas and Philonous*. The rest of Berkeley's life, apart from travels abroad and a curious interlude when he went to America as part of an unsuccessful attempt to establish a missionary college, was spent in the church. He was appointed Dean of Derry in 1724 and Bishop of Cloyne ten years later. He died in Oxford in 1753.

Berkeley was the leading exponent of philosophical 'idealism'. He developed his ideas in critical response to the dominant trends in late seventeenth and early eighteenth century thought, trends which Berkeley believed led towards a materialism and determinism that would necessarily undermine religion and morality. Locke's view of the world as a gigantic Machine, with God relegated to the role of designer and prime mover of a mechanistic universe, Berkeley found intolerable. Locke's view that there were no such things as innate ideas and that ideas were only created by the mind's interaction with material substances in the external world, he felt to be logically inconsistent. Berkeley's solution to the questions posed by Locke and others was a radical one. He denied the existence of matter altogether. Everything we see in the external world, all objects out there, are, in truth, ideas or collections of ideas existing only in minds, either in those of individual, fallible men and women or in the all-encompassing mind of God. As long as these objects 'are not actually perceived by me, or do not exist in my mind or that of any other created spirit they must either have no existence at all, or else subsist in the mind of some eternal spirit.' Berkeley's view of developing scientific method was, necessarily given his other views, a sceptical one. Out of step with most of his contemporaries, he can now be seen, curiously, to foreshadow some twentieth century philosophies of science. Scientific theories could not be seen as true in any absolute sense but they could be viewed as useful fictions which, when they were treated as if they were true, provided, within limits, information about the observed world. That world's only ultimately true existence, however, lay in the minds of the observers.

'All the choir of heaven and furniture of earth – in a word, all those bodies which compose the mighty frame of the world – have not any subsistence without a mind.'

WRITINGS BY BERKELEY

Philosophical Works
Everyman pbk £6.99
0460873431

Principles of Human Knowledge and Three Dialogues
Oxford UP pbk £6.99
0192835491

Principles of Human Knowledge and Three Dialogues
Penguin pbk £6.99
0140432930

Three Dialogues Between Hylas and Philonous
Oxford UP pbk £6.99
0198751494

A Treatise Concerning the Principles of Human Knowledge
Oxford UP pbk £6.99
0198751613

WRITINGS ON BERKELEY

Berman, David
Berkeley
Phoenix pbk £2.00
0753801949

Cambridge Companion to Berkeley
Cambridge UP pbk £16.95
0521456576

Giambattista

VICO

1725

The New Science

Unrecognised outside his native Naples until his death in 1744, Giambattista Vico and his *New Science* remain unjustly neglected, more often quoted than read. Figures as diverse as James Joyce, Karl Marx, Matthew Arnold, Ernst Cassirer and Isaiah Berlin have all hailed Vico as a prophetic father-figure. Perhaps it is precisely this breadth of appeal that has contributed to his obscurity in an age of specialists. Yet Vico's explorations of mythology, poetics, anthropology, jurisprudence, historiography and etymology, revolutionary in themselves, fuse in his masterwork into a challenge to the Cartesian tradition more vital to us than ever before as we struggle to extricate ourselves from the darker practical and philosophical consequences of the scientific revolution.

It seems fitting that the man who taught us to read in Homer's myths the secrets of civilization's genesis should have wrapped his own origins and those of his masterpiece in fable. In his *Autobiography*, having first unaccountably mistaken the year of his birth, Vico attributes both his genius and his irritable temperament to a near-fatal tumble from the top of a ladder at the age of seven. The first printing of *The New Science* he paid for himself through the sale of a ring, an appropriate source of funding for a work in which he expounded the cyclical theory of history which has become the best-known, if not the most valuable, of his ideas.

Born, in fact, in 1668 to a Neapolitan bookseller, Vico's professional life was full of disappointments. Having studied law, his future looked promising when, at the age of eighteen, he successfully defended his father in court. Yet the unorthodox originality of his writings and his lack of political nous left him ill-equipped for success as an academic, and he remained a poorly-paid professor of rhetoric for most of his career.

Like many of his contemporaries, the young Vico was seduced by the new Cartesian philosophy. However he quickly became disillusioned with the assimilation of all knowledge into physical and mathematical models. With an insight one commentator has described as being so revolutionary that full justice could scarcely be done to it until the logicians of our own century transformed conceptions of mathematical reasoning, Vico claimed that formal sciences such as geometry and logic are indeed irrefutable but that this is precisely because they are the creations of our own minds. A creator can understand her creation as an outsider cannot. Thus the natural world necessarily retains an opaqueness in the face of human investigation.

To fully know a thing, he argued, it is not enough to have a clear and distinct idea of its attributes. One must know why it has these qualities, how it came to be as it is, must know it from the inside and identify with it. Influenced by scholastic philosophy's claim that to know is to become what is known, Vico opposed the paucity of the new epistemology with this concept of knowledge *'per causas'* (through causes).

Concluding that since man makes his own history and culture, this is his proper subject of study, Vico embarked on his most ambitious project of all. Ironically it was the conclusive frustration of his academic aspirations (his failure at the age of fifty five to win the prestigious and profitable 'first morning chair of law') that propelled him towards his greatest achievement. Freed from professional ambitions by his disillusionment at losing the competition to a plagiarist with a taste for serving girls, he abandoned academic Latin for his native Italian and relinquished the juridical emphasis of his Universal Law to pursue its deeper, broader, less neatly categorisable implications.

The 'master key' of his science was the discovery that our earliest ancestors were not, as Locke had implied, simply modern men in primitive settings but were irrational giants of the senses, poets of monstrous imagination who made themselves the measure of all things. How did the rational world of the scientific revolution emerge from these irrational beginnings? The originality, significance and daring of this attempt to expose and explore the historicity of not only the supposedly universal truths his age was discovering, but also that of the rational tools it was using to make those discoveries, remain astonishing.

Vico's sense of how humanity's need to comprehend and survive the world transforms both that world and humanity itself made him peculiarly sensitive to historical and cultural differences. Ancient myths he saw not as deliberately allegorical or as twisted descriptions of particular events but as examples of early 'poetic logic' in which were to be found the histories of customs. Hercules, for example, was the embodiment of great labours performed under the demands of family necessities, an archetype in which were subsumed all those noted for such endeavours. Myths were the creations of whole peoples rather than of individuals. Vico was amongst the first to argue that 'the Homeric epics were composed and revised by several hands in several ages', and the power of the masses, rather than the elites, to mould cultures is emphasised throughout the *New Science*.

Vico applied his historicist perspective not only to myth but also to ancient law, religion and language to reveal an 'ideal eternal history' which each nation traversed through time. The explorations and archaeologies of the sixteenth and seventeenth centuries had revealed startling parallels in the patterns of development of diverse societies. Each nation had its own Jove and, as the ancients themselves had done, modern scholars bickered over which civilization could claim to be the oldest, the original which others had imitated.

'If philosophy is to benefit human kind, it must raise and support us as frail and fallen beings, rather than strip us of our nature and abandon us in our corruption.'

Vico rejected this 'conceit of nations' which he saw as equivalent to the 'conceit of scholars' who evaluated other ages and peoples by criteria of their own. Through his ingenious, occasionally erroneous, interpretations of legends, etymologies and laws Vico delineated a necessary cycle through which divine providence, by means of the poetic nature of humanity, propelled each nation individually. The age of gods was followed by the age of heroes which in turn gave way to the age of men. Each age displayed certain linguistic, political and philosophical characteristics. Ultimately the final, democratic age would fall into decadence and collapse, initiating a *ricorso* to the start of the cycle.

The figure of Vico looms large over the philosophy of Hegel and the historical materialism of Marx. He also had a grasp of individual psychology that prompted Joyce to remark that Vico had anticipated Freud. Ultimately it is as the serious philosopher of fantasia, of the cultural and personal significance of the imagination, that Vico remains an exciting thinker to read today.

PATRICK HART,
Waterstone's Charing Cross Road

WRITINGS BY VICO

The New Science
Penguin pbk £9.99
0140435697

The most readily available edition of Vico's most significant and influential work. Cornell University Press also publish an edition (pbk £21.99 0801492653) and keep in print editions of some of Vico's lesser works.

WRITINGS ON VICO

Lilla, Mark
Vico: The Making of an Anti-Modern
Harvard UP pbk £12.50
0674339630

David

HUME   1748

Enquiry Concerning Human Understanding

Of all the empiricist philosophers it is David Hume who had, arguably, the finest philosophical mind. Hume's friendships with other figures of the Scottish enlightenment like Adam Smith and Henry Home made Edinburgh one of the centres of intellectual thought at the time. His popularity abroad with writers and thinkers like Voltaire and Jean Jacques Rousseau (another friend) eventually made him part of, and an influence on, the wider culture of the European Enlightenment.

Although Hume began his philosophical pursuits early in life, publishing his early masterpiece *A Treatise of Human Nature* at the age of 28, it was not until relatively late (and in the case of his religious philosophy posthumously) that his work reached a wide audience. *The Treatise* was published in two instalments (1739/1740) and was received as Hume put it 'Dead born from the press'. Undeterred, he pushed forward with its sceptical empiricism and produced two further volumes that he hoped might popularise his theories: *An Enquiry Concerning Human Understanding* (1748) and *An Enquiry Concerning the Principles of Morals* (1751).

Hume improved upon his forebears Locke and Berkeley by taking their empiricism to its logical extent, not being shy of dealing with unpalatable conclusions (tackling God's non-existence for example) and demonstrating this with a clarity that even now is unsettling in its acuity. Descartes, Locke and Berkeley all accepted that there must be a continuous self, 'I think, therefore I am'. Hume however, pointed out that we cannot know that. If we gain our knowledge through experience, when do we experience the self that underpins our feelings, thoughts etc? We experience only the content not the self. Therefore as we have not experienced it, we cannot with any certainty say that there is a 'self'. We have no way of knowing how subjective experience is connected over time, if it is at all. It would seem therefore, that Descartes's axiom should be revised to say – 'there is a thing that is thinking now' (but it may not be the same thing thinking in a minute's time).

In a similar vein Hume went on to apply his scepticism to the idea of causality. When we see a match lighting after being struck we assume that the striking caused the lighting. We have no right to do so, says Hume, we simply observed one event following another. The fact that they have always followed one another in the past does not logically imply that they must always follow one another in the future. Have we observed any extra thing other than a sequence of events that we might call a cause? Hume observes that just because we have a psychological constant conjunction of two events (I expect to hear thunder, when I see lightning, I expect to see day after night) it

'Custom, then, is the great guide of human life.'

does not logically follow that there is a necessary connection between the two events. Hume's challenge is to say; 'You have experienced the events, now show me where you experienced the necessity of the connection'.

Hume's sophistication comes with his analysis of this world-view. Obviously we do not operate in the world this way, worrying about necessary connections or the temporal continuity of the self, but we do need to realise the difference between reasoned thought and the colouring of our beliefs by our emotions. 'Reason', as Hume famously opined 'is the slave of the passions.' Hume was one of the first philosophers to engage in circumscribing the limitations of philosophical endeavour. He showed that there were clear boundaries between what philosophy and science can reasonably tell us and what is merely wild metaphysical speculation. This sentiment, so prevalent in Hume, profoundly influenced the Utilitarian thinkers Bentham and Mill in the 19th century and emphatically shaped the course of 20th century philosophy through Russell, Ayer and Wittgenstein.

Hume's common sense and persuasive style won him admirers and friends across the continent who valued its directness and rigour. During several periods in France, Hume established several important intellectual friendships, including that with Rousseau for whom he secured political asylum in England in 1766. Rousseau's paranoia soon led to a split when he accused Hume of ruining his reputation, a charge brilliantly refuted by Hume. Hume was much closer in his friendship with the economist Adam Smith and dabbled briefly in economics himself. In the late 1750s he moved away from philosophy and wrote a six-volume history of England, which was to remain a key text until the appearance of Macaulay in the 1840s. Some of his greatest work is contained in his surgical assault on religious belief, *Dialogues Concerning Natural Religion* (1779).

Unlike Descartes or Berkeley, Hume did not use philosophy to create a universe in which God could survive the onslaught of scientific, rational thought. Hume wanted to pursue the argument to its furthest extent and, if the idea of God suffered in that pursuit, then so be it. The dialogues thus became one of the most incisive philosophical critiques of religion in the history of ideas. In Hume's view the arguments levelled at the self and causality operated equally for the existence of the deity. If God has not been observed then God cannot be rationally held to exist. If the claim is that God is the cause or designer of the universe, then where is the observational evidence to support that? Even if the idea of a cause or a designer is allowed then we still cannot be assured of the nature of God. How can we be sure that it is the God of the Christians who is the First Cause or the designer? Hume withheld the publication of this work and it was only published posthumously in 1779. Hume's arguments caused great controversy in the 18th century, so much so that he became known to the Scottish clergy as 'the great infidel'.

Hume may not have had quite the political influence of Locke or the influence on the developing romantic movement that his friend Rousseau had, but, as a stylist and a thinker, he is a classic demonstration of how to conduct philosophical argument; forcefully, logically and with wit. Immanuel Kant wrote of how his reading of Hume awoke him from his 'dogmatic slumbers'. Kant was but one of many. The last word we should leave to Hume: 'When we run over libraries, persuaded of these principles, what havoc must we make? If we take in our hand any volume; of divinity or school metaphysics, for instance; let us ask, Does it contain any abstract reasoning concerning quantity or number? No. Does it contain any experimental reasoning concerning matter of fact and existence? No. Commit it then to the flames: for it can contain nothing but sophistry and illusion.' (*An Enquiry Concerning Human Understanding*).

NOEL MURPHY, *Waterstone's*

WRITINGS BY HUME

Dialogues Concerning Natural Religion
Penguin pbk £6.99
0140445366

Dialogues Concerning Natural Religion and The Natural History of Religion
Oxford UP pbk £6.99
0192838768

An Enquiry Concerning Human Understanding
Oxford UP pbk £5.99
0198752482

An Enquiry Concerning the Principles of Morals
Oxford UP pbk £6.99
0198751842

Political Essays
Cambridge UP pbk £12.95
0521466393

Selected Essays
Oxford UP pbk £6.99
0192836218

Treatise of Human Nature
Oxford UP pbk £8.99
0198245882

WRITINGS ON HUME

Cambridge Companion to Hume
Cambridge UP pbk £16.95
0521387108

Flew, Anthony
David Hume
Blackwell pbk £13.95
0631151958

Ayer, A.J.
Hume
Oxford UP pbk £5.99
0192875280

One of the Oxford Past Masters series.

Quinton, Anthony
Hume
Phoenix pbk £2.00
0753801868

VOLTAIRE | 1759

Candide

Candide, ou l'optisme was a key text of the
Enlightenment, celebrated as a plea for justice,
freedom of speech and reason, in place of the
repression and bigotry of the *ancien regime* of
pre-revolutionary France. *Candide* arguably
established a new literary genre, the *conte
philosophique*, a blend of the literary and the
philosophical, of the entertaining and the
educative. The book was extremely successful,
one of the best-selling books of the eighteenth
century, outselling *Gulliver's Travels*, for
example, by two to one.

Voltaire was born François-Marie Arouet in
1694, into a wealthy Parisian family. Following
his education at a Jesuit school, he took up
legal studies, but soon abandoned the law for
literature. His writings were to range from
poetry to polemical works, history, drama and
philosophy. He was also a brilliant raconteur,
wit and debater. In 1713 a satirical piece was
poorly received and Arouet was forced to leave
France for the first of what were to be many
periods of exile. In 1717 he was imprisoned in
the Bastille, where he assumed the name
Voltaire. Perhaps his most celebrated period of
exile was his sojourn in England from 1726 to
1729, which resulted in the *Lettres
Philosophiques* of 1733 (translated as
Philosophical Letters on the English Nation).
In the *Letters*, Voltaire contrasted favourably
the relative liberalism of England with France,
where the repressive apparatus of church and

state blocked intellectual progress. Voltaire was
heavily influenced in the *Letters* by the
empiricism of John Locke (especially the *Essay
Concerning Human Understanding* of 1690).

Candide is a critique of all philosophical
systems or broad doctrines incapable of
adaptation in the face of evidence. Voltaire
believed that such systems demanded, at the
very least, occasional suspension of rational
thought. Such a willingness to overlook the
facts could lead to appalling evils. 'Those who
can make you believe absurdities,' he warned,
'can make you commit atrocities.' The method
Voltaire is promoting in *Candide* resembles
Locke's: to approach philosophical problems
with a 'plain', open mind, without prejudice or
preconception, and always to take account of
the facts, always to be open to enlightenment.

Following publication of *Candide*, Voltaire's
position on organised religion hardened,
notably in the *Dictionnaire Philosophique* of 1764.
He campaigned vociferously against the superstitions and injustices of the Roman Catholic
church, and even opened his own home to
refugees fleeing the persecution of Rome. For
the rest of his life Voltaire was the embodiment
of the eighteenth century Enlightenment and
his house at Ferney near Geneva became a
place of pilgrimage for those who shared his
beliefs in the power of reason and his distaste
for the entrenched forces of church and state.

> *'Men use thought only as authority for their injustice, and employ speech only to conceal their thoughts.'*

He died in Paris from an illness brought on by the stresses of staging a performance of his tragedy *Irène.*

JOE PONTIN, *Waterstone's Bristol Galleries*

WRITINGS BY VOLTAIRE

Candide and Other Stories
Oxford UP pbk £2.99
0192834266

Candide
Penguin pbk £2.50
0140440046

Letters Concerning the English Nation
Oxford UP pbk £5.99
0192837087

Letters on England
Penguin pbk £6.99
014044386X

Philosophical Dictionary
Penguin pbk £9.99
014044257X

Political Writings
Cambridge UP pbk £13.95
052143727X

Selected Writings
Everyman pbk £6.99
0460876244

Zadig and L'Ingenu
Penguin pbk £6.99
0140441263

WRITINGS ON VOLTAIRE

Gray, John
Voltaire
Phoenix pbk £3.00
0753802120

Jean-Jacques

ROUSSEAU | 1762

The Social Contract

Jean-Jacques Rousseau was born in Switzerland in 1712 and before he began his intellectual career he led a varied career as, amongst other things, an apprentice engraver; a footman, a music teacher; and secretary to the French Ambassador in Venice. Although he had written operas in the 1740s (such as *Le Devin du Village*), he was in his late thirties before his writings began to make an impact on the intellectual world of Enlightenment France where he had taken up residence. In 1762 publication of *The Social Contract*, and shortly after of *Émile*, a treatise on education, caused uproar in France. Rousseau had offended the church, the aristocracy and fellow intellectuals. Anticipating his arrest, he fled the country for his native Switzerland, and thence to England.

Rousseau's life, both before and after this self-exile, was full of controversy and scandal. He quarrelled with many of the most eminent intellectuals of his era, including Hume, Voltaire and Diderot. It was also a life of contrasts. He was, at varying times, both Calvinist and Catholic. His lovers included distinguished ladies and a laundry maid whom he made his wife. He travelled widely and suffered bouts of both physical and mental illness. He was back in France and living in relative poverty, writing largely autobiographical (and often paranoid and self-justifying) works at the time of his final illness and death.

Some of Rousseau's most colourful adventures were set out in his *Confessions*, published posthumously. In addition to *The Social Contract* he wrote several other volumes of political philosophy, contributions to Diderot's prestigious *Encyclopédie* and a successful novel, *Julie, ou La Nouvelle Héloise*.

Probably his most influential work, *The Social Contract* set out Rousseau's theory on the principles of ideal government, based on a covenant binding its participants to protect each other's freedom. Rousseau did not himself regard the social contract as the central concept of his general political theory. *The Social Contract* had originally been part of a much larger work, *Political Institutions*, which Rousseau never completed. Neither was the social contract Rousseau's idea. Thomas Hobbes, John Locke and several legal theorists, including the seventeenth century German jurist Samuel Pufendorf, had also used the expression. These earlier writers argued that the state was the outcome of a covenant in which men exchanged their freedom for the protection of a sovereign. Rousseau's unique contribution was to insist that sovereignty resided permanently with the people (i.e. the individuals participating in the contract) and that the executive was a subordinate institution.

Rousseau's starting point was his theory on the essential nature of man. He set out the conditions under which men had lived in a state of nature. (Unlike some earlier social contract theorists, Rousseau did not claim that the state of nature had existed in fact. This state of nature was inferred, and expressed the essence of pre-social man. If man's actual history differed, reasoned Rousseau, this did not affect his theory.) Rousseau argued that man was essentially solitary. In a state of nature, man need only provide for his own modest needs, and therefore had no motive for conflict; without enemies, man had lived in a state of freedom. (Rousseau defined freedom as an absence of interference by others.)

Yet, argued Rousseau, man in the state of nature was incapable of moral virtue; he was a 'stupid and unimaginative animal'. His so-called freedom was mere independence. Only by combining with others was this animal capable of becoming 'an intelligent being and a man' and of experiencing political and moral freedom. (Why the animal man would enter into a contract that he could not, by Rousseau's own argument understand, is not clear.) Hobbes had argued that in the act of making the social contract, man renounced his freedom. Rousseau countered that this was not logically possible. In making the contract, man had for the first time understood the signifi-cance of freedom. How could he simultane-ously agree to renounce it? The idea was absurd. Thus, Rousseau reasoned, the contract could not logically provide for a permanent transfer of power from the individual to the state. Sovereignty permanently resided with the people. Arrangements for an executive body to administer the law could be made, but the executive was to be subject to regular approval

by the people. Thus Rousseau set out his case that man could in principle be both free and subject to the social bond. Unfortunately, though, existing political societies were wrongly consti-tuted. 'Civilisation' had corrupted the virtues of individuals and the conduct of the state.

Rousseau noted that the challenge posed by 'civilising' influences varied according to the size and material development of the community involved. Instead of setting out an ideal, democratic constitution, Rousseau, therefore, recommended a variety of constitutional arrangements, depending on the circumstances. His favoured system he deemed suitable only for small, semi-agrarian communities. This he based on his native Switzerland, where a series of rural cantons were loosely bound in a confederation, and where the whole male population of each canton gathered together to make laws. Modern, complex societies Rousseau believed too unwieldy for democracy; and so he recom-mended a modified form of aristocracy for a medium-sized state, and of monarchy for a large state.

In making his constitutional recommendations, the existing constitutional models appeared a poor source of inspiration. Rousseau's scepticism toward representative democracy, for example, was probably based on his study of parliamentary democracy in Britain, which was then dominated by landed interests and the monarchy.

Rousseau nevertheless made a valuable contri-bution to the theoretical underpinnings of western democracy. His insistence on the sover-

'Nature made man happy and good, but society corrupts him and makes him miserable.'

eignty of the people, his advocacy of general will as the judge of the common good, and his support for the liberty of the individual in the face of the state were all key elements used by later democratic theorists.

JOE PONTIN, *Waterstone's Bristol Galleries*

WRITINGS BY ROUSSEAU

The Confessions
Penguin pbk £8.99
014044033X

A Discourse on Inequality
Penguin pbk £5.99
0140444394

Discourse on Political Economy and The Social Contract
Oxford UP pbk £5.99
0192835971

Discourse on the Origin of Inequality
Oxford UP pbk £5.99
0192829475

The Discourses and Other Early Political Writings
Cambridge UP pbk £10.95
0521424453

Emile
Everyman pbk £8.99
0460873806

Reveries of the Solitary Walker
Penguin pbk £7.99
0140443630

The Social Contract
Penguin pbk £5.99
0140442014

The Social Contract and Other Later Political Writings
Cambridge UP pbk £7.95
0521424461

WRITINGS ON ROUSSEAU

Wokler, Robert
Rousseau
Oxford UP pbk £5.99
0192876406

Dent, N.J.H.
Rousseau
Blackwell pbk £14.99
0631158839

Dent, N.J.H.
The Rousseau Dictionary
Blackwell pbk £17.50
0631175695

Adam

SMITH 1776

The Wealth of Nations

Smith was born in Kirkcaldy and studied at both Glasgow and Oxford Universities. He spent a number of years as professor of logic and, later, moral philosophy at the former university and in 1759 published *The Theory of Moral Sentiments*. In this influential work he argued that the basis for moral actions was sympathy with others, the pleasure of which worked to overcome the natural urge towards egocentricity and selfishness. In 1764 Smith resigned from his academic positions to tour the Continent as tutor to a Scottish aristocrat. During this tour Smith came to know Voltaire and other leading European intellectuals. On returning to Scotland he settled in his native town and devoted himself to the work that was eventually published in 1776 as *An Inquiry into the Nature and Causes of the Wealth of Nations*. In the same year Smith moved to London where he was a member of the famous literary Club founded by Dr. Johnson. He moved back to Scotland in 1778 and died in Edinburgh in 1790.

The Austrian-American economist Joseph Schumpeter once famously described *The Wealth of Nations* as containing 'no really novel ideas'. Despite this dismissal, Smith is rightly regarded as the founder of the tradition of classical economics. He broke with older traditions of economic value and with the views of the eighteenth century French physiocrats, who persisted in seeing land as the basis of economic wealth. His work established the broad framework for the classical tradition: a concern with the theory of value as a measure of the social product, an analysis of distribution and its relation to economic growth and a general interest in uncovering the laws of development of the new industrial capitalism. Underlying Smith's work was a subtle theory of how the pursuit of individual iniative and interest might result in a cohesive social order where all would benefit. This based the general welfare on allowing the individual to promote his own interest freely so long as 'it did not violate the laws of justice.' In this way the individual can be seen to serve society more effectively when he is not actually conscious of promoting its interest. Thus, in his writings on *The Theory of Moral Sentiments*, Smith developed an account of natural justice. It was only when individual actions were guided by natural justice, according to Smith, that the pursuit of self-interest would be socially beneficial.

'It is not from the benevolence of the butcher, the brewer or the baker, that we expect our dinner, but from their regard to their own interests.'

WRITINGS BY ADAM SMITH

An Inquiry into the Nature and Causes of the Wealth of Nations
Oxford UP pbk £6.99
0192835467

The Wealth of Nations I-III
Penguin pbk £6.99
0140432086

The Wealth of Nations
Everyman hbk £10.99
1857150112

Oxford University Press publish the Glasgow Edition of the Works and Correspondence of Adam Smith in hardback.

WRITINGS ON ADAM SMITH

Raphael, D.D.
Adam Smith
Oxford UP pbk £5.99
0192875582

Adam Smith's The Wealth of Nations: A Critical Companion
Manchester UP pbk £13.99
0719039436

Ross, Ian Simpson
The Life of Adam Smith
Oxford UP hbk £29.95
0198288212

Edward

GIBBON | 1776–88

The Decline and Fall of the Roman Empire

DAVID WOMERSLEY *of Jesus College, Oxford, editor of Penguin's definitive three-volume edition of* The Decline and Fall of the Roman Empire, *and of a one-volume abridgement due out in paperback in June 2000, examines Gibbon's masterpiece and its continuing importance today.*

A heroine of Trollope's is given the semi-medicinal advice to 'take two hours of Gibbon daily.' It is too much to hope that one could ever get *The Decline and Fall* prescribed on the National Health. But equally it would be hard to think of any prescription which would do as much for the intellectual well-being – and good humour – of the nation.

The origins of this monument of sanity and intellectual achievement were not auspicious. Gibbon, a sickly child, was thoroughly miserable when a pupil at Westminster, which he later called a 'cavern of fear and sorrow'. From there his father, who was never particularly sensitive to his son's needs or aversions, decided that he should go to Oxford. On 3rd April, 1752, a slender figure, not yet fifteen, alighted from the coach at Magdalen bridge. As he himself would later put it, 'I arrived at Oxford with a stock of erudition that might have puzzled a Doctor, and a degree of ignorance of which a school boy would have been ashamed.' Neglected by his tutors, he began to read Catholic theology, and, like many other Oxford undergraduates since, he became

fascinated by the ceremonies of Roman Catholicism ('the use of the sign of the cross, of holy oil, and even of images, the invocation of Saints, the worship of relicks'). On his furtive trips to Covent Garden, he passed by the doors of the brothels which drew in his contemporaries, and instead walked on to the premises of 'a Roman Catholic bookseller in Russel-street ... who recommended me to a priest ... and at his feet on the eighth of June, 1753, I solemnly, though privately, abjured the errors of heresy.' Gibbon's father was furious. His chosen remedy was to exile his son to Switzerland. There he might come to understand the error of his ways. So it was that the young Edward Gibbon found himself transplanted from the opulence of Magdalen College to the indigent squalor in which lived the man who was to be his tutor for the next five years, Mr. Pavilliard, a Calvinist Minister of Lausanne.

At the end of his life Gibbon acknowledged that, however he had resented it at the time, this move to Switzerland had been the making of him: 'Such as I am, in Genius or learning or manners, I owe my creation to Lausanne: it was in that school, that the statue was discovered in the block of marble; and my own religious folly, my father's blind resolution, produced the effects of the most deliberate wisdom.' How did this happen? There are I think two points which have to be made about Gibbon's time in Switzerland. The first is that here he began for

> *'The reign of Antoninus is marked by the rare advantage of furnishing very few materials for history, which is indeed little more than the register of the crimes, follies and misfortunes of mankind.'*

the first time in his life a methodical programme of serious reading, in both classical literatures and in more recent European, particularly French, literature. So the chasms and shortcomings of his English education were to some degree repaired in Lausanne. Without the painstaking and thorough grounding he acquired when exiled in Switzerland, it is difficult to imagine that Gibbon could ever have put himself in a position to write *The Decline and Fall*. Secondly, however - and just as importantly for the resulting character of Gibbon's history - this education occurred outside England and English institutions. It did not take an English form, and the values which it instilled were not in the first instance English values. And this European conditioning, in which England was but one part of a broader continental grouping of nations (what Gibbon would later call a 'Christian republic of nations') stayed with him until the end of his life.

That independence of outlook is stamped upon the character of his great history. It leaves its trace even on that most obvious feature of his writing, his ironic wit:

[The younger Gordian's] manners were less pure, but his character was equally amiable with that of his father. Twenty-two acknowledged concubines, and a library of sixty-two thousand volumes, attested the variety of his inclinations; and from the productions which he left behind him, it appears that the former as well as the latter were designed for use rather than for ostentation.

The most serious charges were suppressed; and the Vicar of Rome was accused of only murder, incest, sodomy, rape and theft.

An air of mild indecency hangs around these quotations, and reminds us of Richard Porson's censure of Gibbon's lubricity; 'nor does his humanity ever slumber, unless when women are ravished, or the Christians persecuted ... A less pardonable fault is [a] rage for indecency ... If the history were anonymous, I should guess that these disgraceful obscenities were written by some debauchee, who having from age, or accident, or excess, survived the practice of lust, still indulged himself in the luxury of speculation.' Gibbon could, we know, offend against English standards of propriety. But Porson is wrong, I think, to see in such passages a simple 'rage for indecency'. Gibbon's innocent neglect of customary decorums flowed not from the disposition of a libertine, but from the peculiarities of his upbringing, which had not trained his mind to observe the usual boundaries. Although Gibbon eventually moved in the highest social circles, the anecdotes we have about him - his occasionally comic lack of insight into how others perceived him, his carelessness over his personal hygiene - suggest that, beneath or around the edges of his manifest urbanity, he remained oddly unsocialized.

A similar independence is to be found in the substantive vision of the history. It is often assumed that *The Decline and Fall* is a straightforward lament for departed glory, and that the dominant emotional colouring of the work is that of an elegy. But Gibbon was the enemy of empire as a political form, and a friend to the freedom of nations, for 'there is nothing perhaps more adverse to nature and reason than to hold in obedience remote countries and foreign nations, in opposition to their inclination and interest.' However much Gibbon may have admired the artistic and cultural achievement of Rome, he was no admirer of empire as a political system. This disenchantment with empire influenced Gibbon's assessment of the barbarians who overran the western provinces of the empire in the fifth century. Gibbon's admiration for the barbarians had its limits. He remained convinced that the pastoral state of nations was a condition of intellectual, ethical and material impoverishment. Recounting the atrocities perpetrated by the Thuringian allies of Attila, he distanced himself emphatically from the modish cult of the noble savage, promulgated by contemporaries such as Rousseau: 'Such were those savage ancestors, whose imaginary virtues have sometimes excited the praise and envy of civilized ages!' But barbarians such as the Huns, despite themselves, had created a hinge linking the Roman empire to the civilized republic of commercial states in which the history of that transformation was now itself being written.

And if Gibbon's view of the barbarians was unexpectedly positive, the same could in the end be said for his attitude towards religion. Gibbon is famous for his hostility to Christianity. His ironic treatment of the early Christian church in the fifteenth chapter of *The Decline and Fall* created trouble for him in his own day, and it is probably still his most notorious characteristic as a writer. However, although Gibbon seems not to have enjoyed any lively Christian faith himself (at least after his adolescent brush with Catholicism), he nevertheless saw as an historian that the Christian church had played an important role in keeping civil society alive during the collapse of the Roman empire, and had thereby permitted the transferral of precious elements of culture from the ancient world to the modern. Nowhere is this clearer than in what he says about the incorporation of aspects of paganism into Christianity.

In the long period of twelve hundred years, which elapsed between the reign of Constantine and the reformation of Luther, the worship of saints and relics corrupted the pure and perfect simplicity of the Christian model; and some symptoms of degeneracy may be observed even in the first generations which adopted and cherished this pernicious innovation.

This was, then, a lapse from simplicity into plurality. The unity of the Godhead was divided into the literal fragments which were revered as relics, and the holy and undivided Trinity was refracted into the company of saints. Considered from a purely religious standpoint, the lapse into superstition was indeed degeneracy:

The sublime and simple theology of the primitive Christians was gradually corrupted; and the MONARCHY of heaven, already clouded by metaphysical subtleties, was degraded by the introduction of a popular mythology, which tended to restore the reign of polytheism.

Paganism was thus not annihilated. It was translated into the ceremonies and doctrines of its successor, where it persisted in a way which was theologically unfortunate. But religion can be assessed in terms other than its own, and Gibbon insinuated at the very end of the chapter how the corruption of Christianity, considered purely as a religion, might nevertheless be seen in a positive light. For the recurrence of pagan forms in Christianity was not to be attributed to 'the uniform original spirit of superstition'. It was, rather, a stroke of deliberate and conscious policy, in which theological purity was wisely subordinated to political benefit:

. . . it must ingenuously be confessed, that the ministers of the Catholic church imitated the profane model, which they were impatient to destroy. The most respectable bishops had persuaded themselves, that the ignorant rustics would more cheerfully renounce the superstitions of Paganism, if they found some resemblance, some compensation, in the bosom of Christianity.

The religion of Constantine achieved, in less than a century, the final conquest of the Roman empire: but the victors themselves were insensibly subdued by the arts of their vanquished rivals.

Gibbon encourages us to view the infection of Christianity by the superstitious temper of paganism in a secular, rather than a theological, light. When we do so, it seems that paganism had inoculated Christianity with superstition. For, as we shall see, Gibbon will go on to suggest that Christianity, corrupted into superstition, exerted a benign and protective influence over the fledgling societies which established themselves on the ruins of the western empire. To the extent that Christianity became pagan, it acted as a conduit for a civil order which might otherwise have been lost in the gulf between the ancient and the modern worlds. Those respectable Catholic bishops were both wiser than they knew, and, in all probability, wiser than they wished to be.

Does *The Decline and Fall* still speak to us today? I believe that it does, because we are still living through the consequences of the vast historical process whose beginnings Gibbon analyzed and narrated. The fall of Rome was, for Gibbon, 'the greatest, perhaps, and most awful scene in the history of mankind', and it is possible to see the whole of European history since the collapse of the empire as, in some measure, a playing out of the implications of that episode. Certainly our present discontents connect teasingly with Gibbon's vision. His Europe had been erected on the ruins of empire, protected by superstitious religion, invigorated by barbarian energy, and held together by the bonds arising from the commercial organization it had derived from Byzantium. We now see a European empire being reassembled via the Treaty of Rome, religion either weakening or assuming the forms of fanaticism, and no obvious source of external renewal for a society which seems often to be more brutalized than strengthened by the opera-

tions of commerce. Should a second Gibbon arise, the story he will tell is unlikely to confirm the judgements of his eighteenth-century predecessor.

WRITINGS BY GIBBON

The Decline and Fall of the Roman Empire
Penguin pbk £8.95
0140437649

Abridged edition.

Decline and Fall of the Roman Empire
Allen Lane hbk £75.00
3-volume boxed edition

Decline and Fall of the Roman Empire Volume 1
Penguin pbk £14.99
0140433937

Decline and Fall of the Roman Empire Volume 2
Penguin pbk £14.99
0140433945

Decline and Fall of the Roman Empire Volume 3
Penguin pbk £14.99
0140433953

Memoirs of My Life
Penguin pbk £6.99
0140432175

WRITINGS ON GIBBON

Porter, Roy
Gibbon
Phoenix pbk £9.95
1857993624

Immanuel

KANT   1781

Critique of Pure Reason

Although Kant is, arguably, the most important philosopher of modern times, his life was passed in provincial obscurity in the East Prussian town of Königsberg. It was there that he was born, spent his entire life and it was there that he died in 1804. He entered the University of Königsberg as a student and, after a period as a private tutor, he returned there as a lecturer in 1755. Fifteen years later he was appointed a professor and continued to teach and lecture in the university until his retirement in 1796. Kant led what would today be seen as a highly restricted life. He never married and rarely travelled outside Königsberg. He was so much a creature of routine that it is said that the townspeople felt able to set their watches by Kant's evening constitutional. Yet this provincial academic produced one of the most ambitious and all-encompassing systems of thought in the history of philosophy.

Kant dubbed his own system 'transcendental idealism'. He developed his ideas from the rationalism of Descartes and the empiricism of Locke and Hume. In the *Critique of Pure Reason* he accepts the empiricists' view that there can be no innate ideas - nothing can be known prior to sense experience - but he rejects the idea that all knowledge must be directly derived from experience. This only took into account the object observed and not the observer. Kant proposed that our experience was modified by

two factors: our sensibility ('through which objects are given us') and our understanding ('through which they are thought'). Our understanding was, in turn, composed of twelve categories (such as quality, quantity and causation) through which we made sense of, and drew judgements from, our experience. Thus, for Kant, the external world consists of appearances (phenomena), the causes of which (the noumena or 'things themselves') remain beyond the reach of our knowledge or reason. In this way Kant's system can be seen to be metaphysical, concerned not with the impressions upon which ideas are based (as were the empiricists) but rather with the fundamental and transcendental concepts which underlie a thinking subject's experience of objects.

However the system was never speculative, for Kant is careful to stress that any application of these concepts to anything beyond sense experience is bound to result in contradiction and error. In the sphere of morality this led to his idea of the moral law. Man feels a moral obligation or duty that he cannot always explain through his desires or wishes, or his anticipation that his action will be advantageous to him. This is the 'categorical imperative' which allows us to act in accordance with the moral law. As a practical code it bids us 'to act as if the principle by which you act were about to be turned into a universal law', the implication being that the only test for a moral action is whether it is done in accordance

'*I am never to act otherwise than so that I could also will that my maxim should become a universal law.*'

with, and for the sake of, an innate sense of duty. Consequently Kant is driven to accept the existence of a God from which the moral law of the universe ultimately derives, although he can't 'prove' it by reason since both religion and morality are beyond the scope of knowledge and rely on the human capacity for faith.

WRITINGS BY KANT

Critique of Judgement
Oxford UP pbk £11.99
0198245890

Critique of Pure Reason
Everyman pbk £6.99
046087358X

Critique of Pure Reason
Macmillan pbk £15.99
0333057139

Probably the best student edition, translated and annotated by Norman Kemp Smith.

Critique of Pure Reason
Cambridge UP pbk £14.95
0521657296

Groundwork of the Metaphysics of Morals
Cambridge UP pbk £8.95
0521626951

The Metaphysics of Morals
Cambridge UP pbk £10.95
0521566738

This volume in the series Cambridge Texts in the History of Philosophy comprises two parts: the 'Doctrine of Right' which deals with the rights people can have or acquire and the 'Doctrine of Virtue' which deals with the virtues that people ought to acquire.

Logic
Dover pbk £8.95
0486256502

German Idealist Philosophy
Penguin pbk £8.99
0140446605

This Penguin Classics selection of writings includes works by Johann Gottlieb Fichte (1762 – 1814), Friedrich Schelling (1775-1854) and Hegel, as well as Kant.

Opus Postumum
Cambridge UP pbk £15.95
0521319285

Prolegomena to Any Future Metaphysics
Cambridge UP pbk £10.95
0521575427

Religion Within the Boundaries of Mere Reason
Cambridge UP pbk £11.95
0521599644

WRITINGS ON KANT

Cambridge Companion to Kant
Cambridge UP pbk £16.99
0521367689

Introducing Kant
Icon pbk £8.99
1840460814

Korner, Stephan
Kant
Penguin pbk £8.99
0140134859

Scruton, Roger
Kant
Oxford UP pbk £5.99
0192875779

A Kant Dictionary
Blackwell pbk £16.99
0631175350

Alexander James John
HAMILTON, MADISON, JAY
The Federalist Papers
1787–88

The Constitution of the United States was drawn up by the Federal Constitutional Convention held in Philadelphia in 1787 and came into operation in 1789. A major role in getting the Constitution adopted was played by what came to be known as *The Federalist Papers*. These eighty-five essays in support of the Constitution were originally published in 1787 and the following year as a sequence of letters to a number of New York newspapers. The authors were Alexander Hamilton, James Madison and John Jay.

Hamilton (1757-1804) had been a prominent New York lawyer and had played a major role in the Philadelphia convention. He went on to become one of the leading politicians in the new republic's first decade and would probably have become President had his career not been cut short by a duel with his rival Aaron Burr in which he was fatally wounded.

Madison (1751-1836) *did* become President, elected as the fourth incumbent of the office in 1809. During the Philadelphia convention he had been closely associated with Hamilton and he was later to become the political partner of Thomas Jefferson who, in 1801, appointed him secretary of state. As president Madison served two terms and retired in 1817.

John Jay (1745-1829) was a New York lawyer who was one of the most influential figures in the peace negotiations between Britain and the new America and went on to serve as governor of New York and chief justice of the Supreme Court. Although the letters appeared anonymously, scholars are now more or less agreed that more than fifty were written by Hamilton, a smaller number by Madison and Jay alone and a number by Hamilton and Madison in collaboration.

The importance of *The Federalist Papers* is far more than historical. At the time of their appearance Thomas Jefferson described them as 'the best commentary on the principles of government which ever was written' and the role the letters played in ensuring ratification of the Constitution was significant. Yet, just as the American Constitution itself has shown its resilience and flexibility over more than two centuries, so the *Federalist Papers*, the definitive expositions of that constitution, have continued to speak directly to later generations of Americans about the relationship between state and federal power and the nature of republican government. Over the years they have become an authority on the principles on which American government is based and it is far from unknown for Supreme Court decisions affecting that government to be founded, at least in part, on statements found in them. It is impossible to imagine American

'It has been frequently remarked that it seems to have been reserved to the people of this century, by their conduct and example, to decide the important question, whether societies of men are really capable or not of establishing good government from reflection and choice, or whether they are forever destined to depend for their political constitutions on accident and force.'

democracy, with all its extraordinary powers for good and ill, without the American Constitution. It is almost as impossible to imagine the constitution without *The Federalist Papers*.

WRITINGS BY HAMILTON, MADISON & JAY

The Federalist Papers
Penguin pbk £9.99
01401444955

This edition of the Federalist Papers includes the Constitution as an appendix and an insightful introduction by Professor Isaac Kramnick.

Edmund

BURKE | 1790

Reflections on the Revolution in France

Born in Dublin in 1729 Burke, was educated at Trinity College there and came to London in 1750 to enter Middle Temple. He practised at the Bar for a short while before turning to a career in literature and politics. By 1765 he had become the Private Secretary to Rockingham, the prime minister of the day. Out of office in the 1770s, Burke proved an able opponent of North's administration. He denounced the abuse and corruption of the government, expressing sympathy with the American colonies in their struggle with the authorities in London. Before 1790 Burke wrote works on aesthetics (*A Philosophical Inquiry into the Origin of our Ideas of the Sublime and the Beautiful*) and much on the political issues of the day. By a long way the most significant political issue of the century began in 1789 - the French Revolution.

The Bastille was stormed in July. *The Declaration of the Rights of Man* was adopted by the National Assembly. October saw the Royal Family move from Versailles to Paris, escorted by the mob. France was convulsed. British radicals were ecstatic. In their eyes, events in France were the fruits of Enlightenment principles. It was through the application of rational thought that the individual could achieve liberty, free from the oppressions of traditional religion and government. The *ancien regime* in France had been judged by Reason and found wanting. Radical voices in Britain clamoured

for reform. On 4th November 1789, the anniversary of the 1688 Revolution in England, Richard Price gave a sermon associating contemporary events in France with 1688. He proclaimed the right of the people both to choose its government and to remove it. He urged Britons to assert their sovereignty.

Reflections on the Revolution in France was a reply to Price and his fellow radicals. Burke saw nothing but danger in the French Revolution and he warned against reformist zeal. The work was addressed to the British political nation, presented as a study of the Revolution. *Reflections* was immediately hailed as masterful work of political theory. It is now recognised as being the classic exposition of conservative thought. Burke proffers the view that society is akin to an organism. Complex in its nature, it cannot properly be understood through reason alone. Rationalism is too blunt an instrument to apply in reforming society; it takes no account of human instincts and emotions, the subtleties of human interaction. From such interaction, through such shared experience, derives a wisdom that governs human affairs. It is a wisdom inherited and added to by each generation. Society is not an abstract entity; it is real, reaching back to the dead and forward to those unborn. A generation should not consider itself free to embark upon experimental political reforms.

'People will not look forward to posterity who never look backward to their ancestors.'

Burke extols continuity. Through continuity come expectation and habit. In turn, there come confidence and shared values that bond individuals. Violent change disrupts that process; it destroys the social fabric, diminishing men's lives. Society's institutions have evolved over time. Their innate value has been tested by the years, men have become accustomed to them.

Burke berates radicals for basing reform on the abstract. Such men and women fail to heed the limitations of the individual intellect. Men cannot fully understand the complexities of humanity, the workings of society. Having recognised as much, men must respect and have due regard to what has been left to them by countless predecessors. The past acts as a guide for each generation in determining society's path. Accordingly, change must be organic. It must come from within, moving at a pace so that '...in what we improve, we are never wholly new; in what we retain we are never wholly obsolete.' The radical alternative, that of experimental reforms, of subjecting institutions to the scrutiny of human reason (limited as it is), is madness. It risks throwing out the good with the bad.

Burke praises the British experience. The English Revolution of 1688 saw the removal of the monarch, not the monarchy. It is presented as an example of cautious, constitutional and effective reform. The French example is very different. Its sweeping and free-spirited change would lead to the wholesale destruction of institutions and traditions, with an accompanying collapse of social custom and habit. Anarchy would prevail. As it was, France descended into factional strife and terror. Out of that turmoil came Napoleon. To many British eyes, Burke was vindicated.

The accuracy of Burke's prognosis helped secure his influence in British political life. In the following two hundred years, the idea of continuity, of gradual, evolutionary and restrained reform has prevailed. Universal suffrage came about after several progressive extensions of the franchise. The monarchy, the aristocracy, the church, all remain, their power and position altered through the years. Socialism expressed itself through the Trade Union movement and ultimately the Parliamentary Labour Party. In contrast with many European neighbours, Britain has experienced no popular revolutions, no momentous and destructive civil unrest.

Burke's conservatism displays no pessimism, no fear of human nature. Society will progress, the individual's lot will improve so long as harmonious social conditions prevail. Burke's concern is that such harmony be maintained, not endangered by the arbitrary imposition of some untested ideology. His vision of an organic, developing society, one not to be subjected to the experiments of rational revolutionaries, has survived into a political world very different to the eighteenth century one he inhabited.

CLAIRE MILBURN, *Waterstone's*

WRITINGS BY BURKE

**A Philosophical Inquiry Into
the Origin of Our Ideas of the
Sublime and Beautiful**
Oxford UP pbk £5.99
0192835807

**A Philosophical Inquiry Into
the Sublime and Beautiful &
Other Pre-Revolution Writings**
Penguin pbk £6.99
0140436251

Pre-Revolutionary Writings
Cambridge UP pbk £12.95
0521368006

**Reflections on the Revolution
in France**
Penguin pbk £6.99
0140432043

**Reflections on the Revolution
in France**
Oxford UP pbk £5.99
0192818449

Oxford UP publish a multi-
volume hardback edition
of Burke's writings and
correspondence.

WRITINGS ON BURKE

Robinson, Nicholas
Edmund Burke: A Life in Caricature
Yale UP hbk £30.00
0300068018

O'Brien, Conor Cruise
Edmund Burke
Random House pbk £12.99
1856196984

Thomas

PAINE | 1791–92

The Rights of Man

Born into a Quaker family from Norfolk in 1737, Thomas Paine first worked, like his father, as a corset maker. He then tried his hand as a sailor, teacher, and an excise man. He was dismissed from the latter occupation following a protest over pay. Whilst in London Paine met Benjamin Franklin and travelled to America in 1774, finding work there as a journalist. Fighting between British soldiers and colonists broke out the following year. In 1776, Paine published his first great pamphlet. Denouncing monarchy, asserting equality of rights, and calling unequivocally for an independent America, the pamphlet was entitled *Common Sense*. It was a title brilliant in its simplicity, indicative of Paine's innovative and wholly original style. *Common Sense* was an unparalleled success, selling over 100,000 copies and providing robust and plain-speaking propaganda for the American Revolution.

Having served in the colonial army and sitting as Secretary to the Congress Committee on Foreign Affairs, Paine returned to Britain in 1787, primarily to seek backing for a bridge that he had designed. Engineering was an interest, politics a passion, and Paine was soon embroiled in further political controversy, this time as a leading voice in the growing debate between the radical and the traditional. The French Revolution polarised British politics. In 1790, Edmund Burke published *Reflections on the Revolution* in France. Burke upheld the

British constitution, unwritten and based on convention, as a guarantor of security and sustainable change. The alternative, the sudden removal of the established order, he argued, would lead only to anarchy, rule by the 'swinish multitude'.

Paine was one among many radical thinkers who responded to Burke and he was, by far, the most effective. Again, Paine gave his work a straightforward title, understandable and accessible to all. Burke offered reflections addressed to office holders and other learned gentlemen who could properly concern themselves with politics. Paine's audience was all men, because all men, he argued, have rights. *The Rights of Man* was published in two parts. It caused a sensation, selling over 200,000 copies among a population of 10 million. (Moreover, this was an age when books were read out to fellow patrons in coffee houses and public houses.) Paine inspired ordinary men, filling them with the realisation that they too could understand, and participate in, political affairs. Paine's style of writing played an integral part in the success of *The Rights of Man*. Occasionally scurrilous, always provocative, Paine's writing has a vibrancy that sets it apart from other polemics of the time. Burke is lampooned and lambasted. Paine also writes scornfully of monarchy and the principle of hereditary government, a notion 'as absurd as an hereditary wise man; and as ridiculous as an hereditary poet-laureate.'

Part One of *The Rights of Man* was a defence of the French Revolution and an exposition of its guiding principles. Paine asserts popular sovereignty. Each generation has the right to choose its government, unfettered by the actions of its predecessors - a direct riposte to Burke. The individual is free to do that which hurts no other, constrained by the Law. The Law is an expression of the popular will as laid down by elected representatives. Paine was advocating ideas that today seem orthodox but were exceptionally radical for the 1790s. Part Two went further. Paine envisaged a classless society with progressive taxation, state pensions, and state education, a truly novel concept. It would be a republic governed by popularly elected representatives. Paine was, perhaps, the first to write of democracy in its modern sense. There would be no monarchy: true government has no use for such 'a silly, contemptible thing.' The aristocrats, 'the mere consumers of rent', would crumble, their existence no longer justified by an extravagantly expensive royal court.

Such sentiments and language could not be tolerated by the British government. Seditious libel became a capital offence. A writ was taken out against Paine, alleging defamation of the King. Faced with political persecution, he fled to France. There he fell victim of factional intrigue and spent several months in prison, ironically facing the threat of execution. Before returning to America he published *The Age of Reason*. With its attack on conventional Christianity and the Bible (the Old Testament, according to Paine was made up of little but

'obscene stories and voluptuous debaucheries' and the account of the Virgin Birth was 'hearsay upon hearsay') it was to prove as controversial and as provocative as his other writings. Its perceived atheism cost him many friends. He returned to America in 1802 where he died in 1809, isolated and unnoticed.

It was a sad death for a man who played a pivotal role in the development of modern democracy. He may not have devised concepts of universal rights and suffrage but he was the first to write of them in a popular manner. That, perhaps more than anything, was Paine's outstanding contribution. He took politics to the ordinary man. The Corresponding Societies, established in the 1790s by working men inspired by *The Rights of Man*, were seen as subversive and quickly suppressed by the British government. However, from that moment on, popular political movements took a new form. Ordinary men, Paine's sought-after audience, now believed that they could understand and rightfully influence political events. That was Thomas Paine's greatest legacy.

CLAIRE MILBURN, *Waterstone's*

> *'Of more worth is one honest man to society and in the sight of God, than all the crowned ruffians that ever lived.'*

WRITINGS BY PAINE

Common Sense
Penguin pbk £5.99
0140390162

The Rights of Man
Penguin pbk £5.99
0140390154

The Rights of Man, Common Sense and other Political Writings
Oxford UP pbk £5.99
0192835572

The Thomas Paine Reader
Penguin pbk £8.99
0140444963

A wide-ranging selection from Paine's writings, edited by Michael Foot and Isaac Kramnick.

Pickering & Chatto publish a five-volume Works of Thomas Paine in hardback

WRITINGS ON PAINE

Philp, Mark
Paine
Oxford UP pbk £5.99
019287666X

Keane, John
Tom Paine
Chatto hbk £20.00
0701137371

Mary

WOLLSTONECRAFT | 1792

A Vindication of the Rights of Women

A Vindication of the Rights of Woman, central to the understanding of the birth of modern feminism, was written in just six weeks at the latter end of 1791 and published the following year. The American and French Revolutions had brought the rights of man to the forefront of political thought but the rights of woman were overlooked. Mary Wollstonecraft took upon herself the task of championing these rights and placing them within the larger context of contemporary social upheaval. She has been hailed by recent scholars as 'the first modern feminist'; to some of her contemporaries, less flatteringly, she was a 'hyena in petticoats.'

Influenced by the political climate of the time, *Vindication* also emerged from the circumstances of Wollstonecraft's own life and her quest for personal and financial independence. Born in London, she worked as a teacher and governess before becoming a journalist and writer and entering the world of political dissenters and radical authors and artists such as Richard Price, Thomas Paine, Henry Fuseli and William Godwin. Many of these men were influenced strongly by Rousseau and, while Wollstonecraft was also inspired by the writings of the Swiss *philosophe* (particularly his ideas on education) she disagreed strongly with his view that a woman's role was 'to please men' and 'be useful to them.' Her most famous work was a bold and passionate attempt to correct the balance in

radical thought. She threw down her 'gauntlet' and fiercely attacked the political and moral systems responsible for the inferiority of women's education and their political and legal rights.

Wollstonecraft condemned marriage as 'domestic tyranny', restricting any freedom of choice or independence. So it is an unhappy irony that, after the publication of *Vindication*, her own emotional and romantic life was in stark contrast to the ideals she espoused. Deserted by her American lover Gilbert Imlay, and left with an illegitimate child, she fell into such a state of despair that she threw herself off Putney Bridge. However she survived this emotional turmoil and, in 1796, again pregnant, she married the novelist and political philosopher William Godwin. The marriage was to be short-lived. Just months after the wedding Wollstonecraft died of septicemia, twelve days after giving birth to her second daughter Mary, later to win fame as the author of *Frankenstein*. The following year Godwin published *Memoirs of the Author of A Vindication of the Rights of Woman,* exposing her personal life to public scrutiny. Her political ideals were interpreted in the light of what were seen as the faults of her personal life, and the public did not give *Vindication* or Wollstonecraft's other writings the recognition they deserved. For a long time she was mercilessly criticised and even some of those in the

> *'The divine right of husbands, like the divine right of kings, may, it is hoped, in this enlightened age, be contested without danger.'*

developing feminist movements of the nineteenth and early twentieth centuries, who might have been expected to turn to her work for inspiration, scorned it.

In truth Wollstonecraft's writings were years ahead of their time. Throughout the nineteenth century feminists and champions of the rights of women turned their attentions on specific issues (poverty, rape, suffrage for women) but it was only Wollstonecraft's book of 1792 that continued to offer a sustained and wide-ranging critique of women's position in society and to demand a complete and radical overhaul of social values. Wollstonecraft was a pioneer and only in the last few decades has *Vindication* been recognised as the foundation stone of modern feminism. Over 200 years, however, it has inspired other great thinkers – from John Stuart Mill to Germaine Greer, Emma Goldman to Simone de Beauvoir. In her original introduction to *Vindication* Wollstonecraft wrote that 'intellect will always govern' and the history of her book's influence offers some hope that this might, indeed, be the case.

SHARON ROWE, *Waterstone's Cardiff*

WRITINGS BY WOLLSTONECRAFT

'Mary' and 'The Wrongs of Woman'
Oxford UP pbk £5.99
019283536X

'Mary' and 'Maria'
Penguin pbk £7.99
0140433716

This volume in the Penguin Classics series includes these two novels by Mary Wollstonecraft and also 'Matilda', a novel by her daughter Mary Shelley.

Political Writings
Oxford UP pbk £5.99
0192823116

A Short Residence in Sweden, Norway and Denmark/Memoirs of the Author of 'The Rights of Woman'
Penguin pbk £7.99
0140432698

A Vindication of the Rights of Men
Prometheus, UK pbk £4.50
1573921068

A Vindication of the Rights of Woman
Penguin pbk £5.99
0140433821

This Penguin Classics edition is the most readily available edition of Wollstonecraft's best-known work. There are also editions published by Everyman's Library in hardback (£7.99 1857150864) and Everyman in paperback (£5.99 0460876155).

A seven-volume edition in hardback of all Mary Wollstonecraft's known writings is published by Pickering & Chatto in hardback.

WRITINGS ON WOLLSTONECRAFT

Tomalin, Claire
The Life and Death of Mary Wollstonecraft
Penguin pbk £9.99
0140167617

Schneir, Miriam (ed)
The Vintage Book of Historical Feminism
Vintage pbk £8.99
0099597810

This interesting anthology brings together work by Wollstonecraft and other pioneers of feminism including George Sand, Emma Goldman and Clara Zetkin.

Thomas

MALTHUS 1798

An Essay on the Principle of Population

Born in Dorking, Surrey, Malthus attended Cambridge where he distinguished himself as a mathematician and was elected a fellow of Jesus College. After a short career in the church, during which time his most influential writings were undertaken, he was appointed professor of political economy at the East India College at Haileybury in 1805. He remained there until his death. Initially Malthus was stimulated to write *An Essay on the Principle of Population* by what he saw as the baseless and dangerous optimism of radicals such as William Godwin, who believed that, if only change was made to the social structure, the ills of man could be eradicated. Published anonymously in 1798, and substantially revised and expanded in an 1803 edition, the *Essay* argued that such beliefs could not be sustained in the face of what Malthus saw as an unvarying law of population growth. There was a natural and unavoidable tendency of population (which grew geometrically) to outstrip the means of subsistence (which grew only arithmetically). Thus, whatever social structures were in place, poverty, disease and famine were inevitable. Indeed they were more than inevitable. They were necessary evils which acted as checks on the population growth.

Unsurprisingly Malthus's work was vigorously attacked by those very radicals, like Godwin, whose rosy view of man and nature had originally driven him to write it. However, it was immensely influential throughout much of the nineteenth century. Combined with the *laissez-faire* economics of writers like Adam Smith and David Ricardo, Malthus's theories provided the underpinning for arguments (of varying degrees of sophistication) against state intervention in the market or in social structures.

More rewardingly and interestingly in the long term, Malthus's ideas about rapid increase in population provided an essential stimulus to Darwin's thinking. Such rapid increase necessarily led to a struggle for existence. In his *Autobiography* Darwin made his debt to Malthus explicit. 'In October 1838 I happened to read for amusement Malthus on Population, and being well-prepared to appreciate the struggle for existence which everywhere goes on from long-continued observation of the habits of animals and plants, it at once struck me that under these circumstances favourable variations would tend to be preserved, and unfavourable ones to be destroyed. The results of this would be the formation of a new species. Here then I had at last got a theory by which to work.'

'Population, when unchecked, increases in a geometrical ratio. Subsistence only increases in an arithmetical ratio.'

WRITINGS BY MALTHUS

An Essay on the Principle of Population
Oxford UP pbk £6.99
0192830961

An Essay on the Principle of Population
Penguin pbk £7.99
014043206X

Edited by Anthony Flew, this volume of the Penguin Classics also includes *A Summary View of the Principle of Population*

An Essay on the Principle of Population
Cambridge UP pbk £8.95
0521429722

One of the Cambridge Texts in the History of Political Thought.

Pickering and Chatto publish an eight-volume edition of the Complete Works of Malthus.

WRITINGS ON MALTHUS

Petersen, W.
Malthus: Founder of Modern Demography
Transaction Publications pbk £19.95
0765804816

Three Great Economists
Oxford UP pbk £9.99
0192876945

A collction of three of the Past Masters series which includes Malthus as well as Adam Smith and Keynes.

Georg Wilhelm Friedrich

HEGEL   1807

The Phenomenology of Spirit

Born in Stuttgart in 1770, Hegel studied theology at the University of Tübingen where he met the future poet Hölderlin and the younger but precocious philosopher Friedrich Schelling. After graduation Hegel spent a number of years as a private tutor before moving, in 1801, to Jena where Schelling had become professor of philosophy while still in his early twenties. At this time Hegel and Schelling were working in close collaboration (indeed Hegel's first philosophical work compared Schelling's ideas favourably with those of the older philosopher Fichte) but their friendship came to an abrupt end in 1807 when Schelling took exception to something Hegel had written in his *Phenomenology of Spirit*. By the time this book was published Hegel, because the Napoleonic victory outside the town had resulted in the closure of the University of Jena, was working as a newspaper editor in Bamberg. For eight years between 1808 and 1816 he was the headmaster of a *gymnasium* in Nuremberg and he was then successively Professor of Philosophy at Heidelberg and, in 1818, at the University of Berlin. He remained there until his death in 1831.

Hegel was one of the great systematisers in the history of philosophy and his work can be alarmingly obscure. Yet the fundamental driving-force behind his system is relatively easy to grasp. In Hegel's system the dualism that had marked the work of Kant was healed and apparent opposites reconciled in a totality in which they are seen as merely different manifestations of the same phenomenon. Yet it is these polarities which allow for development in the system. Each proposition or 'thesis' is by itself inadequate and from this inadequacy emerges its polar opposite or 'antithesis'. This is itself inadequate and thesis and antithesis together engender the 'synthesis' from which the inadequacies of both have been eliminated. At this point a new thesis can emerge and the whole dialectical process can begin again. When applied to history, Hegel's ideas produced an intelligible pattern in which each nation or people developed its own spirit or 'mind' (Volkgeist). The culmination of this process would be the Weltgeist or 'world-mind'- very close to the 'absolute-mind', produced in the ideal synthesis of objective mind (society) and subjective mind (the individual) which finally, in Hegel's view, resolves all divisions between spirit and matter. Purged of their spiritual dimension and re-christened 'dialectical materialism', Hegel's ideas were taken and transformed by Marx. They have thus contributed a major influence to the most powerful political philosophy to emerge from the nineteenth century. Hegel's writings about art and religion, with their emphasis on them as modes of thought rather than just expressions of feeling, as ways (albeit inferior to philosophy) of apprehending reality, have also been influential in the years since his death.

'In history, we are concerned with what has been and what is; in philosophy, however, we are concerned not with what belongs exclusively to the past or to the future, but with that which is, both now and eternally – in short, with reason.'

1807 **Georg Wilhelm Friedrich Hegel** The Phenomenology of Spirit

WRITINGS BY HEGEL

Aesthetics: Lectures on Fine Art Vol.I
Oxford UP pbk £19.95
0198238169

Aesthetics: Lectures on Fine Art Vol.II
Oxford UP pbk £19.95
0198238177

Encyclopedia of the Philosophical Sciences: Logic
Oxford UP pbk £13.95
0198245122

Encyclopedia of the Philosophical Sciences: Philosophy of Mind
Oxford UP pbk £14.95
0198750145

Introduction to the Lectures on the History of Philosophy
Oxford UP pbk £12.99
0198249918

Introductory Lectures on Aesthetics
Penguin pbk £7.99
014043335X

Lectures on the Philosophy of World History
Oxford UP pbk £12.95
0521281458

The Phenomenology of Spirit
Oxford UP pbk £17.50
0198245971

The Philosophy of History
Dover pbk £9.95
0486201120

The Philosophy of Right
Oxford UP pbk £16.50
0195002768

Political Writings
Cambridge UP pbk £14.95
0521459753

The Hegel Reader
Blackwell pbk £15.99
0631203478

WRITINGS ON HEGEL

Cambridge Companion to Hegel
Cambridge UP pbk £16.95
0521387116

Singer, Peter
Hegel
Oxford UP pbk £5.99
0192875647

Plant, Raymond
Hegel
Phoenix pbk £2.00
075380185X

Hegel for Beginners
Icon pbk £8.99
1874166447

Arthur

SCHOPENHAUER | 1819

The World as Will and Representation

Arthur Schopenhauer occupies a rather uneasy place in the western philosophical canon. Although he is certainly regarded as one of the greatest philosophers of the nineteenth century he has had as much impact on literature and other arts as on academic philosophy. His work was enthusiastically embraced by Wagner who saw in his championing of music a cause for celebration. Ironically Schopenhauer was not a fan of Wagner's work. Thomas Hardy, Joseph Conrad and Thomas Mann were all impressed by his glamourisation of despair. His descriptions of biological development are seen by many as a precursor to Darwin and his ideas on both memory and sexual desire would inspire Freud. Wittgenstein would rather ostentatiously place Schopenhauer's (by then deeply unfashionable) tomes on the empty shelves of his Cambridge rooms. But if one name is inextricably linked with Schopenhauer it is that of Friedrich Nietzsche. It could be argued that Nietzsche whose own work would ultimately overshadow his, never really escaped the influence of Schopenhauer. Yet, like his famous disciple, Schopenhauer would remain unread for the majority of his own lifetime.

Fame came late in life and seemed to do little to disburden him of his dark outlook. Schopenhauer's pessimism appears to have formed early in life. His mercantile father had forced him to pursue a business appren-ticeship and at seventeen Schopenhauer claimed to have been 'gripped by the misery of life'. While Leibiniz held that this world was the best of all possible worlds, for Schopenhauer this world would always be the worst of all possible worlds. His own academic career was only possible after his father's death, itself an act of suicide. While this death was certainly fortuitous for Schopenhauer, he blamed and resented his mother for her part in his father's demise and then for her subsequent fame as a novelist. Perhaps unsurprisingly his writings are littered with scathing attacks on women. Bryan Magee, in his book on Schopenhauer, has even gone so far as to suggest that he was a repressed homosexual.

The completion of his magnum opus *The World as Will and Representation* was met with unanimous indifference but it did gain him an assistant position at the university of Berlin. Here he rather foolishly decided to schedule his own lectures at the same time as those of Hegel, then seen as the inheritor of both Kant's philosophy and his place in German philosophy. Schopenhauer's failure to seduce students away from Germany's most renowned idealist led him to renounce lecturing forever. This decision is typical of both his arrogance and the steely determination with which he conducted his life. While his writings may have advocated renouncing the horrors of existence, his daily routine seemed to show

'The will in us is certainly a thing-in-itself, existing for itself . . . It is nonetheless not capable of self-knowledge; because it is actually something that merely wills, not something that knows.'

little signs of adhering to such doctrines. Each morning he would leave the seclusion of his Frankfurt home to read *The Times* in the public library; later he would embark on a walk, regardless of the weather, before indulging in an evening of flute playing or attending the theatre. Guests would have to quickly adapt to such rituals or receive a brush with his well-developed temper. Despite such a stony façade, he had something of a reputation as a witty conversationalist.

Schopenhauer's philosophy, like that of so many of the contemporaries he despised, begins by espousing many of the metaphysical conventions conceived by Kant. Immanuel Kant held that the everyday world, the world given in sense-perception, is a mere representation, a creation of the human mind quite different from the reality or 'world-in-itself' that underlies it. As a biological survival mechanism the human brain presents the world to us in a useful rather than coincidental way. We have to experience the world in time and space; we have to experience causal connections that persist through time. So it follows that if objects must exist in space and in time for us to experience them we must also be enduring mental substances. Schopenhauer, unlike the idealists who chose to abandon Kant's troublesome concept of the thing-in-itself in favour of a world of pure ideas, believed we could form ideas about the true nature of things-in-themselves. This for him was possible because we not only experience the phenomenal world through space and time but as a body. We therefore experience ourselves not only like other external objects of perception but also from within as a will to live.

It is this will that is the primal reality of our universe. It is outside of time and space and all reason is subject to what he sees as its pernicious striving.

So while the everyday phenomenal world is subject to the *principium individuationis* i.e. it is a world of individuals, 'the will' beneath is beyond plurality i.e. one singular entity. It is this illusion of difference that leads us to experience the world as an evil, viciously competitive place; we are therefore compelled by the character of existence to cause one another suffering. The will has only one goal (that of perpetuating its very existence) and Schopenhauer's state of nature, much like that of Hobbes, is a state of perpetual conflict. This primacy of the life force or 'will' over the mind would have a profound influence on psychoanalysis.

It is only through aesthetic contemplation that we can escape this dreadful reality. True works of art offer us rare moments of metaphysical insight and penetrate, to use Schopenhauer's Upanishad-inspired phrase, the 'veil of Maya'. We realise that we are not individuals but part of a universal whole and cease, briefly, to strive. He feels that the noblest form of art is tragedy because through it we become most keenly aware of the 'supersensible side of our nature'. Music has a special place in his system for while the other arts offer us representations of individuals or events of reality that provide insights into the will, music gives us an immediate copy of the will. He derives this view from music's immediate and seemingly abstract character. Opera becomes problematic for Schopenhauer, as it seems to imply that the purest form of music is instrumental and it is with some reluctance that this Rossini-loving thinker states that opera is 'an unmusical invention for the benefit of unmusical minds'.

While art can offer us welcome respite from the striving of the will, Schopenhauer contends that it is only through embracing an almost Buddhist rejection of life that we can find peace. Some would contend that suicide would appear to be a more appropriate course of action. For Schopenhauer, relentlessly pessimistic though he is, this is not an enlightened form of rejection but just the will asserting its insidious aims again.

TRAVIS ELBOROUGH, *Waterstone's*

WRITINGS BY SCHOPENHAUER

Essays and Aphorisms
Penguin pbk £6.99
0140442278

On the Basis of Morality
Hackett pbk £8.95
1571810536

The World as Will and Representation
Dover pbk £11.95
0486217612

Essay on the Freedom of The Will
Cambridge UP pbk £9.95
0521577667

WRITINGS ON SCHOPENHAUER

Magee, Bryan
The Philosophy of Schopenhauer
Oxford UP pbk £15.99
0198237227

Tanner, Michael
Schopenhauer
Phoenix pbk £3.00
0753804425

Sir Charles

LYELL | 1830–33

Principles of Geology

Born in Scotland, Lyell was educated at Oxford where he originally studied law. While at the university he attended the lectures of William Buckland, whose discoveries in the Kirkdale cave in North Yorkshire were soon to establish palaeontology as a scientific discipline. Buckland stimulated a burgeoning interest in geology and, although Lyell was called to the Bar, he devoted himself to scientific study. In the early 1830s he was professor of geology at King's College, London and it was at this time that he published the first edition of his monumental *Principles of Geology*. He was to revise the work eleven times in the next forty years and it became one of the most influential books of the nineteenth century, second only to *The Origin of Species* in its effects on Victorian views of the earth and its history. Darwin himself became a close friend and Lyell was one of those who persuaded him to present his ideas to a wider public. Lyell became one of the great public figures of Victorian science. He was knighted in 1848 and made a baron sixteen years later.

Lyell's great achievement was to establish clearly the antiquity of the earth and to show that natural processes still at work could, over huge stretches of time, have produced the geological phenomena we see today. When he began his work the prevailing theory in geology was catastrophism which claimed that only major catastrophes (the Biblical flood, for example) could make fundamental changes to the earth's surface. The advantages of catastrophism, in a religious age, were that it could be reconciled with the Bible's account of the Creation and it could accommodate the idea of an earth that had been in existence only a few thousand years. Using the ideas of the eighteenth century geologist James Hutton as a starting point, Lyell built up the opposing theory of uniformitarianism. Uniformitarianism emphasised the power of natural forces to effect gradual geological change over long periods of time and Lyell in *Principles of Geology* and other books like *The Elements of Geology* and *The Geological Evidences of the Anitiquity of Man* amassed a great body of evidence in the shape of geological observations to support his ideas. By the time he died, it was virtually impossible for any but the most diehard fundamentalist to cling to Biblical accounts of the earth's creation. The late Victorian intellectual was obliged to inhabit an earth that was hundreds of thousands, perhaps millions of years old and his own, previously privileged position in the grander scheme of things had to be radically questioned.

'The mind was slowly and insensibly withdrawn from imaginary pictures of catastrophes and chaotic confusion such as haunted the imagination of earlier cosmogonists. Numerous proofs were discovered of the tranquil deposition of sedimentary matter and the slow development of organic life.'

WRITINGS BY LYELL

Principles of Geology
Penguin pbk £9.99
014043528X

Abridged edition. Complete
multi-volume edition published
by University of Chicago Press.

WRITINGS ON LYELL

Stephen Jay Gould
Time's Arrow, Time's Cycle
Penguin pbk £7.99
0140135723

Includes much material about the
history of geology and the ways
that people have envisaged the
earth's past. Gould writes interestingly and engagingly on a wide
variety of topics, including the
work of James Hutton and of Sir
Charles Lyell

Carl Von

CLAUSEWITZ | 1832

On War

Born into a genteelly impoverished family in Magdeburg, Prussia, Clausewitz joined the Prussian army when he was still a boy and spent his teens serving in that army during the Napoleonic Wars. In 1801 he entered the War College in Berlin where he came under the influence of the forward-thinking General von Scharnhorst. Following the disastrous battle of Jena and the subsequent campaign Clausewitz spent time as a prisoner of the French and then returned to Berlin to join Scharnhorst's drive to reform the Prussian army. During Napoleon's invasion of Russia, Clausewitz worked as a staff officer attached to the Russian forces and, after Napoleon's defeat, became a general and administrative head of the War College. The twelve years in which he held that position were the years in which he worked on his ideas about the conduct and strategy of warfare which were to be published as *Vom Kriege* (On War). In 1830 Clausewitz was transferred from the War College to regular forces stationed at Breslau.There he contracted cholera and died on November 16th 1831. His work was edited by his widow and appeared posthumously.

As well as *On War* Clausewitz wrote extensively on Napoleon's campaigns and used examples from them and from the military successes of Frederick the Great in his strategic writings. His writings are tied to a specific historical period yet have transcended that period to become possibly the most influential writings on the subject of war ever published. Throughout the nineteenth century his influence was felt, both in Prussia and in other European countries, and the leading generals of both the World Wars this century were steeped in the thought of Clausewitz and his followers. Even in an age of smart bombs and warfare at a distance, Clausewitz's strategic concepts and realism about the nature of war have their relevance. It is this unflinching realism and refusal to romanticise the terrible violence of war that distinguished Clausewitz. Rejecting eighteenth century views, which tended to see war as some kind of elaborate chess-game, he emphasised the need for decision by battle as the prerequisite of a military campaign. Tactics and strategy should be single-mindedly concentrated on the destruction of enemy forces. 'We do not hesitate to regard as an established truth,' Clausewitz wrote, 'that in strategy more depends on the number and the magnitude of the victorious combats than on the form of the great lines by which they are connected.' Yet it must be acknowledged, he felt, that military action did not take place in a social and political vacuum. Military and political strategy had to march together. The successful general needed to face up to the destruction and violence of war, and realise that it was only through them that a nation imposed its will on another, but also to acknowledge that they were a means to an end that was essentially political.

'War is nothing but a continuation of politics by other means.'

WRITINGS BY CLAUSEWITZ

On War
Penguin pbk £8.99
0140444270
Abridged edition

WRITINGS ON CLAUSEWITZ

Howard, Michael
Clausewitz
Oxford UP pbk £5.99
0192876074

Paret, Peter
Clausewitz and the State
Princeton UP pbk £15.95
069100806X

Paret, Peter
Understanding Clausewitz
Princeton UP pbk £11.95
0691000905

Soren
KIERKEGAARD | 1843
Either/Or

If Hegel is the leading example in the first half of the nineteenth century of a philosopher interested in large abstractions and vast systems, then Kierkegaard is the philosopher of the fragmentary and the individual. He takes a stand against the rational humanism of the time and proposes a philosophy which has its origin in passion and religious feeling, in the inner life of the individual, as much as it has in the intellect. Kierkegaard was born in Copenhagen into a family dominated by the brooding melancholy of his oppressively religious father. This melancholy was confirmed by family tragedies. Before Kierkegaard was 21 his mother and five of his six siblings had died. He was to inherit his father's temperament, in many ways, and wretchedness and despair were lifelong companions. In his journal in March 1836, he wrote, 'I have just returned from a party of which I was the life and soul; wit poured from my lips, everyone laughed and admired me – but I went away – and the dash should be as long as the earth's orbit ———— and wanted to shoot myself.' In 1841 he broke off his engagement to Regine Olsen, largely because he believed it would be unfair to inflict his black moods on her. Although he had already published some articles and papers before, it was in 1843 that he began the series of works on which his reputation rests. *Either/Or* was published in February of that year, *Fear and Trembling* in the October and *The*

Concept of Anxiety the following June. For the rest of his short life Kierkegaard was an astonishingly prolific writer, producing books and pamphlets under his own name and various pseudonyms. Although a passionately idiosyncratic Christian himself, he launched a series of attacks on the dogmas and hidebound rituals of the organised church. On his deathbed, in October 1855, a pastor asked Kierkegaard if he wished to take Holy Communion. True to his principles, even at the last, Kierkegaard replied, 'Yes, but not from a parson.'

Kierkegaard may have had little impact outside his native country during his lifetime but he has been an enormously influential figure on philosophers and thinkers in this century. Because of his distrust of Hegelian systematising and his belief in the importance of choices made by the individual, he has been called the first existentialist and figures as diverse as Sartre and Buber owe something to him. It is choice, choice made as a kind of leap of faith, that is at the centre of Kierkegaard's philosophy. 'Through having ventured to take a decisive step,' he wrote in *Concluding Unscientific Postscript*, 'in the utmost intensity of subjective passion and with full consciousness of one's eternal responsibility... one learns something else about life, and learns that it is quite a different thing from being engaged, year in and year out, in piecing together

'Life is not a problem to be solved but a reality to be experienced.'

something for a system.' His belief in intense subjectivity ('The thing is to find a truth which is true for me, to find the idea for which I can live and die.') and his skill as a writer have ensured that Kierkegaard remains read when many of the systematisers whose work he so hated, have not.

WRITINGS BY KIERKEGAARD

The Concept of Anxiety
Princeton UP pbk £11.50
0691020116

**Concluding Unscientific Postscript
to 'Philosophical Fragments'**
Princeton UP pbk £25.00
0691020833 (2 Vols.)

The Diary of a Seducer
Pushkin P pbk £8.00
1901285235

Eighteen Upbuilding Discourses
Princeton UP pbk £17.75
0691020876

Either/Or
Penguin pbk £9.99
0140445773

Either/Or: Part I
Princeton UP pbk £16.75
0691020418

Either/Or: Part II
Princeton UP pbk £12.95
0691020426

Papers and Journals: A Selection
Penguin pbk £9.99
0140445897

Parables of Kierkegaard
Princeton UP pbk £8.50
0691020531

The Sickness Unto Death
Penguin pbk £9.99
0140445331

Works of Love
Princeton UP pbk £17.95
0691059160

The above list includes only a selection of the many volumes of Kierkegaard's writings available from Princeton UP.

WRITINGS ON KIERKEGAARD

**Cambridge Companion
to Kierkegaard**
Cambridge UP pbk £16.95
0521477190

**Gardiner, Patrick
Kierkegaard**
Oxford UP pbk £5.99
0192876422

Kierkegaard: A Critical Reader
Blackwell pbk £15.99
0631201998

Karl   Friedrich

MARX & ENGELS | 1848

The Communist Manifesto

ALEX CALLINICOS, *Professor of Politics at the University of York and author of many books, including* Marxist Theory *(Oxford UP) and* A Social Theory *(Polity Press), explains why the Communist Manifesto remains essential reading.*

Karl Marx wrote the Manifesto of the Communist Party, drawing on a draft by his friend and collaborator Friedrich Engels, at the beginning of 1848. The party of which it was ostensibly the programme did not exist, merely a group of squabbling German *emigrés* with whom Marx and Engels soon broke. 1848 proved to be a year of revolutions throughout Europe, and the Manifesto reflects the mood which gave birth to these upheavals. In its supremely confident style it is evidently the work of young men (Marx and Engels were in their late twenties) exhilarated by their discovery of what they conceived to be the driving forces of history.

What reason is there still to read the Manifesto? Surely, as A.J.P. Taylor suggested more than a generation ago, it is hopelessly dated: 'What strikes a historian is how deeply the Communist Manifesto is rooted in the circumstances of its own time.' When Taylor wrote these words, large parts of the world were ruled by regimes that derived their legitimacy from the ideology of 'Marxism-Leninism'. In the autumn of 1989 these regimes were swept from power in Eastern

Europe in a revolutionary outburst as spectacular as anything that occurred in 1848. Two years later the Communist Party of the Soviet Union fell, bringing down with it the state over which it had presided. The collapse of the Communist regimes marked the apparently definitive triumph of the liberal capitalism of North America and Western Europe. What place could Marx's thought have in this world?

It is, however, the very extent of capitalism's domination of the globe that makes the Manifesto still worth reading. When Marx wrote it, industrial capitalism had only begun to establish itself in portions of north-western Europe and the north-east sea-board of the United States, though the rest of the world was starting to feel its gravitational pull as international trade in manufactured goods took off. What is remarkable about the Manifesto is the extent to which Marx grasped the logic of this system when it was still taking its first steps.

Thus, reading the first few pages of the opening chapter, one is likely to be struck less by the rather ornate language and occasionally obscure contemporary references than by the freshness and contemporaneity of the analysis of capitalism it offers. Though Marx is capitalism's greatest critic, he nevertheless highlights the 'most revolutionary part' it plays:

'The philosophers have merely interpreted the world in various ways; the point, however, is to change it.'

The bourgeoisie cannot exist without constantly revolutionizing the instruments of production, and thereby the relations of production, and with them the whole relations of society. Conservation of the old modes of production in unaltered form, was, on the contrary, the first condition of existence for all earlier industrial classes. Constant revolutionizing of production, uninterrupted disturbance of all social conditions, everlasting uncertainty and agitation distinguish the bourgeois epoch from all earlier ones. All fixed, fast-frozen relations, with their train of ancient and venerable prejudices and opinions are swept away, all new-formed ones become antiquated before they can ossify. All that is solid melts into air, all that is holy is profaned, and man is at last compelled to face with sober senses, his real conditions of life and his relations with his kind.

The portrait Marx paints of capitalism is compelling because of its modernity. The Manifesto anticipates the analyses offered by, among others the sociologist Anthony Giddens, of what it has become fashionable to call 'globalization': 'The bourgeoisie has through its exploitation of the world market given a cosmopolitan character to production and consumption in every country.' This is a cultural as well as an economic process: Marx proclaims the emergence of 'a world literature'. But it is, in the main, economic competition which provides the main driving force: 'The cheap prices of its [the bourgeoisie's] commodities are the heavy artillery with which it breaks down all Chinese walls. It compels all nations, on pain of extinction, to adopt the bourgeois mode of production. In a word, it creates a world after its own image.' Today we

are more likely to think of cheap Asian goods breaking into Western markets than the other way round, but the relentless process of international competition Marx describes is very familiar.

Equally striking is his account of capitalism's subversion of traditional social relations: it 'has left remaining no other nexus between man and man than naked self-interest, than callous 'cash payment'.' For example, 'the bourgeoisie', he claims, 'has reduced the family relation to a mere money relation'. Here too we are on familiar ground. Over the past generation Western societies have experienced both major changes in family structures and a great surge in possessive individualism as what Thomas Carlyle called the 'cash nexus' comes to shape ever more aspects of social life. Conservative and centre-left politicians strongly committed to the free market are seeking desperately to restore traditional family life. The Manifesto implies that this is a Utopian project – allowing the market to reign supreme necessarily undermines institutions that can only function effectively if money is not the measure of everything.

Of course, there is much more to the Manifesto than this compelling portrait of capitalism. In the first place, the latter rests on the materialist theory of history Marx and Engels which developed in the mid-1840s and which is sketched out at the beginning of the first chapter. According to this theory, historical change is driven by the conflicts that develop within social production, and in particular those between exploiting and exploited classes. Hence the famous opening

sentence: 'The history of all hitherto existing society is the history of class struggle.' Secondly, the Manifesto, as its title suggests, outlines the programme of a political movement that seeks to rid the world of all forms of class domination, and to establish a communist society where 'the free development of each is the condition for the free development of all.'

What connects these two aspects of the Manifesto is Marx's effort to show that real historical forces are working towards the overthrow of capitalism: the chief fault of his socialist predecessors, he believed, lay in their tendency to allow fantasies about the future substitute for hard-headed analysis. Capitalism, like earlier modes of production, is a self-limiting system. It rests on the exploitation of wage-labour and so 'produces, above all, its own grave-diggers' in the shape of an increasingly militant and organized working class. Moreover, capitalist relations of production, geared to the competitive pursuit of profit, are increasingly fetters on the further development of the productive powers of humankind. What economists now call the 'business cycle' of boom and slump 'is but the revolt of modern productive forces against modern conditions of production, against the property relations that are the conditions for the existence of the bourgeoisie and of its rule'. Out of this combination of social conflict and economic crisis would emerge a revolution of a new kind for the first time in history 'the self-conscious, independent movement of the immense majority, in the interest of the immense majority'.

Even this brief summary indicates the gulf separating Marx's conception of communism from what, until the upheavals of 1989 and 1991, was known as 'existing socialism' in Eastern Europe and the USSR: he would later call socialism 'the self-emancipation of the working class' – a necessarily democratic process in which the exploited free themselves. But it also highlights the contrast between Marx's expectations and the course of world history since 1848.

To make sense of this discrepancy we must take into account the evolution of Marx's own views. The economic analysis of his great work *Capital*, reflecting two additional decades of research, is considerably more nuanced than the relatively crude theory on offer in the Manifesto: thus he later rejected the so-called 'iron law of wages', according to which wages cannot rise above a bare subsistence minumum. It is also worth keeping in mind that he regarded the working class as comprising all those compelled to live by selling their ability to work in exchange for a wage, not just those performing manual labour or working in factories.

Marx, moreover, was the founder of a tradition. His successors had to grapple with questions he ignored or merely touched on. Take, for example, the Manifesto's most obvious error: 'National differences and antagonisms are daily more and more vanishing.' Later Marxists - for example, Lenin and Rosa Luxemburg - had to address the political reality of the nation in all its complexity and destructive potential.

Yet even thus modified and developed, Marx's thought must still face a world profoundly at odds with it. The paradox is that its portrayal of capitalism offers what is still the best account we have of what drives this world. As long as capitalism exists, the Manifesto will be read.

WRITINGS BY MARX

Capital Volume I
Penguin pbk £15.99
0140445684

Capital Volume II
Penguin pbk £12.99
0140445692

Capital Volume III
Penguin pbk £14.99
0140445706

The Communist Manifesto
Penguin pbk £2.99
0140444785

The Communist Manifesto
Oxford UP pbk £2.99
0192834371

The Communist Manifesto
Verso pbk £9.00
1859848982

An edition published to mark
the 150th anniversary of the first
appearance of the manifesto, with
an introduction by Eric
Hobsbawm.

Early Writings
Penguin pbk £11.99
0140445749

**The German Ideology:
A Student's Edition**
Lawrence & Wishart pbk £6.99
0853152179

Grundrisse
Penguin pbk £17.00
0140445757

Later Political Writings
Cambridge UP pbk £10.95
0521367395

**Political Writings:
The Revolutions of 1848**
Penguin pbk £8.99
0140445714

**Political Writings:
Surveys from Exile**
Penguin pbk £7.99
0140445722

**Political Writings:
The First International**
Penguin pbk £11.00
0140445730

Selected Writings
Oxford UP pbk £17.99
0198760388

Lawrence & Wishart publish a
fifty volume, definitive edition of
the Collected Works of Marx and
Engels, including their extensive
correspondence. Each volume is
hardback and priced between
£25.00 and £45.00.

WRITINGS ON MARX

Althusser, Louis
For Marx
Verso pbk £10.00
1859841465

Rius
Introducing Marx
Icon pbk £8.99
1840460555

Elster, Jon (ed)
Karl Marx: A Reader
Cambridge UP pbk £15.95
0521338328

Blumenberg, Werner
Karl Marx: An Illustrated History
Verso hbk £18.00
1859847056

McLellan, David
Karl Marx: A Biography
Macmillan pbk £10.00
0333639472

Singer, Peter
Marx
Oxford UP pbk £5.99
0192875108

McLellan, David
Marx
Fontana pbk £6.99
0006861075

Henry David

THOREAU 1854

Walden

Thoreau was born in Concord, Massachusetts and educated at Harvard. A friend of the essayist and poet Ralph Waldo Emerson, Thoreau has often been described as a leading member of the Transcendentalist movement, so important in Emerson's life and in the intellectual life of mid-nineteenth century America. Thoreau certainly shared many beliefs in common with the Transcendentalists but, to see him primarily in the context of the movement, is to lessen and diminish his individuality and importance. During his lifetime Thoreau made little money from his writings (he earned his living in trades as various as teacher and pencil-maker) and he published only two books, *A Week on the Concord and Merrimack Rivers* (1849) and *Walden* (1854). He also published a number of essays including the highly influential 'Civil Disobedience' in which he argued that the individual had the right to listen to his own conscience and to refuse to pay taxes if he felt that the purpose to which they would contribute was an immoral one. (He followed his own argument and spent a brief period in jail, having refused to pay taxes in a protest against slavery in the Southern states.)

Walden, which describes Thoreau's two years of attempted self-sufficiency in a wooden hut he had built on the edge of Walden Pond, is amongst the most important of American books and amongst the most wide-ranging in its influence throughout the century and a half since its first publication. It is a book that is an extraordinary mixture of the practical and the visionary. Like Emerson and others, Thoreau advocates the quasi-religious properties of the natural world and the possibilities of achieving a mystical union with nature. He also describes his domestic economy, his agricultural experiments and his very precise observations of the plants and animals around him. He questions the materialism of the age and the work ethic that drives it yet he never loses sight of the 'real' world of civilisation to which he later returned. Thoreau's work combines philosophy, political thought and natural history and he can be seen, without too much anachronism, as the forerunner of today's ecological movement. Many volumes of his journals and uncollected writings have been published since his death.

'If a man does not keep pace with his companions, perhaps it is because he hears a different drummer. Let him step to the music which he hears, however measured or far away.'

1854 Henry David Thoreau Walden

WRITINGS BY THOREAU

Cape Cod
Princeton UP pbk £8.50
069100076X

The Maine Woods
Princeton UP pbk £12.95
0691014043

Political Writings
Cambridge UP pbk £10.95
0521476755

The Portable Thoreau
Penguin pbk £9.99
0140150315

Walden and Civil Disobedience
Penguin pbk £6.99
0140390448

A Week on the Concord and Merrimack Rivers
Penguin pbk £7.99
0140434429
(due summer 2000)

WRITINGS ON THOREAU

Harding, Walter
The Days of Henry Thoreau
Princeton UP pbk £13.95
0691024790

Sayre, Robert F.
New Essays on Walden
Cambridge UP pbk £12.95
0521424828

Peck, Daniel
Thoreau's Morning Work
Yale UP pbk £9.95
0300061048

See also
Emerson, Ralph Waldo
Selected Essays
Penguin pbk £7.99
0140390138

Waterstone's Guide to Ideas **127**

Charles

DARWIN | 1859

The Origin of Species

Darwin was born in Shrewsbury in 1805. His grandfather was the doctor, poet and polymath Erasmus Darwin whose poem, *The Loves of the Plants*, first published in 1789, contains some hints of the kind of evolutionary theory his grandson was later to elaborate. Charles Darwin was educated at Edinburgh University and Christ's College, Cambridge and then, in 1831, made what was the most significant decision of his life when he chose to embark as naturalist on the Beagle in its voyage to South America. In the course of a five-year voyage Darwin had the opportunity to study a wide variety of flora and fauna, as the Beagle sailed to the Cape Verde Islands, the South American mainland, the Galapagos, Tahiti and New Zealand, and it was during these years that the first seeds of his ideas about natural selection and the evolution of species were sown. Returning to England in 1836 Darwin published a *Journal of Researches into the Geology and Natural History of the Various Countries Visited by HMS Beagle* three years later and this, together with a number of scientific papers, established his reputation. He married his cousin Emma Wedgwood in 1839 and, in 1842, he moved to Down House, Down in Kent, where, supported by private means, he lived the life of a country gentleman and, despite years of ill-health, continued to address the problem of the origin of the species. For two decades Darwin developed and refined his ideas but they were unknown outside a small circle of friends and fellow-scientists. It is possible that he would not have published his theories in his lifetime had not a younger naturalist called Alfred Russel Wallace, living in the Far East, roused him to action by sending him a paper which made it clear that he, Wallace, was moving towards similar conclusions. Darwin, encouraged by his friends Hooker and Lyell, put together a paper which, together with Wallace's, was read at an epoch-making meeting of the Linnean Society in 1858. The following year Darwin published *The Origin of Species by Means of Natural Selection*. The book aroused great controversy from which Darwin, a shy and modest man, shrank. It was left to more assertive personalities like T.H. Huxley ('Darwin's Bulldog') to defend the idea of natural selection against the attacks of outraged churchmen and others. For the rest of his life Darwin continued to live and work at Down, producing books which ranged from the equally controversial *The Descent of Man* (1871), which extended his ideas to man's origins, to books on far less contentious issues such as *The Formations of Vegetable Mould through the Action of Worms* (1881). He died in 1882.

Darwin's central argument has been described by the American philosopher Daniel Dennett as 'the single best idea anyone has ever had.' Yet it is an extraordinarily simple and elegant explanation of the variety and richness of nature which had so impressed Darwin on his

Beagle voyage. Different members of the same species have different characteristics. Some of these accidentally occurring variations allow the individual which possesses them an adaptive advantage. Those individuals which have the variation, marginally more suited to their environment than those which do not have it, are more likely to survive and reproduce. Thus the next generation will have more individuals possessed of that adaptive advantage. And so on. Over a long period of time natural selection operates on random mutation and what was once a characteristic of a few individuals becomes a widespread characteristic of a species now better adapted to its environment. And, over an even longer period of time, natural selection allows for the evolution of one species into another. Species are not fixed forever. They change over time and individual variation leads to the death of some and the creation of new ones.

'I have called this principle, by which each slight variation, if useful, is preserved, by the term Natural Selection.'

WRITINGS BY DARWIN

The Origin of Species
Penguin pbk £5.99
0140432051

The Origin of Species
Oxford UP pbk £5.99
019283438X

The Descent of Man
Princeton UP pbk £21.50
0691023697

The Voyage of the Beagle
Penguin pbk £5.95
014043268X

The Expression of the Emotions in Man and Animals
pbk £9.99
0006387349

A recent edition of a book Darwin first published in 1872 in which he discussed similarities and differences between human and animal behaviour and their expression.

Darwin's Letters
Cambridge UP pbk £9.99
0521566770

A selection of letters Darwin wrote from 1825, when he was at Edinburgh University, miserably studying medicine, to 1859, when *The Origin of Species* was first published. With a foreword by Stephen Jay Gould.

A Darwin Selection
Fontana pbk £7.99
0006863213

A selection of Darwin's most important writings, chosen and put into context by Matt Ridley, author of *The Red Queen*.

The Autobiography of Charles Darwin
Dover pbk £9.95
0486204790

Autobiographical writings by Darwin gathered together originally by his son Francis.

Pickering and Chatto publish a set of Darwin's complete published writings in 29 hardback volumes.

WRITINGS ON DARWIN

Desmond & Moore
Darwin
Penguin pbk £12.00
0140131922

Browne, Janet
Darwin : Volume 1: Voyaging
Pimlico pbk £12.00
0712673059

Browne, Janet
Darwin : Volume 2
J. Cape hbk £20.00
0224042122

The first volume of what promises to be the standard biography of Darwin for the foreseeable future was published in hardback in 1995 and covers the years from childhood to the publication of *The Origin of Species*. The second volume appeared in hardback in the autumn of 1999.

Darwin
Oxford UP pbk £5.99
0192875566
One of the invaluable Past Masters series published by Oxford which encapsulates Darwin's ideas in less than a hundred pages without trivialising or over-simplifying them.

Miller, Jonathan
Darwin for Beginners
Icon Books pbk £8.99
1874166013
Another book which introduces the reader to Darwin's thought in simplified form. One of a series of books which use the format of a comic book but employ the talents of experts (in this case Jonathan Miller) to provide a text of some depth.

DARWIN AND DARWINISM TODAY

Darwin's ideas, modified by the discoveries of the past century, continue to form the basis of biological thought today. There are several excellent books available which give the general reader an overview of the position of Darwinism in contemporary science and thought:

Daniel Dennett
Darwin's Dangerous Idea
Penguin pbk £10.99
014016734X

Niles Eldredge
Reinventing Darwin
Everyman hbk £16.99
0460861468

The two writers who have done most to make Darwin and Darwinism comprehensible to the general reader are Stephen Jay Gould and Richard Dawkins. Although they disagree profoundly about the nature and implications of current Darwinian thought, they share the ability to write lucid expositions of often complex theories and arguments. Gould's range of reference and Dawkins's capacity for illuminating metaphor ensure that their books are rewarding reading for anyone seeking to know more about how Darwin's ideas continue to influence scien-

tists today. Gould's most accessible books are the collections of essays he has been publishing at regular intervals for more than a decade. The three most recent collections are:

Eight Little Piggies
Penguin pbk £8.99
0140179941

Dinosaur in a Haystack
Penguin pbk £8.99
0140256725

Leonardo's Mountain of Clams and the Diet of Worms
Jonathan Cape pbk £17.99
0224050435

Wonderful Life (Penguin pbk £8.99 0140133801) is a full-length study of the fossils found in the Burgess Shale and what they tell us about the nature of evolution and of history.

Dawkins, currently Professor for the Public Understanding of Science at Oxford, has written a number of best-selling popular science titles. His most recent book, **Unweaving the Rainbow** (Penguin pbk £8.99 0140264086) eloquently argues that science, far from disenchanting nature, works, if properly understood, to enhance the poetry and wonder of the natural world. **The Blind**

Watchmaker (Penguin pbk £8.99 0140144811) and **Climbing Mount Improbable** (Penguin pbk £8.99 0140179186) both offer very clear explanations of contemporary evolutionary thought and state the arguments of those who have been called 'Ultra-Darwinists', largely geneticists who see the individual creature as a vehicle for the ongoing transmission of 'the selfish gene'. It was Dawkins who invented that memorable phrase and **The Selfish Gene** (Oxford UP pbk £8.99 0192860925), although it was first published nearly twenty years ago, remains a trenchant statement of the 'ultra-darwinist' position.

Michael

FARADAY | 1859

Experimental Researches in Chemistry and Physics

Michael Faraday was born on September 22nd, 1791 in the Surrey village of Newington Butts, the area of London now known as Elephant and Castle. His father was a blacksmith whose long periods of ill health ensured that Faraday's childhood was a poor one. The whole family drew great spiritual comfort from their membership of a small Christian sect called the Sandemanians, who believed in the literal truth of the Bible and their own assured salvation. Faraday received only the rudiments of an education at Sunday school. At the age of fourteen he was apprenticed to a bookseller to learn the skill of bookbinding. Taking the opportunity to read the texts he had to bind, the young Faraday was particularly engaged by the article on electricity in the third edition of the *Encyclopaedia Britannica*. In 1812 he was offered tickets to attend lectures given at the Royal Institution by Humphry Davy. The intense young man caught Davy's attention by sending him bound notes of these lectures and in March 1813 Faraday was engaged by Davy as his assistant.

It has been said that Michael Faraday was Davy's greatest discovery. At his side, Faraday was trained primarily as an analytical chemist. As such he enjoyed remarkable success. In 1823 he became the first person to liquefy chlorine, and went on to liquefy over twenty gases in all, which provided the theoretical basis for the technology of refrigeration. He also isolated and described benzene, the simplest of the aromatic hydrocarbons and widely used today in the manufacture of plastics, dyes and detergents. Faraday's two laws of electrochemistry still hold good today, and it was his work which introduced into the language the terms electrolysis, anode, cathode and ion.

Yet Faraday is perhaps best remembered for his work on the relationship between electricity and magnetism. In 1820 Hans Christian Oersted had demonstrated that, when a magnetic compass needle was held across a wire carrying an electric current, the needle is deflected to point at a right angle to the wire. This effect was baffling in that it differed from the expected Newtonian model of straightforward attractive or repulsive effects as observed with static electricity, magnetism and gravity. Faraday understood that there was a circular force around the wire. In a famous experiment he demonstrated that a wire carrying a current could be made to rotate around a fixed magnet, and that likewise a magnet could be made to rotate around the fixed wire. Without declaring it as such, Faraday had constructed the first primitive electric motor. This discovery of electromagnetic rotation was published in October 1821, and the effect was studied all over Europe. Electric trains were in service on two continents only sixty years later.

It was ten years later that Faraday made his next significant advance in this field. Attempting to reproduce an electromagnetic phenomenon that had been reported by Francois Arago, Faraday wound two lengths of wire around the opposite sides of a soft iron ring. When a current was passed through one of the wires, a galvanometer detected a momentary current in the second wire. Faraday is therefore credited with the discovery of electromagnetic induction. He went on to realise that if he pushed a magnet into a coil of wire a current was induced in the wire, and likewise when the magnet was withdrawn. No current was induced when the magnet was stationary. Surmising that motion was necessary, Faraday conducted an experiment in which he rotated a copper disc between the poles of a magnet and discovered that a steady current flowed in the disc from its centre to its edge. By thus converting mechanical energy into electrical energy, Faraday constructed the world's first rotary electric generator, or dynamo. Perhaps no other single discovery played a greater role in transforming electricity during the Victorian age from a scientific curiosity into the power that has shaped the modern world. The Prime Minister, Robert Peel, visited Faraday and asked him what use his discovery of the dynamo effect might have. Faraday replied, 'I know not, but I wager that one day your government will tax it'.

It has been speculated that had Nobel Prizes been awarded in his lifetime, Faraday's work would have merited as many as six. Yet for all the international plaudits, his most profound contribution to scientific understanding was little recognised until after his death. The prevailing model of the universe in the nineteenth century was still that of Newtonian mechanics. Matter was understood as consisting of particles or points of force, the interaction between bodies being explained by the concept of action at a distance. Faraday was dissatisfied with this model as an explanation of how forces such as electricity and magnetism are communicated across space. His work on electromagnetic conduction led him to conceive of a magnet exerting lines of force which link its two poles and extend beyond the physical boundary of the magnet and across space. The influence of the magnet can then be explained by the field of force it generates. Matter itself, he suggested, was constructed not of particulate atoms but simply of centres of concentration within fields. James Clerk Maxwell studied Faraday's work on lines of force, and was intrigued by Faraday's theory that light could be explained in terms of vibrations in electric lines of force. Maxwell's equations gave mathematical form to Faraday's theories and are rightly regarded as the crowning achievement of nineteenth century science. Yet it is to Faraday's eternal credit that classical field theory was born not from the advanced mathematics of theorists, but from his intuitive grasp of reality, derived from a series of practical experiments a schoolchild can understand. A year after Faraday's death in 1867, his colleague John Tyndall wrote, 'I think it will be conceded that Michael Faraday was the greatest experimental philosopher the world has ever seen; and I will add the opinion, that the progress of future research will tend, not to dim or diminish, but to enhance and glorify the labours of this mighty investigator'.

ANDY WALKER,
Waterstone's Charing Cross Road

'How wonderful it is to me, the simplicity of nature when we rightly interpret her laws, and how different the convictions which they produce to the mind, in comparison with the uncertain conclusions which hypothesis or even theory present.'

WRITINGS BY FARADAY

The Forces of Matter
Prometheus, UK pbk £7.50
0879758112

The Philospher's Tree
Institute of Physics
pbk £16.99
075035711

A selection from Faraday's writings, linked by a commentry.

WRITINGS ON FARADAY

Cantor, Geoffrey
Michael Faraday:Sandemanian and Scientist
Macmillan pbk £16.99
0333588029

This book looks at the relationship between Faraday's scientific achievements and the religious beliefs of the small sect to which he belonged, and expands into a broader study of science and religion in the nineteenth century.

Guillen, Michael
Five Equations That Changed the World
Abacus pbk £7.99
0349110646

Includes the story of Faraday in an examination of five of the most significant scientific achievements of the last few centuries. The book also looks at Einstein, Newton, Clausius and Bernoulli.

John Stuart

MILL   1859

On Liberty

Earlier thinkers had given the concept of liberty an important role in their theories, including John Locke, Thomas Hobbes, Jean-Jacques Rousseau, Adam Smith and Thoreau. Each of these writers nonetheless proposed significant limitations on liberty, when individual freedom clashed with other ends deemed superior, such as morality, religion, or even social expediency.

John Stuart Mill, in contrast, made human liberty an absolute. An individual's freedom was, or should be, limited only by the obligation not to diminish others' freedom. 'The object of [On Liberty],' declared Mill, 'is to assert one very simple principle. That principle is, that the sole end for which mankind are warranted in interfering with the liberty of action of any of their number, is self-protection.'

This doctrine seems so familiar now – to those brought up in the latter half of the twentieth century – that it is easy to underestimate its radicalism. 'Over himself, over his body and mind, the individual [is] sovereign,' argued Mill. He thus undermined the pillars of mid-Victorian Britain: neither the church, nor the state, nor even parents were justified in interfering with the freedom of an individual, as long as his behaviour harmed no others.

Mill was responding in part to the institutional

shortcomings of the British parliamentary system. He went on to propose a number of reforms in his *Considerations on Representative Government* (1861). From 1865 to 1868 Mill served as Liberal Member of Parliament for Westminster, where he campaigned for several major reforms, notably the enfranchisement of women. But the real motive in publishing *On Liberty* was to demand a loosening of what Mill regarded as the suffocating constraints of society. He believed that people were increasingly intolerant of non-conformity. Society risked stifling intellectual and moral freedom, ending up 'like China'. (Mill had good personal reasons to resent the confining customs and norms of Victorian society).

Mill intended *On Liberty* to be widely read. It was a short, simplified statement of his doctrine, expressed with maximum clarity and force. The result is a fluent and highly readable book. Critics claimed that Mill had sacrificed philosophical rigour for the sake of rhetoric. If so, this can hardly have been accidental: *On Liberty* was the most carefully composed and thoroughly reworked piece Mill ever published. Despite the many criticisms of the essay, it was never revised or amended in any of the six editions published in Mill's lifetime.

Some of Mill's philosophical preoccupations probably reflected his personal life. Much of his work can be seen as a response to his father. James Mill was an eminent supporter of the radical doctrine of utilitarianism. He was a disciple and friend of the guru of utilitarianism, Jeremy Bentham. Put simply, utilitarianism held that the single criterion for morality was the principle of utility, defined as the greatest happiness of the greatest number. In deciding whether an action was right or wrong, one must determine scientifically where the balance of benefits and disbenefits lay. Key elements of utilitarianism included a hedonistic psychology which regarded men's sole motivation to be the pursuit of their own personal welfare; religious scepticism; and support for representative government and freedom of speech.

Although John Stuart Mill read none of Bentham's works until he was 15 years old, he was educated under what he later described as the 'Benthamite system'. Mill's father was his tutor, and Bentham his frequent visitor. Mill quickly excelled; he could read Greek by the age of three. He later insisted that his early progress had been purely due to his father's educational method, and that his own natural abilities were merely average. By the age of 16 Mill had established the Utilitarian Society and shortly after he joined the East India Company, working in the same office as his father.

When he was 20 Mill had a personal crisis. He was struck with the conviction that even the perfect realisation of utilitarianism could not guarantee happiness. He became severely depressed. Despite the brilliance of his education, he was at a loss to understand his own emotional state. His father's emotional coolness had left him ill-prepared for adult life. Bentham and James Mill had set out a design for the external circumstances of human life, but had failed to consider the internal dynamics of individuals. Mill determined to understand men's own emotional needs and to place these needs at the heart of his own philosophical system. His *Utilitarianism* of 1861 made clear how far his own mature thinking had modified and altered Benthamism.

In 1830 Mill met a married woman, Harriet Taylor. She became his close friend and confidante. The pair continued their unorthodox relationship for twenty years, despite the risk to the reputation of both parties. Although Mill insisted that the relationship was proper, he came under pressure to sever contact with Mrs Taylor. Only after the death of Harriet's first husband was Mill able to marry her. Mill lavished praise on his 'brilliant' partner, even crediting her with joint authorship of some of his works. She died in 1858, and *On Liberty* was published only a year later. By that time Mill was the dominant intellectual figure of his era. Much of his later life, including his years in Parliament, were devoted to the cause of women's suffrage. Inspired by his late wife's views on the discriminations inflicted on women in Victorian society, he wrote *The Subjection of Women*, a classic statement of nineteenth century feminism. Mill's *Autobiography* was published in 1873, the year of his death in Avignon where his wife lay buried.

JOE PONTIN, *Waterstone's Bristol Galleries*

'The sole end for which mankind are warranted, individually or collectively, in interfering with the liberty of action of any of their number, is self-protection.'

WRITINGS BY MILL

Autobiography
Penguin pbk £6.99
0140433163

On Liberty
Penguin pbk £2.99
0140432078

On Liberty and Other Essays
Oxford UP pbk £2.99
0192833847

Principles of Political Economy
Oxford UP
pbk £7.99
0192836722

Selected Writings
Norton pbk £6.95
0393970094

This volume in the Norton Critical Editions series provides annotations to many of Mill's most notable essays and includes a number of assessments of his work by leading critics.

Utilitarianism and Other Essays
Penguin pbk £6.99
0140432728

Routledge publish the Collected Works of John Stuart Mill in 33 hardback volumes.

WRITINGS ON MILL

Cambridge Companion to Mill
Cambridge UP pbk £13.95
0521422116

Stafford, William
John Stuart Mill
Macmillan pbk £12.99
0333628527

Ryan, Alan
The Philosophy of John Stuart Mill
Macmillan pbk £16.99
0333727193

Probably the best essay in Isaiah Berlin's *Four Essays on Liberty* (Oxford UP pbk £9.99 0192810340) is entitled 'John Stuart Mill and the Ends of Life'.

Gregor

MENDEL | 1865

Experiments in Plant Hybridization

One of the most significant publications in the history of science appeared in an 1865 edition of the journal *Proceedings of the Natural Science Society of Brno*. It was the work of an Augustinian monk from Brno who had conducted a series of experiments over more than twenty years, using pea plants grown in the garden of his monastery. The paper, appearing in an obscure journal, written by an obscure monk, was scarcely noticed. Mendel was increasingly involved in administrative work at the monastery and found difficulty in continuing his scientific work. (And, when he did, he was led increasingly down scientific dead-ends.) When Mendel died in 1884 no-one realised the importance of his work. It was sixteen years after his death that his experiments were re-discovered and only then did biologists begin to see that Mendel had laid the foundations for the science which came to be known as genetics. One of the questions which had exercised Darwin for years after the publication of *The Origin of Species* (What was the mechanism by which hereditary traits were passed from generation to generation?) had been answered by a Moravian monk only six years after Darwin's work had appeared.

Mendel was born in what is now the Czech Republic, the son of a farming family, and entered the Augustinian monastery in Brno at the age of nineteen. Apart from some time at the University of Vienna and several brief trips abroad he spent the rest of his life there. He began his experiments with plants in the mid-1840s and continued with them until 1868. By crossing pea plants which had clear differentiations in height, colour etc. and carefully logging the results, Mendel was able to formulate the basic principles behind heredity. He realised that it wasn't the characteristics themselves but the factors that determined them (what were later called 'genes') that were passed on and he appreciated that these units of inheritance were two in number for each characteristic, one coming from each parent. He also realised that there were both 'dominant' and 'recessive' genes and that characteristics which were not present in one generation (because the gene responsible for it was recessive) could return in later generations. Since the re-discovery of Mendel's work, and Bateson's naming of the new subject as 'genetics', the science has expanded at an enormous rate. But it owes its beginning to a Moravian monk patiently working in a monastery garden.

'My scientific labours have brought me a great deal of satisfaction, and I am convinced that before long the entire world will praise the result of these labours.'

WRITINGS BY MENDEL

**Experiments in
Plant Hybridization**
Harvard UP pbk £6.50
0674278003

WRITINGS ON MENDEL

**Jones, Steve
Genetics for Beginners**
Icon Books pbk £8.99
1874166129

Mendel in 90 Minutes
Constable pbk £3.50
0094771200

John

RUSKIN 1871–78

Fors Clavigera

When Ruskin is remembered today it is largely as an art critic. We remember the man who was the champion of Turner and one of the first supporters of the Pre-Raphaelites. We remember the great arbiter of taste whose power in the Victorian art world was ironically celebrated by the comic versifier Shirley Brooks in the lines he wrote in the assumed persona of a Royal Academician:

I takes and paints
Hears no complaints
And sells before I'm dry.
Till savage Ruskin
He sticks his tusk in
Then nobody will buy.

Ruskin was all of these things but he was also much more. He was one of the great social and cultural critics of his age and the legacy of his critical stance to the achievements and values of the Victorian era is still with us. Only Thomas Carlyle had the same kind of stature in nineteenth century British culture and he now seems a figure of purely historical interest. Without Ruskin and his disciples we would not have many of the institutions for the preservation of our past, at least not in the form which they now take. Indirectly it could be argued that, without Ruskin, the modern heritage industry and our particular attitudes to the past, both liberating and constricting, would not have taken the shape they have.

Ruskin was born in London, the son of a wealthy wine merchant, and it was on his family's regular and leisurely trips to the continent that he first acquired his love and wide-ranging knowledge of European art and architecture. He studied at Christ Church, Oxford where he won the Newdigate Prize for poetry. He continued to write late Romantic verse for a number of years and also devoted much time to drawing and watercolours but, with the publication of the first volume of *Modern Painters* in the mid-1840s, his career as a critic had begun. Further volumes appeared over the next decade and a half. In 1848 he married Effie Gray but the marriage was a disaster and was annulled seven years later. Effie went on to marry the Pre-Raphaelite painter John Millais. (Ruskin's personal life remained unfulfilled. As he grew older he developed a number of unrequited attachments to younger women, most importantly Rose La Touche, whose death in 1875 contributed to a severe breakdown in Ruskin's mental health.)

The first volumes of *Modern Painters*, followed by books like *The Seven Lamps of Architecture* (1849) and *The Stones of Venice* (1851), made Ruskin's reputation as a critic. To Ruskin the relationship between a society, its morality and its art was paramount. In the Gothic architecture which he loved he saw an ideal integration of the spiritual and the artistic. The

'Life without industry is guilt, and industry without art is brutality.'

society and art of his own time, by contrast, seemed too often ugly and morally corrupt. Increasingly Ruskin's concerns became as much social as artistic. His antagonism to the spirit of the age and his disgust with unbridled competition and selfishness, his longing for a return to the values of a largely idealised past, were expressed in a series of powerful polemics. *Fors Clavigera*, a series of 'Letters to the Workmen and Labourers of Great Britain', which were issued at irregular intervals between 1871 and 1878, were perhaps the most notable of these. Ruskin died in the Lake District in 1900 after nearly a decade in which he had written nothing and had been increasingly slipping into a world of mental darkness. By that stage his disciples had taken his message, in various forms, out into a wider world. William Morris had taken it into the new Arts and Crafts movement, into a particularly English form of Socialism and into a developing conservation movement. Arnold Toynbee had taken it into the world of workers' education and into the slums of the East End. Through them, and thousands of others, Ruskin's ideas about industrial society have been passed on to ourselves.

WRITINGS BY RUSKIN

Selected Writings
Penguin pbk £8.99
0140433554

Includes excerpts from most of the major works including *Modern Painters* and *Fors Clavigera*.

The Lamp of Beauty
Phaidon pbk £9.99
0714833584

WRITINGS ON RUSKIN

Dixon-Hunt, John
The Wider Sea:
A Life of John Ruskin
Phoenix pbk £14.99
0753801388

Wiener, Martin
English Culture and the
Decline of the Industrial Spirit
Penguin pbk £7.99
0140136967

A general account of English distrust of the very industrialism on which nineteenth century society was based, this includes a full and interesting discussion of Ruskin's contribution to the cultural debate.

James Clerk

MAXWELL 1873

Treatise on Electricity and Magnetism

Born in Edinburgh, James Clerk Maxwell had the precociousness asociated with many mathematical and scientific geniuses and presented his first paper to the Royal Society of Edinburgh, *On the Description of Oval Curves and those having a plurality of foci,* at the age of 14. Two years later he began to attend classes at Edinburgh University and then went on to Cambridge where his great gifts as a mathematician and scientist were soon recognised. He graduated from Trinity in 1854 and was awarded a fellowship at the college. His early work on giving mathematical formulation to Faraday's theories of electricity and magnetic lines of force was undertaken at Cambridge in 1855 and 1856. In the latter year Maxwell's father died and he moved back to Scotland where he became professor at Aberdeen. In 1860, newly married, he was appointed to the chair of Natural Philosophy at King's College, London and it was there, over the next six years, that much of his most lasting work was undertaken. Through experiments conducted when he was in London he came to the epoch-making conclusion that light was, in fact, an electromagnetic phenomenon. In 1871 Maxwell was offered the opportunity to become the first Cavendish professor of physics at Cambridge. In this role he was largely responsible for the organisation of the Cavendish Laboratory which was formally opened in June 1874. Maxwell's great *Treatise on Electricity and Magnetism* was published in

1873. It was in the *Treatise* that he gave the fullest version he ever gave of what came to be known as Maxwell's Equations. These consisted of a set of partial differential equations that described and predicted the behaviour of electromagnetic waves. They expanded upon and formalised earlier work by Faraday, Ampère and the German mathematician Johann Gauss. Einstein once remarked of the work of James Clerk Maxwell that it was 'the most fruitful that physics has experienced since the time of Newton.' He himself drew enormously on Maxwell's work and it continues to be the foundation of modern electromagnetic theory.

'We can scarcely avoid the conclusion that light consists in the transverse undulations of the same medium which is the cause of electric and magnetic phenomena.'

WRITINGS BY MAXWELL

Treatise on Electricity and Magnetism Vol. 1
Oxford UP pbk £20.00
0198503733

Treatise on Electricity and Magnetism Vol.2
Oxford UP pbk £20.00
0198503741

Treatise on Electricity and Magnetism
Dover pbk £12.95
0486606368

WRITINGS ON MAXWELL

Harman, Peter
The Natural Philosophy of James Clerk Maxwell
Cambridge UP hbk £37.50
0521561027

Unfortunately the only readily available book solely on Maxwell's work is this hardback volume published in 1997. It is, however, a comprehensive account of his science and worldview.

Laidler, Keith
To Light Such a Candle
Oxford UP hbk £25.00
0198500564

Also only in hardback, this looks at a number of significant periods in the history of science and includes chapters on both Faraday and James Clerk Maxwell.

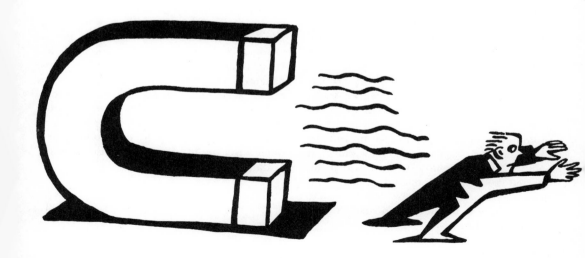

Leo
TOLSTOY | 1879–82

A Confession

Tolstoy is known as one of the greatest of all European novelists, the author of *War and Peace* (1863-69) and *Anna Karenina* (1873-77). He was much more. His novels, like all his works, are shot through with his own moral fervour and his search for a way to live in the world that would satisfy his own most stringent demands. Born into the Russian aristocracy, Tolstoy spent time at Kazan University and, in 1851, served in an artillery regiment in the Caucasus. It was there that he began to write. During the Crimean War he was active in the defence of Sebastopol before returning to St. Petersburg, where his stories based on his military experiences and his autobiographical trilogy (*Childhood, Boyhood* and *Youth*) made him a literary celebrity. In 1862 he married Sophie Behrs and settled on his family estate where he combined the writing of *War and Peace* with his attempts to run the estate on progressive lines. *Anna Karenina* followed but in the early 1880s Tolstoy was engaged in a profound moral struggle in which his writings so far came to seem increasingly vain and empty. This spiritual crisis, in which he rejected both institutionalised religion and private property (thereby earning the displeasure of both church and state), is best described in *A Confession*.

Tolstoy's ethical writings all revolve around a belief in the overwhelming efficacy of love (towards God and humanity) as a moral principle. Evil was not to be directly resisted, private property was to be renounced and governments and churches, which stifled the soul, were to be abolished. Tolstoy himself made over his fortune to his wife and, increasingly, he took upon himself the dress and lifestyle of the peasants he admired. Further writings such as *What I Believe* and *What Is Art?* confirmed the severe asceticism of his beliefs, which also colour the fiction (*The Kreutzer Sonata, Resurrection*) he continued to write. Sophie found her new role as wife to a latter-day prophet a difficult one to sustain and Tolstoy's last decades were ones of increasing moral stature in the wider world and increasing disharmony in his domestic life. In October 1910 the octogenarian writer left the family home, accompanied only by one of his daughters and by a personal physician. He caught a chill and died at a railway station, stubbornly refusing to the last to see his wife. His estate at Yasnaya Polyana became a place of pilgrimage and his ideas lived on to influence other advocates of non-violent resistance such as Gandhi.

'The highest wisdom has but one science – the science of the whole – the science explaining the whole creation and man's place in it.'

FICTION BY TOLSTOY

Anna Karenina
Penguin pbk £4.99
0140440410

Childhood, Boyhood, Youth
Penguin pbk £7.99
0140441395

The Death of Ivan Ilych and other stories
Penguin pbk £5.99
0140445080

How Much Land Does a Man Need and other stories
Penguin pbk £6.99
0140445064

The Kreutzer Sonata and other stories
Penguin pbk £6.99
0192838091

Master and Man and other stories
Penguin pbk £6.99
0140443312

The Raid and other stories
Oxford UP pbk £4.99
0192815849

Resurrection
Penguin pbk £6.99
0140441840

The Sebastopol Sketches
Penguin pbk £6.99
0140444688

War and Peace
Penguin pbk £7.99
0140444173

NON-FICTION BY TOLSTOY

What is Art and other essays
Penguin pbk £7.99
0140446427

A Confession and other Religious Writings
Penguin pbk £6.99
0140444734

Friedrich
NIETZSCHE
1883–85
Thus Spoke Zarathustra

Nietzsche was born, the son of a Lutheran pastor, in Saxony and received his early schooling at the famous Schulpforta, which had been founded at the time of the Reformation. He was an outstanding student and, after periods at the Universities of Bonn and Lepizig, he was appointed Professor of Classics at Basel in Switzerland at the age of only 25. He took Swiss citizenship in 1872. It was at this time that Nietzsche was at the height of his admiration for Richard Wagner whose operas, he believed, would rescue German art from mediocrity and rival the drama of Ancient Greece. He became a friend of the composer but Wagner's arrogance and anti-semitism soon became too much for Nietzsche and the pair broke irrevocably in 1876. (Nietzsche later wrote a swingeing critique of Wagner.) Nietzsche suffered from poor health and, in 1879, he resigned from his professorship.

For the next ten years he was a kind of itinerant scholar and thinker, drifting from Sicily to Nice, Leipzig to Turin, and working on the aphoristic, unclassifiable books he published under titles like *Also Sprach Zarathustra* (Thus Spoke Zarathustra) and *Jenseits von Gut und Böse* (Beyond Good and Evil). It was in Turin, in 1889, that Nietzsche's mind gave way. He collapsed in the street at the sight of a horse being flogged and was to spend the last years of his life clinically insane. (The insanity could well have been syphilitic in origin.) Nietzsche's rather sinister sister Elizabeth acted as his nurse in the years before he died and jealously guarded his reputation after his death. Elizabeth, who lived a long life, was to become an enthusiast for Hitler and her inextricable links with her brother's work have meant that Nietzsche, who was a strong opponent of anti-semitism and narrow nationalism, has often been seen, unfairly, as a proto-fascist.

Nietzsche was the very reverse of a systematic philosopher. His works do not pursue insight through pages of carefully argued text but seize upon it with devastatingly precise and resonant aphorisms and *aperçus*. He touches upon dozens of subjects from art and music to science and morality. Yet, despite the range and seeming disjointedness of his most characteristic books, certain themes emerge clearly from his writing. Nietzsche challenged many of the ruling assumptions and ideas of his time. He rejected Christianity as the morality of the slave, with its emphasis on humility and submission to an objectively existing God. Influenced by Schopenhauer, Nietzsche believed instead in an extreme form of subjective idealism; that we live in a self-created world which is the projection of our own minds. There is no objectively existing 'reality' beyond the creative powers of the human will.

'I teach you the superman. Man is something to be surpassed.'

Nietzsche is best known for his cult of the *Übermensch* (Superman) - who has overcome human nature and transcended the limitations placed upon it - and, although his ideas have been highly influential, the extremity and solipsism of his position have not always made him popular. He has also exerted considerable influence on aesthetics, with important work on the 'metaphysical solace' of tragedy and his memorable distinction, introduced in his 1872 book *The Birth of Tragedy*, between 'Apollonian' art (characterised by order and harmony) and 'Dionysian' art (characterised by turbulent passion).

WRITINGS BY NIETZSCHE

Beyond Good and Evil
Penguin pbk £7.99
0140445137

Beyond Good and Evil
Oxford UP pbk £6.99
0192832638

The Birth of Tragedy
Penguin pbk £6.99
0140433392

**The Birth of Tragedy and
Other Writings**
Cambridge UP pbk £12.95
0521639875

Daybreak
Cambridge UP pbk £12.95
0521599636

Ecce Homo
Penguin pbk £6.99
0140445153

Human, All Too Human
Penguin pbk £7.99
0140446176

**Human, All Too Human/A Book
for Free Spirits**
Cambridge UP pbk £13.95
0521567041

A Nietzsche Reader
Penguin pbk £7.99
0140443290

On the Genealogy of Morals
Oxford UP pbk £5.99
019283617X

Selected Letters
Hackett pbk £14.95
0872203581

Thus Spoke Zarathustra
Penguin pbk £7.99
0140441182

Twilight of the Idols
Penguin pbk £6.99
0140445145

Twilight of the Idols
Oxford UP pbk £6.99
0192831380

Untimely Meditations
Cambridge UP pbk £12.95
0521585848

WRITINGS ON NIETZSCHE

**Cambridge Companion to
Nietzsche**
Cambridge UP pbk £16.95
0521367670

**Gilman, Sander
Conversations with Nietzsche**
Oxford UP pbk £15.99
0195067789

This collection of memoirs,
anecdotes and recollections
constitutes a life of Nietzsche in
the words of his contemporaries.

Introducing Nietzsche
Icon pbk £8.99
184046075X

**Tanner, Michael
Nietzsche**
Oxford UP pbk £5.99
0192876805

**Sedgwick, Peter
Nietzsche: A Critical Reader**
Blackwell pbk £17.99
0631190457

Gottlob

FREGE 1884

The Foundations of Arithmetic

Frege spent nearly all of his working life in the mathematics department of the University of Jena and produced much of his ground-breaking work in mathematical logic and the philosophy of language while in relative isolation. (He was, however, in correspondence with Bertrand Russell who was interested in similar areas of logic and mathematics.) Frege died in a German spa town, Bad Kleinen, in 1925, three years after Wittgenstein had written approvingly of his achievements in the *Tractatus*.

As early as 1879 Frege had produced the *Begriffschrift,* a book which has since been acknowledged as heralding the beginning of modern logic and he followed this in 1884 with *Grundlagen der Arithmetik (The Foundations of Arithmetic).* In this book he examined, and demolished, various accounts of the nature of arithmetic and then set out his own case, that, if the system of formal logic was elaborated, it could be seen that arithmetic and arithmetical operations possessed an affinity with that logic. Central to *The Foundations of Arithmetic* is Frege's definition of number. Indeed it has been said that the work is Frege's answer to two questions. What are numbers? What is arithmetical truth? *Grundgesetze der Arithmetik (The Basic Laws of Arithmetic)* in 1893 continued his investigations of these questions, although Russell, much to Frege's dismay ('arithmetic totters', he wrote), pointed out a logical paradox in the German's theory. As well as his interests in mathematics

and logic, indeed as a necessary consequence of them, Frege was concerned with semantic problems, the meanings of words and their relationships to the objects to which they are applied. In a series of papers he set out many of the debates and formulated many of the concepts which have dominated philosophical investigations into language this century. It is hard to imagine Wittgenstein's work in this field without his responses, both positive and negative, to Frege. Similarly logical positivism, the dominant school of thought in English philosophy for many decades this century, owes a huge debt to Frege.

'If it is one of the tasks of philosophy to break the domination of the word over the human spirit by laying bare the misconceptions that, through the use of language, often almost unavoidably arise . . . then my ideography can become a useful tool for the philosopher.'

WRITINGS BY FREGE

The Foundations of Arithmetic
Blackwell pbk £15.99
0631126945

WRITINGS ON FREGE

Cambridge Companion to Frege
Cambridge UP pbk £16.99
0521624797

Weiner, Joan
Frege
Oxford UP pbk £5.99
0192876953

One of the Past Masters series.

Prince Peter

KROPOTKIN 1892

The Conquest of Bread

Kropotkin was a Russian nobleman, born with the rank of prince, who became the leading intellectual figure in the anarchist movement of the late nineteenth and early twentieth centuries. After attending an elite military academy in St. Petersburg, the young Kropotkin was a personal page to the Tsar Alexander II before spending five years (1862-1867) serving in a Cossack regiment in Siberia. During this time, when he was undertaking administrative responsibilities in the region to which he had been assigned, he became increasingly frustrated by official corruption, bureaucratic inefficiency and political conservatism, and rapidly disillusioned with the apparatus of the tsarist state. His chief interest during his period in Siberia lay in the geological expeditions he undertook and the scientific work he began. This continued when he returned to St. Petersburg to study mathematics. He acted as secretary of the Russian Geographical Society and, in 1871, led an expedition into Scandinavia to examine geological and glacial phenomena there. In his political views, Kropotkin was growing increasingly troubled by the contrast between the life of the poor, culturally and educationally as well as materially impoverished, and the life of privilege led by the class from which he sprang. He moved further and further to the left, becoming a supporter of the radical Populist movement, which favoured small, self-governing communes. In 1874 Kropotkin was arrested and jailed, escaping two years later to Britain and then to Switzerland. In 1881 anarchists assassinated Tsar Alexander II and Kropotkin, despite misgivings, went into print to defend their actions. The Swiss authorities jailed him for three years. On his release he settled in London where he was to stay until the time of the Russian Revolution.

The Conquest of Bread was published in 1892 and revised in 1913. Kropotkin derided the state as merely an agent of repression, and demanded its immediate abolition. It should be replaced with small communities, self-sufficient in all material needs, and linked only by voluntary agreement. As the institutions of state dissolved, a communal sense of justice, long suppressed, would emerge. *The Conquest of Bread* set out Kropotkin's brand of anarcho-communism, in which capitalism was to be repleced with communally organised means of production and distribution. Despite favouring a mainly agrarian economy, with fairly frugal rewards for its workers, Kropotkin, himself a scientist, was not tempted by Luddism. In contrast, he advocated the use of the most modern technology in the production process.

Like Marx, Kropotkin claimed his theories were scientifically based and he was particularly influenced by Darwin's *The Origin of Species*. He believed that the ideal society set out in *The Conquest of Bread* would best meet

'There are those like ourselves who see the State, both in its present form, in its very essence, and in whatever guise it may appear, as an obstacle to the social revolution, the greatest hindrance to the birth of a society based on liberty and equality, as well as the historic means designed to prevent this blossoming.'

the basic needs of human beings. Unlike Marx he rejected the idea of a political party organising and leading a forthcoming revolution. This would merely prolong the existence of the state. Instead the revolution should be a mass and spontaneous uprising.

Kropotkin's success as an anarchist theorist owed much to his accessibility. He was well-read, fluent and not overly technical. He intended his works for the widest possible audience. In addition to *The Conquest of Bread*, Kropotkin wrote and published books on a range of subjects. *Mutual Aid* (scheduled for publication as a Penguin Classic in 2001) was an account of the development of the modern state, which stressed the evolutionary importance of co-operation over competition. Other works included the autobiographical *Memoirs of a Revolutionist* (1899), *Fields, Factories and Workshops* of the same year and *The Great French Revolution* (1909), which stressed the role of the masses in the revolution.

Kropotkin returned to Russia immediately after the February 1917 revolution. He died in February 1921 and his funeral was attended by 20,000 mourners. Just a month later the Bolshevik government suppressed the Russian anarchist movement. The movement may have been suppressed in Russia but it has continued to play its role in 20th century politics, perhaps most notably in the Spanish Civil War where anarchists fought side by side with republicans and communists in defence of the Republic. Today, in a time of disillusionment with traditional politics, Kropotkin's anarchist libertarianism still speaks to people.

JOE PONTIN, *Waterstone's Bristol Galleries*

WRITINGS BY KROPOTKIN

Mutual Aid
Penguin pbk £8.99
0140445676 (due 2001)

The Conquest of Bread and Other Writings
Cambridge UP pbk £14.95
0521459907

WRITINGS ON KROPOTKIN

Marshall, Peter
Demanding the Impossible
HarperCollins pbk £12.99
0006862454

A general history of anarchism which has a thorough examination of Kropotkin's life and ideas.

Emile

DURKHEIM | 1895

The Rules of Sociological Method

Born in the French province of Lorraine, Durkheim inherited a dual intellectual legacy - the rationalist tradition of France and the Talmudic learning of his Jewish background. He was originally intended by his family to become a rabbi but he is remembered as one of the founding fathers, together with Max Weber, of modern sociology. The University of Bordeaux established a chair in the subject for him in 1887 and he later taught for many years at the Sorbonne.

Durkheim believed that people are, necessarily, products of their society and that their feelings and attitudes, which seem to them personal attributes, are conditioned by social forces. Society itself is more than the sum of its parts and collective beliefs and behaviour cannot be explained in terms of individual psychology. His major works consist of both general expositions of the principles and methods of the new social science he was so instrumental in creating and studies of specific social phenomena.

The Rules of Sociological Method (1895) defined the data of this new science as consisting of 'social facts' – customary ways of acting and feeling to which an individual in a society feels compelled to conform. *Suicide* (1897) is a pioneering study of the relation between the rate of suicide in a society and the structure of that society. Towards the end of his life

Durkheim planned two major and complementary works on the role of religion in society and on the role of moral education within society. He completed only the one, *The Elementary Forms of Religious Life* (1912). In it he examines the ways in which religious beliefs and concepts in a society can be examined not as expressions of ultimate truth or falsity but as products of specific social conditions.

'The first and fundamental rule is to consider social facts as things . . . a social fact is every way of acting which is capable of exercising an external constraint upon the individual.'

WRITINGS BY DURKHEIM

The Rules of Sociological Method
Macmillan pbk £14.99
0333280725

The Elementary Forms of the Religious Life
Simon & Schuster pbk £14.99
0029079373

Suicide
Routledge pbk £14.99
0415045878

WRITINGS ON DURKHEIM

Craib, Ian
Classical Social Theory
Oxford UP pbk £14.99
0198781172

An examination of the ideas of Durkheim and other founding fathers of social thinking.

Sigmund

FREUD | 1900

The Interpretation of Dreams

DARIAN LEADER *is a psychoanalyst and author of* Why Do Women Write More Letters Than They Post, Promises Lovers Make When It Gets Late *and* Freud's Footnotes, *all published by Faber and Faber. Here he examines Freud's greatest book and what it reveals about his theories of the conscious and unconscious mind.*

It is difficult to think of any modern thinker apart from Sigmund Freud whom the twentieth century has expended so much energy in trying to forget or discredit. His theories about how the broken romances of our childhoods shape our lives, and the practice of psychoanalysis that he invented, are just as disturbing today as they were in the 1890s. Born in Moravia in 1856, he would study medicine in Vienna, specialising in neuroanatomy and neuropathology, before formulating his properly psychoanalytical models of how the human mind functions. When Freud died in London in 1939, he left a vast body of theoretical work and a practice which continues to respond, through listening and interpreting, to the very real problems of human distress.

Many thinkers before Feud had spoken about the unconscious, but it was Freud who showed not only its dynamic, sexual nature but also how our attempts to distance ourselves from unconscious material organise our daily lives, our love, our work and all our endeavours.

Freud's interest in hypnosis in the 1880s and 1890s had drawn his attention to a strange phenomenon. A subject under hypnosis might be convinced that certain features of their environment did not exist. Told that there is no furniture in the room and then instructed to walk over to the opposite wall, the subject will walk carefully around the furniture. When asked why that particular route had been chosen, rather than the more obvious passage which would have involved collision with the 'non-existent' furniture, rationalisations will be produced to explain their behaviour: 'A picture over there attracted me', 'I saw someone I knew' etc. Freud called these explanations 'false connections.'

Rather than seeeing the production of false connections as an isolated phenomenon of hypnosis, Freud argued that this was the central characteristic of the human ego. We spend our lives creating false realities and deceiving both ourselves and others as to the real reasons for our actions. We do this in order to avoid the pain of confronting the failed love stories of our childhood and the sexual and murderous desires that these involve. Ideas which would generate unbearable pain or pleasure are separated from the sequence of ideas to which they belong, and then the ego busies itself with building up false realities to cover over these initial distortions. Freud spent many years investigating the particular mechanisms by which we remove such ideas from consciousness, and correlating these mechanisms with different forms of human suffering.

Central to Freud's project was an attention to whatever seemed to have no place in our supposed control of our daily lives. Physical and mental symptoms are the most obvious examples of this but also, Freud argued, slips of the tongue, laughter and dreams. These apparently nonsensical phenomena could provide clues to the working of the unconscious and, if taken seriously, could be followed through to the unconscious complexes that govern our lives without us knowing it.

Dreams have always held a certain mystery. We can have a dream and be perplexed, even haunted by it, without understanding what it actually means. But we tend to think, despite this, that dreams must mean something. They seem to be the bearers of a knowledge from which we are cut off. Hence the appeal, from century to century, to certain privileged figures who will be able to interpret our dreams for us. To suppose that a dream has meaning implies that we 'know' more than we know consciously: the dream is ours yet its meaning eludes us. In his monumental work on dreams, the *Traumdeutung, (The Interpretation of Dreams)* published in 1899 but dated 1900, Freud claimed that the unravelling of the associations to our dreams could allow an access to this knowledge, which consisted of chains of repressed ideas.

Freud's approach to dreams is often misunderstood. He was interested primarily less in the experience of dreaming than in the telling of dreams. This meant enlarging the very definition of the dream: a dream consisted not simply in the telling of what we remembered of it, but also in the associations which we might have to it. It was through the unravelling of these networks of associations that the meaning of dreams could be approached. The method of free association, in which the patient says whatever it is that comes into his or her head, was the privileged route to this unravelling. By saying whatever was in their mind, what wasn't in their mind – the unconscious complex – would distort the material in such a way that its content could be interpreted.

Freud's argument in *The Interpretation of Dreams* is frequently caricatured with the slogan, 'A dream is the fulfilment of a wish.' But Freud's argument is much more subtle. He distinguished the manifest content of dreams – more or less, what we dream – from the latent dream thought, the idea that lies concealed beneath its complicated façade. As an example we could take a dream involving a rendezvous with the dentist. A long and circuitous journey to their office is followed by a series of incidents which prevent us finally from keeping the appointment. We wake up feeling slightly relieved. The details of the journey and the various incidents would make up the manifest content of the dream, and then we might suppose that the latent dream thought is indeed a wish, the simple wish not to have to visit the dentist.

This might very well be the case. We might have gone to bed that night worried about an

'The interpretation of dreams is the royal road to a knowledge of the unconscious activities of the mind'

approaching visit to the dentist. The dream would then have granted our wish not to go, by staging a narrative which continually defers the dreaded moment. Freud does not deny that, in this sense, a dream seems to gratify a wish. But his thesis about dreams goes beyond this simple reasoning. What interests him is less the initial wish, which could be a conscious one, and the manifest dream, than the difference between them. What has happened between the wish to avoid a dental appointment and the dream's details, the particularities of the journey and the incidents en route. Why were those exact details chosen and not others?

This is where Freud sees the presence of unconscious desire. He argues that our unconscious complexes are on the look out for means of expression, and the often conscious wishes we might have during the day preceding the dream are chosen as their vehicles. He compares this to the relationship between a capitalist and an entrepreneur. To get a project going, the entrepreneur needs capital, and so the unconscious complex will seize upon the initial dream wish as its means of both expression and disguise. Since the unconscious desires in question will be unbearable, revolving around our failed love claims to a parent and the prohibition against incest, they cannot enter consciousness undisguised. It is the dream wish which will allow the unconscious desire to dissimulate itself, and hence the importance of the tiny, apparently insignificant details in the telling of the dream. There is thus a difference between the dream wish, and the desire which uses this wish for its own ends.

So what happens between the latent dream wish and the manifest dream? As an unconscious complex latches onto the wish, the wish becomes caught up in a network of condensations and displacements, linguistic, ciphering mechanisms which make the dream seem so opaque to us. Freud calls this process the dream work, and it is in this ciphering that he sees the royal road to the unconscious. Although Freud was fond of searching for symbolism in dreams, it was the mechanisms of this ciphering process that held the key to unconscious desire. Dreams cease to be academic objects of interest, to which we apply our minds with a Freudian key, but they unravel our minds themselves as we become engaged in the process of association.

The Interpretation of Dreams is a rich and perpetually challenging book, and it is surprising that since its publication there has been very little psychoanalytic research on dreams. Freud's early students were keen on finding hidden symbolism, but wrote hardly anything about the actual processes of ciphering or, indeed, the experience of dreaming. The notion of desire being articulated in the dream work remained more or less undeveloped until the pioneering work of the French psychoanalyst Jacques Lacan, starting in the 1950s. Lacan was a careful reader of *The Interpretation of Dreams* and devoted many of his seminars to trying to extract from Freud's work a theory of desire and its functionings. As Freud had focused on linguistic mechanisms in the dream work, so Lacan elaborated a theory of how human desire is generated by language, as we become immersed in the world of speech and language from our infancy.

Since the practice of psychoanalysis is based on an analysand speaking to an analyst, it is difficult to understand why the study of language was neglected for so long by the post-Freudians. Reading *The Interpretation of Dreams* today we can see how, on almost every page, Freud is grappling with the problem of how the mechanisms of language forge our subjectivity and our experience. It is thus a book that defines so much of the twentieth century's fascination with language and interpretation. But it is also more than that. Freud's work shows that the question of language cannot be separated from that of human pain and suffering. Although there is a great deal of research on how language shapes our lives, this programme of 1899 has still not been taken up by today's sciences of the mind. It is thus a book not just for the last century, but for the next one.

WRITINGS BY FREUD

Penguin Freud Library

1. Introductory Lectures on Psychoanalysis
Penguin pbk £10.99
0140137912

2. New Introductory Lectures on Psychoanalysis
Penguin pbk £8.99
0140137920

3. Studies on Hysteria
Penguin pbk £11.99
0140137939

4. The Interpretation of Dreams
Penguin pbk £11.99
0140137947

5. The Psychopathology of Everyday Life
Penguin pbk £11.00
0140137955

6. Jokes and Their Relation to the Unconscious
Penguin pbk £9.99
0140137963

7. On Sexuality
Penguin pbk £10.99
0140137971

8. Case Histories Volume I
Penguin pbk £8.99
014013798X

9. Case Histories Volume II
Penguin pbk £10.99
0140137998

10. Inhibitions, Symptoms and Anxiety
Penguin pbk £11.00
0140138005

11. On Metapsychology
Penguin pbk £10.99
0140138013

12. Civilisation, Society and Religion
Penguin pbk £9.99
0140138021

13. The Origins of Religion
Penguin pbk £10.99
014013803x

15. Historical and Expository Works on Psychoanalysis
Penguin pbk £11.00
0140138056

Complete Letters of Freud to Wilhelm Fliess
Harvard UP pbk £11.95
0674154215

Complete Correspondence of Freud and Ernest Jones
Harvard UP pbk £17.50
067415424X

The Essentials of Psychoanalysis
Penguin pbk £10.99
0140136665

A one-volume distillation of Freud's theories, selected from his writings by his daughter Anna.

The Freud/Jung Letters
Penguin pbk £9.99
0140184449

The Freud Reader
Vintage pbk £9.95
0099577119

Two Short Accounts of Psychoanalysis
Penguin pbk £6.99
0140136541

The most comprehensive edition of Freud's writings, translated into English, is the 24-volume, hardback collection published by Hogarth Press.

WRITINGS ON FREUD

Cambridge Companion to Freud
Cambridge UP pbk £17.95
052137779x

Ferris, Paul
Dr.Freud: A Life
Pimlico pbk £15.00
0712666982

Wollheim, Richard
Freud
Fontana pbk £7.99
0006862233

Storr, Anthony
Freud
Oxford UP pbk £5.99
0192822101

Elliott, Anthony
Freud 2000
Polity P pbk £13.95
0745619096

Gay, Peter
Freud: A Life for Our Times
Papermac pbk £12.00
0333486382

Bettelheim, Bruno
Freud and Man's Soul
Penguin pbk £7.99
0140147578

Brown, J.A.C.
Freud and the Post-Freudians
Penguin pbk £7.99
0140136649

Appignanesi, Richard
Introducing Freud
Icon pbk £8.99
1840460547

Gay, Peter
Reading Freud
Yale UP pbk £12.95
0300051271

Sigmund Freud: His Life in Words and Pictures
Norton pbk £17.95
0393318753

Stafford-Clark, David
What Freud Really Said
Penguin pbk £7.99
0140136827

Leader, Darian
Freud's Footnotes
Faber hbk
(Due January 2000)

William

JAMES 1902

The Varieties of Religious Experience

The son of the leading exponent of Swedenborgian ideas in America and the elder brother of the novelist Henry James, William James, after a false start as an art student, entered Harvard to study medicine in 1861. He was to spend nearly all the rest of his life attached to the university in some capacity, firstly as a lecturer in anatomy, later as a professor of philosophy and of psychology. In the late 1870s James's life was set on a new path. He married in 1878; he was contracted to produce a textbook which grew in scope until it became the monumental *The Principles of Psychology*, finally published in 1890; and he established what was, in effect, the first experimental laboratory of psychology in the US. Ironically, James himself had no enthusiasm for laboratory work and the 1890s were a period spent on metaphysical questions of God, survival after death and religious belief. Characteristically James did not approach these questions as abstract speculation but strove to investigate them empirically. He collaborated with psychical researchers to look into the possibility of survival after death and examined the nature of religious belief by looking at the records of religious experience. The culmination of this period was the book *The Varieties of Religious Experience*. The first decade of the twentieth century saw the publication of James's most directly philosophical work, including the book *Pragmatism*, which appeared in 1907, the same year in which he retired from Harvard. In the last years of his life James, by now the most famous philosopher in America, continued to write and lecture to a wide audience. He died in 1910.

In philosophy James was a radical empiricist who opposed the idealism of Kant and Hegel by positing pure experience as the sole source of our knowledge. He was also a leading exponent of a brand of pragmatism which claimed abstract ideas are only valuable if experience proved that they worked. His most famous work is *The Varieties of Religious Experience*, which began life as two courses of lectures and was published in 1902. James's focus in the work is on the individual's experience of religion rather than the rituals of any church. After analysis of personal accounts, he concludes that the validity of religious experience lies with the emotional fulfilment it provides the individual rather than in its objective 'truth'. The particulars of faith are 'true' insofar as they supply the emotional needs. The book was one of the earliest and most intellectually distinguished works in the psychology of religion.

'The visible world is part of a more spiritual universe from which it draws its chief significance; union with the higher universe is our true end; spiritual energy flows in and produces effects within the phenomenal world.'

WRITINGS BY JAMES

**The Varieties of
Religious Experience**
Penguin pbk £7.99
0140390340

**Pragmatism and the
Meaning of Truth**
Harvard UP pbk £10.50
0674697375

Selected Writings
Everyman pbk £6.99
0460875574

WRITINGS ON JAMES

**The Cambridge Companion
to William James**
Cambridge UP pbk £15.95
0521459060

Max

WEBER 1905

The Protestant Ethic and the Spirit of Capitalism

Weber was one of the most wide-ranging thinkers in the social sciences of the twentieth century, with interests in subjects as diverse as the nature of bureaucracy and the religions of the East. He was born in the university town of Erfurt into a professional family and studied law at a number of German universities. Appointed professor of political economy at Freiburg and then Heidelberg, he suffered a severe nervous breakdown in the late 1890s and was unable to teach again until the last few years of his life. Indeed, for a number of years, Weber was rendered incapable of serious intellectual work. In 1907 he came into an inheritance and, his mental health largely restored, he worked as an independent scholar. He died in the great influenza epidemic that swept Europe at the end of the First World War, killing more people than the war itself had.

Weber's work is tremendously ambitious in its scope but it is possible to highlight three main strands in his thought. Firstly, he was interested in authority within society and the various forms it could take. He distinguished between authority based on the traditions of the past and the wisdom of the elders, authority based on the personal charisma of an individual political or religious leader and authority based on the structure of laws and behavioural rules which have evolved in society. The more complicated Western society became the more it was based on the latter kind of authority.

Similarly social actions could be classified by type. In older societies actions would be guided by customary habits of thought, by motives rooted in emotional rather than rational causes and by what Weber called the *wertrational*, a rational approach to the attainment of what was essentially a non-rational goal. In modern Western society the primary motivation for social action was what Weber called the *zweckrational*, a goal-oriented approach to specific purposes.

Linked with this was Weber's interest in religion and the ways in which religious ideas interacted with economic and social activities within a society. This interest is evinced most clearly in his most famous work *The Protestant Ethic and the Spirit of Capitalism*. Weber was fascinated by the question of why capitalism had developed in the way it had, in the countries it had and driven forward by the particular social groups which had led it. He found his answers in the differences between Catholicism and Protestantism. In Catholic societies economic activities were not given a high priority, the profit motive was not highly esteemed and the values of what he had elsewhere called the *wertrational* were promoted. The 'Protestant ethic' was different. In Protestant societies, emphasis was upon the individual and his own efforts, both to attain salvation and to win social position. Work was seen as a calling of

'Economic acquisition is no longer subordinated to man as the means for the satisfaction of his material needs. This reversal of what we should call the natural relationship . . . is evidently a leading principle of capitalism as it is foreign to all peoples not under a capitalist influence.'

value and the path was open to the employment of the *zweckrational*, the purposive form of rationality which now characterised the most advanced capitalist countries.

WRITINGS BY WEBER

The Agrarian Sociology of Ancient Civilizations
Verso pbk £14.00
1859842755

From Max Weber
Routledge pbk £15.99
0415060567

Selections in Translation
Cambridge UP pbk £14.95
0521292689

The Protestant Ethic and the Spirit of Capitalism
Routledge pbk £10.95
0415084342

The Russian Revolutions
Polity P pbk £13.95
0745617522

Political Writings
Cambridge UP pbk £11.95
0521397197

WRITINGS ON WEBER

Cambridge Companion to Max Weber
Cambridge UP pbk £16.95
052156753X

Craib, Ian
Classical Social Theory
Oxford UP pbk £14.99
0198781172

An examination of the ideas of Weber and other founding fathers of sociological thinking, Marx, Durkheim and Georg Simmel.

Kasler, Dirk
Max Weber
Polity P pbk £13.95
0745602150

Turner, Bryan
Max Weber: From History to Modernity
Routledge pbk £14.99
0415103878

Osbourne, Richard
Introducing Sociology
Icon pbk £8.99
1840460679

Ferdinand de

SAUSSURE 1915

Course in General Linguistics

Born in Geneva, Saussure studied in Leipzig and Berlin and published his earliest work in comparative philology when he was 21. After teaching in Paris for a number of years he returned to Geneva in 1891 and taught there for the rest of his life. His most influential work, the *Course in General Linguistics*, was pieced together by students from notes from several series of lectures and published in Paris two years after Saussure's death. Much of his influence has been posthumous and it has not been restricted to linguistics.

Within linguistics Saussure made crucial differentiations between synchronic linguistics (the study of a language at a given moment of time) and diachronic linguistics (the historical study of a language) and between *langue* and *parole*, language as a complete system and language as the individual manifestations used by individual speakers. Probably his greatest achievement, and the one which led some decades after his death to the developments in literary criticism and social sciences known as 'structuralism' stemmed from his view of a language as a system of signs.

Within a language there are signifiers and the signified, the word and the meaning, and there is no intrinsic link between them. Thus the word 'dog' has only an arbitrary, rather than a necessary, connection with the barking, tail-wagging quadruped that is also known as man's best friend. Furthermore individual units of language can not be understood in isolation but only in relationship with other units in the total language system. Thus 'dog' is, amongst other things, what is not meant by 'dig', 'dug', 'bog', 'log' etc. Each item in the total language system defines other items and is defined by them. This is the idea that, transferred to fields where Saussure may have been surprised to find it used, has proven most influential in twentieth century thought. Levi-Strauss, in developing structural anthropology, attempted to see social systems in the same way that Saussure saw language. In these also, nothing could be defined in isolation but only in relationship to other rituals, behaviours, modes of thought etc. In literary and cultural criticism many practitioners, from Roland Barthes onwards, have found Saussure's ideas of the signified and the signifier and of the arbitrariness of their connection illuminating.

'In language, there are only differences.'

WRITINGS BY SAUSSURE

Course in General Linguistics
Duckworth pbk £13.95
0715616706

WRITINGS ON SAUSSURE

Harris, Roy
Reading Saussure
Duckworth pbk £14.99
0715621750

Thibault, Paul
Re-Reading Saussure
Routledge pbk £18.99
0415104114

Culler, Jonathan
Saussure
Fontana pbk £6.99
000686032X

Holdcroft, David
Saussure
Cambridge UP pbk £15.95
0521339189

Gordon, Terrence
Saussure for Beginners
Writers and Readers pbk £8.99
0863161952

Albert

EINSTEIN 1916

Relativity

The man who, more than anyone since Newton, changed our understanding of the universe, was born in Ulm in 1879 and, as a teenager, moved with his family to Milan. His education was completed at the Zurich Polytechnic and, taking Swiss citizenship, he worked for three years at the Swiss Patent Office. His two paradigm-busting works were published in 1905 (the special theory of relativity) and 1916 (the general theory of relativity). Appointed to a professorship in Zurich in 1909, he later worked in Prague and, from 1914 to 1933, as director of the Physical Institute in Berlin. In 1919 he had the satisfaction of seeing results predicted by his theories confirmed by Sir Arthur Eddington's observations of a solar eclipse. Einstein had said that the wavelength of light emitted by atoms should be influenced by gravitational fields and Eddington showed that light rays from distant stars did indeed bend when passing through the sun's gravitational field. Hitler's rise to power forced Einstein, who was Jewish, out of Berlin and he spent most of the rest of his life in America. In 1940 he became an American citizen and was appointed to a professorship at Princeton. The previous year he had written to Roosevelt warning that an atomic bomb was a feasibility and that the Germans might steal a march on the Americans in pursuit of it. After the war, and the explosions at Hiroshima and Nagasaki which so horrifically confirmed that atomic destruction on a vast scale was possible, Einstein was one of those who called for international control of atomic weapons. In his last years, and since his death, Einstein has become an iconic figure, a symbol throughout Western culture of the power of the intelligence.

Ironically this elevation into a twentieth century icon took place long after Einstein had done his most productive work. His enormous importance in the history of science and of man's understanding of the universe rests on the two papers of 1905 and 1916. Einstein's work destroyed the concepts, inherent in Newtonian mechanics, of absolute time and absolute space.

His insight, essentially, was that observation and measurement were not fixed qualities but varied according to the person doing the observing or measuring. Thus space and time are not absolute but relative. They vary according to the speeds at which observers are travelling. Of course, for the speeds at which observers do travel, the difference in the appearance of space and time are so infinitesimal as to be unnoticed but, mathematically, it can be shown to exist.

'The most incomprehensible thing about the world is that it is at all comprehensible.'

WRITINGS BY EINSTEIN

Ideas and Opinions
Modern Library Hbk £12.95
0679601058

The Principle of Relativity
Dover pbk £7.95
0486600815

Relativity
Routledge pbk £9.95
0416676006

Sidelights on Relativity
Dover pbk £3.95
048624511X

The Theory of Relativity
Citadel P   pbk £7.95
0806517654

The World As I See It
Citadel P pbk £9.99
080650711X

WRITINGS ON EINSTEIN

Clark, Ronald W.
Einstein
Sceptre pbk £9.99
0340665653

Brian, Dennis
Einstein:A Life
Wiley pbk £15.99
0471193623

Gribbin & White
Einstein: A Life in Science
Pocket Books pbk £6.99
0671010441

Whitaker, Andrew
Einstein, Bohr and the
Quantum Dilemma
Cambridge UP pbk £18.99
0521484286

Fritzsch, Harald
An Equation That
Changed the World
University of Chicago P pbk £12.75
0226265587

Schwartz, J.
Introducing Einstein
Icon pbk £8.99
1840460601

Highfield & Carter
The Private Lives of
Albert Einstein
Faber pbk £8.99
0571171702

Pais, Abraham
Subtle Is the Lord
Oxford UP pbk £12.99
0192851381

$$E = mc^2$$

Ludwig

WITTGENSTEIN 1922

Tractatus Logico-Philosophicus

TERRY EAGLETON, *Warton Professor of English Literature at Oxford University and author of the screenplay for Derek Jarman's film about Wittgenstein, writes about the philosopher's life and language games.*

Widely acclaimed as the greatest philosopher of twentieth century Britain, Ludwig Wittgenstein led a life in some respects as courageous, intriguing and unorthodox as his thought. He was born in Vienna in 1889, the youngest child of one of the wealthiest industrialists in Austria, and grew up in a highly cultivated home frequented by the composers Brahms and Mahler. After being a school classmate of Adolf Hitler, Wittgenstein studied aeronautical engineering at Manchester University, where he proved himself something of an inventor, and came to study philosophy at Cambridge with Bertrand Russell. With scarcely any background in philosophy he nonetheless impressed Russell as a great philosopher in the making. When war broke out in 1914, he enlisted in the Austrian army, requested to be posted to positions of particular military danger, and was taken prisoner of war in Italy. He carried in his knapsack the manuscript of the only philosophical book he published in his lifetime, the *Tractatus Logico-Philosophicus*, which was to appear in English in 1922.

After the war, Wittgenstein worked briefly as a village schoolteacher in Austria, and later took a job as a monastery gardener near Vienna. He also designed a house for his sister in Vienna, which is a classic of high-modernist architecture. In 1929 he returned to Cambridge, where he taught and worked until his death in 1951. But he disliked academia and in the 1930s tried unsuccessfully to emigrate to the Soviet Union, a society he admired, in order to train as a medical doctor there. He spent some time living alone in a hut in Norway and, after resigning his Cambridge Chair in 1947, went to live by himself in a remote cabin on the west coast of Ireland. It was here that he completed the major work of his later philosophy, the *Philosophical Investigations*, though, like all his later works, it was not published in book-form in his lifetime. Wittgenstein gave away most of the considerable fortune he inherited from his father and, though secretly a practising homosexual, lived in other respects an austere, monastic life. He read little of the great philosophers, preferring detective stories and third-rate American movies, and urged his students to abandon the study of philosophy for some more useful pursuit. Imperious and uncompromising in his behaviour, he demanded impossibly exacting moral standards of both himself and his friends, and sought in his life for a Tolstoyan simplicity and holiness.

Wittgenstein's philosophy centres largely on the nature of language, though his views on the subject were in some respects to change a good deal. The early *Tractatus Logico-Philosophicus*, published in the same year as James Joyce's *Ulysses* and T.S. Eliot's *The Waste Land*, argues that the problems of philosophy will be resolved once the 'logic of language' is understood. What this turns out to mean, however, is that once philosophy has drawn attention to the limits of our language, indicating what can be clearly and intelligibly said within it and what cannot, we will come to recognise that many of the topics which philosophers have commonly treated are, in fact, spurious, or are genuine moral and metaphysical problems about which the philosopher *qua* philosopher has nothing particularly significant to say. Philosophy goes awry when it trespasses on regions which are no part of its remit, and accordingly tries to say the unsayable. Matters such as ethics, aesthetics and religion are, for Wittgenstein, by no means nonsensical; indeed, they constitute the most vital questions of human life. What is nonsensical is the attempt to say anything about them, since our language can only describe or 'picture' the world, rather than pass judgements of these kinds upon it.

What can be said, for Wittgenstein, is the same as what can be thought, so that, as a celebrated aphorism in the *Tractatus* has it, 'the limits of my language are the limits of my world.' The book tries to mark out, inevitably from within language, the frontiers of language itself, and thus to intimate the crucial but inarticulable realms which lie beyond it, to which Wittgenstein gives the title of the 'mystical.'

Language has an underlying logical structure, which determines what we can intelligibly say; and the logical structure of a proposition can be viewed as a kind of picture of a state of affairs in the world. Language and the world share a common underlying structure. But ethical, religious and other such questions of value lie outside the world - outside the realm of facts and states of affairs - and thus cannot be intelligibly discussed. They can, in Wittgenstein's words, be 'shown' but not 'stated'. The logical form of our language is disclosed in it, but we cannot use language to talk about it. Language, as it were, 'gives' us the world; but it cannot tell us how it does this, and we cannot use language to comment on language's relation to the world. But if this is true, then it follows that the *Tractatus's* own attempts to do this must be finally nonsensical. In this sense, the work must logically cancel itself out, rather like a certain kind of self-consuming modernist art-work. The book, so Wittgenstein writes, is a kind of ladder which the reader must climb only to throw away, so that he can then see the world aright.

What the *Tractatus* has done, then, is to allow what is really important to 'manifest' itself negatively, by marking the points at which our language must necessarily trail off into silence. Wittgenstein's later work, however, rejects the *Tractatus's* assumption that there is only one way in which language and the world fit together. In more pluralist spirit, the *Philosophical Investigations*, *The Blue and Brown Books*, *Zettel*, *On Certainty* and other later writings imagine our language as made up of a whole series of 'language games', which cannot be reduced to a single logical form, and

'Philosophy is a struggle against the bewitching of our minds by means of language.'

which are made up of the rules by which we use words in particular ways for particular purposes. The later Wittgenstein is much concerned to show that all of this is a public affair, in which 'everything lies open to view'. Meaning, intending, promising, expecting and the like are not to be grasped as psychological states of affairs private to an individual and necessarily hidden from others, but as determined by the public criteria of various language games, which are in turn bound up with those cultural activities which Wittgenstein rather vaguely terms 'forms of life'. The idea of a private meaning or private language is shown to be radically incoherent, partly by demonstrating that these things involve following and applying rules, and following rules is a necessarily public affair. Language does not 'represent' mental processes within our heads; on the contrary, the meaning of a word is not some private experience I may have, but the rules which govern its various uses in a specific form of social life. Understanding is a matter of being able to do something – in the case of meaning, of being able to do things with words.

The later Wittgenstein nevertheless continued to hold the view, expressed in his early work, that philosophical problems arise from confusions in language. But whereas the *Tractatus* sees such confusion as trying to 'eff the ineffable', in the words of Samuel Beckett, the later work sees it chiefly in our confusing of one kind of language game with another. I might, for example, worry about quite whereabouts inside me my soul is located; but this is only because seductive similarities of grammar lead me to mistake 'soul language' for, say, the language game of physical objects.

Philosophical or metaphysical problems thus need to be dissolved rather than resolved. They are illusions thrown up by our language games and the only important task of the philosopher is to demystify these illusions by reminding us of how language is actually used. Philosophy is not there to transform the world, invent new ways of speaking or solve our moral problems for us: it is essentially an elucidation of language games which are perfectly in order themselves. There is nothing wrong with 'ordinary language.'

This latter view has led some commentators to accuse the later Wittgenstein of a certain complacent conservatism. What we say is ultimately governed by what we do - by the behaviours and institutions of our practical form of life. But just as for the Wittgenstein of the *Tractatus* language could not be used to comment upon language, so for the later Wittgenstein it would seem that a 'form of life' cannot pass judgement upon itself, since only by virtue of belonging to such a form of life do we derive the criteria for such judgements in the first place. And this then raises the spectre of cultural relativism. Wittgenstein is in this sense an 'anti-foundationalist' thinker, for whom what our community happens to do can be backed by no further metaphysical warranty. As a man, however, he would seem to have sharply rejected the 'form of life' in which he found himself and spent a good deal of his time trying to escape it. His life and later thought are thus somewhat in tension, just as the generous pluralism of the later writing, which is concerned to explore differences rather than identities, is intriguingly at odds with the implacable, ruthlessly single-minded absolutist which the man Wittgenstein apparently was.

WRITINGS BY WITTGENSTEIN

The Blue and Brown Books
Blackwell pbk £16.99
0631146601

Cambridge Letters
Blackwell pbk £16.99
0631207589

Culture and Value
Blackwell pbk £13.99
0631205713

Last Writings on the Philosophy of Psychology: Volume I
Blackwell pbk £15.99
0631171215

Last Writings on the Philosophy of Psychology: Volume II
Blackwell pbk £15.99
0631189564

Lectures and Conversations
Blackwell pbk £14.99
0631095802

On Certainty
Blackwell pbk £15.99
0631169407

Philosophical Grammar
Blackwell pbk £17.99
0631118918

Philosophical Investigations
Blackwell pbk £16.99
0631146709

Philosophical Remarks
Blackwell pbk £17.99
0631191305

Remarks on the Philosophy of Psychology: Volume I
Blackwell pbk £19.99
0631130616

Remarks on the Philosophy of Psychology: Volume II
Blackwell pbk £19.99
0631130624

Remarks on the Foundation of Mathematics
Blackwell pbk £19.99
0631125051

Tractatus Logico-Philosophicus
Routledge pbk £9.99
0415028256

Zettel
Blackwell pbk £16.99
0631128239

WRITINGS ON WITTGENSTEIN

Introducing Wittgenstein
Icon pbk £8.99
1840460709

Monk, Ray
Ludwig Wittgenstein
Vintage pbk £9.99
0099883708

Grayling, A.C.
Wittgenstein
Oxford UP pbk £5.99
0192876775

Wittgenstein
Routledge pbk £14.99
0415119448
(Arguments of the Philosophers)

Hacker, P.M.S.
Wittgenstein
Phoenix £2.00
0753801930

Pears, David
Wittgenstein
Fontana £6.99
0006860125

Kenny, Anthony
A Wittgenstein Reader
Blackwell pbk £15.99
0631193626

Martin

BUBER 1923

I and Thou

The German-Jewish religious philosopher Martin Buber was one of the most intellectually challenging and demanding interpreters of the relationship between God and man the twentieth century produced. Although he worked from within a rich tradition of Jewish thinking on the subject, his influence has been at least as great on Christian thought as it has upon modern Judaism.

Born in Vienna, he was brought up largely by his grandparents in Lemberg, then part of the Austro-Hungarian empire, now the town of Lviv in the Ukraine. Buber studied philosophy and the history of art at a number of German-speaking universities, receiving his Ph.D at Berlin in 1904 for a dissertation on the work of two medieval mystics. He joined the Zionist movement as early as 1898 and, three years later, was invited by the Zionist leader Alexander Herzl to become editor of the newspaper *Die Welt*. In the next three decades and more he became one of the cultural leaders of German-speaking Jewry, founder and editor of the important monthly *Die Jude* and a wide-ranging author on the Jewish religious and mystical (Hasidic) tradition. From 1923 he was professor of Jewish philosophy of religion and the history of religion at the University of Frankfurt. By 1938, despite his international reputation as a scholar, Buber's position in Nazi Germany had become untenable and he emigrated to Palestine. There he took up an academic position at the Hebrew University in Jerusalem. Buber was an enormously productive scholar. He published works on Hasidism, translated the Hebrew Bible into German and wrote extensively on Biblical subjects and on the wider philosophy of religion.

His most influential book was *Ich und Du* (I and Thou) which appeared in 1923. The book expresses with great complexity and poetic power Buber's most original thinking about the relationship between the individual ego and that which is outside of it. In most relationships it is not the full person that engages with the outside world but only a small part of it. These relationships, in which only a fraction of the individual is engaged, Buber calls I-It relationships, ones in which other beings are, to a greater or lesser extent, objectified rather than seen fully. Between individual human beings the I-Thou relationship, in which those concerned enter in the fullness of their being, is rare, only occurring at moments of great love. Between God, the great Thou, and man any form of I-It relationship, in to which God is turned into a set of dogmas or into an unbending moralist and legislator, is to be avoided. God can only be approached truly through an I-Thou relationship. Buber recognised that the I-Thou relationship was an ideal infrequently attained but he calls for such a relationship whenever possible. The moral

'Through the Thou a person becomes I.'

struggle of the individual is to reach a balance between the I-It relationships which are an inevitable part of mundane life and the I-Thou relationships which are always potential.

WRITINGS BY BUBER

I and Thou
T & T Clark pbk £9.95
0567220605

The Knowledge of Man:
Selected Essays
Humanities P pbk £10.95
0391035460

The Letters of Martin Buber
Syracuse UP pbk £15.95
0815604203

On Judaism
Schocken pbk £8.99
0805210504

On the Bible
Schocken pbk £9.99
0805206914

On Zion: The History of an Idea
Syracuse UP pbk £13.50
0815604823

Tales of the Hasidim
Schocken pbk £14.99
0805209956

WRITINGS ON BUBER

Moore, Donald
Martin Buber
Fordham UP pbk £14.95
0823216403

Avnon, Dan
Martin Buber: The Hidden
Dialogue
Rowman & Littlefield pbk £13.95
0847686884

Carl Gustav

JUNG — 1923

Psychological Types

The son of a Lutheran pastor, Carl Gustav Jung was born in Switzerland and studied medicine in Basel. While working with the psychiatrist Eugen Bleuler at the Burghölzli mental hospital in Zurich, Jung came across the work of Freud (then little-known outside Vienna) and was immediately enthralled. He met Freud in 1907 and, in the next few years, was the older man's most devoted and admiring collaborator. In his turn, Freud, who had a number of professional relationships in his career that seemed as much those between a father and a son as those between colleagues, was enormously impressed by Jung's intelligence and ebullient energy. Jung travelled to America with Freud in 1909 and was elected President of the Psychoanalytical Association the following year. Unfortunately the relationship between the two men did not remain at this peak for very long. A rift soon occurred, as it was to do whenever one of Freud's most favoured disciples showed too great an independence of mind. Jung, most certainly, did not possess the temperament of the ideal disciple and his own independent research led him to believe that Freud was wrong in ascribing an exclusively sexual nature to the libido. A split was inevitable, painful though it would be for both men, and the break occurred in 1913. It seemed especially painful for Jung and it was exacerbated in the next few years by his horror at the destructiveness and precariousness of civilization revealed by the First World War. He entered a period of intense self-examination, indeed self-torment. On several occasions he seemed poised himself on the brink of a complete breakdown but he emerged with the path clear before him to move towards the wide-ranging ideas of his own mature Analytical Psychology. The rest of his long life was spent in working out some of the meanings and implications of those ideas.

Jung developed his idea of the 'psyche', the whole personality, which contains the personal unconscious (forgotten or repressed individual experiences) and the collective unconscious, the residue of ideas and images shared by all human beings (archetypes). This led him into a widely diverse study of religion, folklore, mythology, astrology and mysticism. The idea of the collective unconscious is most clearly outlined in *The Archetypes and the Collective Unconscious* which posits a set of symbols shared in common by all individuals, whatever their cultural background. This notion may be controversial (is there any real evidence that such an unconscious exists?) but it has proved fruitful and given rise to innumerable 'Jungian' interpretations of myth and literature. Even more than Freud and other psychoanalysts Jung placed considerable emphasis on dreams. A book such as *Dreams* brings to the discussion of the subject a wealth of allusion to mysticism, religion, culture and

'As far as we can discern, the sole purpose of human existence is to kindle a light of meaning in the darkness of mere being.'

symbolism. In *Psychological Types*, a classic 1923 work, Jung originated the theory of introverted and extroverted personalities. His popularity today (he is much more widely read amongst a 'lay' audience than Freud) rests, to some extent, on his pioneering work with mental disorders but also on his writings on the occult, the idea of synchronicity (a theory of meaningful coincidences Jung developed in the book of the same name) and his use of the terms 'animus' and 'anima' to explore the male and female traits present in each sex. *Aspects of the Feminine*, for example, is a collection of his writings on marriage, Eros, the mother, the maiden and the whole anima/animus concept. Jung also left two works which are readily accessible to an ordinary reader. *Memories, Dreams, Reflections* is a fascinating, autobiographical account of his intellectual and spiritual journey through life. *Man and His Symbols*, deliberately written for the general reader, is a clear and well-illustrated summation of ideas which have been a potent source for others throughout much of the century.

WRITINGS BY JUNG

Aion: Researches into the Phenomenology of the Self
Routledge pbk £16.99
0415064767

Analytical Psychology
Routledge pbk £10.99
0744800560

Answer to Job
Routledge pbk £10.99
0744800196

The Archetypes and the Collective Unconscious
Routledge pbk £16.99
0415058449

Aspects of the Feminine
Routledge pbk £10.99
0744800544

Aspects of the Masculine
Routledge pbk £10.99
0744800927

C.G. Jung on Active Imagination
Routledge pbk £15.99
0415138434

The Development of Personality
Routledge pbk £16.99
0415071747

Dreams
Routledge pbk £10.99
0415136571

Essays on Contemporary Events
Routledge pbk £10.99
0744800870

The Essential Jung
Fontana pbk £8.99
0006861261

Flying Saucers
Routledge pbk £8.99
0744800625

Four Archetypes
Routledge pbk £10.99
074480034X

Jung on Elementary Psychology
Routledge pbk £14.99
0710003439

Jung on Evil
Routledge pbk £15.99
0415089700

**Jung on Synchronicity
and the Paranormal**
Routledge pbk £15.99
0415155096

Man and His Symbols
Arkana pbk £17.99
0140193162

Modern Man in Search of a Soul
Routledge pbk £10.99
0415208393

On the Nature of the Psyche
Routledge pbk £10.99
0744800889

The Practice of Psychotherapy
Routledge pbk £16.99
0415102340

**The Psychogenesis of
Mental Disease**
Routledge pbk £16.99
0415071755

Psychological Reflections
Routledge pbk £10.99
0415151317

Psychological Types
Routledge pbk £16.99
0415071771

Psychology and Alchemy
Routledge pbk £16.99
0415034523

Psychology and the East
Routledge pbk £10.99
0744800552

Psychology and the Occult
Routledge pbk £10.99
074480065X

Psychology and Western Religion
Routledge pbk £10.99
0744800919

**The Psychology of the
Transference**
Routledge pbk £10.99
0415151325

The Science of Mythology
Routledge pbk £9.99
0415104866

**The Spirit of Man in Art
and Literature**
Routledge pbk £10.99
0744800080

Synchronicity
Routledge pbk £10.99
0415136490

**Two Essays on Analytical
Psychology**
Routledge pbk £16.99
0415080282

The Undiscovered Self
Routledge pbk £10.99
0415051517

The most comprehensive edition
of Jung's writings, translated into
English, is the eighteen-volume
hardback collection published by
Routledge.

WRITINGS ON JUNG

Cambridge Companion to Jung
Cambridge UP pbk £16.95
0521478898

**McLynn, Frank
Carl Gustav Jung: A Biography**
Transworld pbk £12.99
0552995622

**Hyde, Maggie
Introducing Jung**
Icon pbk £8.99
1840460628

**Storr, Anthony
Jung**
Fontana pbk £6.99
0006860311

**Stevens, Anthony
Jung**
Oxford UP pbk £5.99
0192876864

**Stevens, Anthony
On Jung**
Penguin pbk £8.99
0140267867

Mahatma

GANDHI 1925–29

An Autobiography

Gandhi was born to a privileged Hindu family in western India in 1869. *An Autobiography* was published in two volumes in 1925 and 1929 and covers the period to 1921, well before its author's historic political achievements. Although Gandhi continued to write prolifically, notably in the *Young India* journal, the autobiography remains the best single statement available of Gandhi's core beliefs.

'For me, truth is the sovereign principle', Gandhi wrote in the introduction to *An Autobiography*. Gandhi's search for truth, or *Satya* (in Gandhi's native Gujarati), was an attempt to grasp man's essential nature. Gandhi believed in the fundamental unity of men; that their similarities were more significant than their differences. The search for unity and harmony among men was the search for truth or *Satya*. Gandhi's aim was an alternative to the oppression, conflict and division which had dominated human relations throughout history. His campaigns for Hindu-Muslim unity and for reform of the Hindu caste system (including abolition of untouchability) both sprang from this source. His asceticism was an attempt to strip himself of all pretension and vanity, to confront the world as his pure self. Gandhi led a life of prayer and fasting, and famously abandoned western dress in favour of a simple peasant *dhoti* and shawl (a gesture which won him such popularity that he became known as Mahatma, or 'great soul').

Gandhi held two fundamental principles throughout his life. *Satya* was one; the other was non-violence, or *Ahimsa*. 'The only means for the realization of Truth,' wrote Gandhi, '[was] *Ahimsa*.' His 'experiments with truth'are his attempts achieve *Satya* through *Ahimsa*. Thus throughout the long campaign for Indian independence, and despite beatings and imprisonment, Gandhi refused to contemplate the use of violence, even in self-defence.

This brings us to a third key concept in Gandhi's thought, and to Gandhi's unique contribution to politics. *Satyagraha*, a term coined by Gandhi and, literally, meaning truth-force, referred to the raft of innovative methods by which *Satya* could be achieved: broadly, passive resistance, civil disobedience and non-cooperation. If one engaged in *Satyagraha* one should be prepared for the ultimate sacrifice. Gandhi himself was close to death in a series of hunger strikes, and eventually fell victim to an assassin. In 1947, having helped persuade the British to quit India, Gandhi launched a campaign against Muslim-Hindu violence; his pacifism incensed some militant Hindus, and one of his co-religionists murdered him.

Gandhi's ideas had been influenced by his relatively cosmopolitan early life. As a young man, Gandhi had studied law in London, where he was exposed to liberal values, particularly the ideas of Henry David Thoreau and John Ruskin. He also

'I wanted to avoid violence. Non-violence is the first article of my faith. It is also the last article of my creed.'

read the religious works of both east and west. The asceticism of Leo Tolstoy's writings appealed to him. Having briefly returned to India to practise law, Gandhi moved to South Africa in 1893. He soon became a leader of the Indian community there. Horrified by the discrimination of the regime, Gandhi launched his first campaign of passive resistance, against the Transvaal government. He also launched an experimental community, Tolstoy Farm, in 1910.

Gandhi returned to India in 1915. His first serious clash with the authorities there occurred in 1919 when he led protests against the Rowlatt acts. He launched the *hartal* or general strike, during which protestors devoted themselves to prayer and fasting. To Gandhi's horror, the protests led to violent clashes, culminating in the Amritsar massacre, in which over 1,000 people were killed by troops under British command. For a period, Gandhi withdrew from politics and travelled India preaching. But Gandhi had returned to the fray by 1925, when he was appointed president of the pro-independence party, Indian National Congress. He was imprisoned several times before Indian independence was finally achieved on 15 August 1947.

Gandhi's achievements drew glowing praise. Viscount Louis Mountbatten, the last British Viceroy of India, wrote that 'Mahatma Gandhi [would] go down in history on a par with Buddha or Christ.' Gandhi's enduring influence was acknowledged by Martin Luther King Jr., who claimed that Gandhi had provided 'the only morally and practically sound methods open to oppressed people in their struggle for freedom.' King also wrote that 'Man [had] thought twice in our century, once with Einstein, then with Gandhi.

Einstein's thought transformed our understanding of the physical world, Gandhi's thought transformed understanding of the political world.'
JOE PONTIN, *Waterstone's Bristol Galleries*

WRITINGS BY GANDHI

An Autobiography
Penguin pbk £8.99
0140066268

Gandhi on Non-Violence
Shambhala pbk £4.99
1570622434

Selection edited by Thomas Merton

Hind Swaraj and Other Writings
Cambridge UP pbk £13.95
0521574315

WRITINGS ON GANDHI

Parekh, Bikhu
Gandhi
Oxford UP pbk £5.99
0192876929

Clement, Catherine
Gandhi: Father of a Nation
Thames & Hudson pbk £6.95
0500300712

Fischer, Louis
The Life of Gandhi
HarperCollins pbk £8.99
0006388876

Chadha, Yodesh
Rediscovering Gandhi
Arrow pbk £10.00
0099795019

Martin

HEIDEGGER | 1927

Being and Time

Heidegger was born in Messkirch in the German province of Baden-Württemberg and entered the Jesuit order as a young man. He left the order and turned to the study and teaching of philosophy during the First World War. Appointed Professor of Philosophy at Marburg in 1923 he succeeded his old teacher Husserl at Freiburg five years later. During the first year of the Nazi regime there was an unfortunate incident when Heidegger, as rector of the university, appeared to endorse wholeheartedly Hitler's rise to power but the nature of the regime soon became only too apparent. Heidegger never repeated his support but, even so, was suspended from teaching after the Second World War and spent his last decades in private study. The stigma of Nazi association is one which clings, undeservedly, to Heidegger's name.

Heidegger's most ambitious work was *Sein und Zeit* (Being and Time) which was published in 1927. The book concerns itself with the question, What do we mean by the verb 'to be'? Plato had asked this question over 2000 years before, and Heidegger places his work in a critical dialogue with the origins of the western tradition of philosophy in order to uncover this sense of being. The question with which he begins is a deceptively simple one: 'Do we in our time have an answer to the question of what we really mean by the word "being"?' The question of being may seem to us to be a frivolous, abstracted topic. Why should we bother ourselves about 'being' when there is so much else in the world that requires thought? As Heidegger points out, every understanding of what there is in the world assumes a familiarity with the meaning of 'is', the third person participle of the verb 'to be': our understanding of being already shapes our sense of ourselves, the world, and the other beings with which we share it. Whether we take it to be self-evident or claim that it is superfluous, we still presuppose its meaning. The question of being is all the more pressing because it has been forgotten. Heidegger sets himself the task of bringing this question back to thinking.

Heidegger is not peddling in semantics. The guiding theme for this renewal of the question of being is one that reaches back through Kant and Descartes to Plato and Aristotle: what is man? what is it to be human? 'We are ourselves the beings to be analysed.' When we ask about the meaning of being it is the fact of human existence, or *Da-sein* (literally 'there-being'), that faces us. Although *Dasein* sounds strange to non-German ears, it is simply an everyday term for 'existence', and thus serves as a way of uncovering the understanding of being that lies within our everyday actions and interactions in the world. 'The essence of *Dasein* lies in its existence.' Dasein is a being which, in its very existence, has an understanding of being. Heidegger lays out this unacknowledged understanding of being in terms of our 'being-in-the-world', the network of relations with our environment, equipment, and other beings. These relations are existential in the sense that we exist in and through them: I am not a solitary 'ego', but share the world with other *Daseins* as well as other kinds of beings.

Fundamental to this shared concern with being as 'being-in-the-world' is time. Two years after the publication of *Being and Time*, Heidegger wrote that 'the "and" in this title conceals within itself the central problem'. This is no glib phrase. The ambition and originality of his existential analytic of *Dasein* lies in the way that two hitherto separate themes in the history of philosophy - the questions of time and of being - are explicitly linked in a single problem: the temporality of being. The meaning of *Dasein's* being is nothing other than temporality. We make plans; we hurry or take our time; we look forward to the future or back into the past; we desire and we fear. These are all thoroughly temporal phenomena. We are not 'in' time as one way of being among others (such as the eternal or supra-temporal). The significance of the temporality is far more fundamental: it is only from this position of time that we can interpret something like being. 'Time is the horizon for all under-standing of being.' Our relation to our own deaths is pivotal to grasping this meaning. Existence is a 'being-towards-death': death is our ultimate possibility which cannot be outstripped. This realisation is neither a suicidal nor a courageous one, but rather it means that death informs everything we do or plan to do, all our possibilities. It is the sense of always being on the way to an end that informs

all of our 'being-in-the-world-with-others' as the inescapable horizon of our own existence.

The question of the meaning of being is one that Heidegger never answers to his own satis-faction. His *magnum opus* remains incomplete. *Being and Time* consists of the first two divisions of the three that he had planned to make up only the first half of the treatise. He eventually gave up the project as fundamentally incom-pletable. However, the book not only forms the touchstone for all his subsequent writings (even as he comes to problematise it), it has had a profound influence on the direction and development of twentieth century thought.

RICHARD STAMP, *Waterstone's Leamington Spa*

> '*The question of the meaning of Being must be* **formulated**. *If it is a fundamental question, indeed* **the** *fundamental question, it must be made transparent.*'

WRITINGS BY HEIDEGGER

Basic Writings
Routledge pbk £10.99
0415101611

Being and Time
Blackwell pbk £18.99
0631197702

The Concept of Time
Blackwell pbk £12.99
0631184252

An Introduction to Metaphysics
Yale UP pbk £10.95
0300017405

WRITINGS ON HEIDEGGER

Cambridge Companion to Heidegger
Cambridge UP pbk £17.95
0521385970

Inwood, Michael
Heidegger
Oxford UP pbk £5.99
0192831925

One of the Past Masters series.

Ree, Jonathan
Heidegger
Phoenix pbk £3.00
0753804417

Collins & Selina
Introducing Heidegger
Icon pbk £8.99
1840460881

Mulhall, Stephen
Heidegger and 'Being and Time'
Routledge pbk £8.99
0415100933

Walter

BENJAMIN 1928

One-way Street

Born into a Jewish middle-class family in
Berlin, Walter Benjamin proved to be a
brilliantly wide-ranging and original student,
as interested in the Kabbalistic tradition as he
was in the great texts of German literature. His
thesis on German 17th century drama, later
published as *The Origin of German Tragic Drama*,
was recognised by many as an exceptional
piece of work but nonetheless failed to gain
him an academic post. Benjamin began the
fragmented and precarious career as a
freelance journalist and cultural critic that he
was to pursue for the rest of his life. During the
twenties he moved towards Marxism, although
very much his own version of it, and began a
friendship with Brecht whose ideas on theatre
he championed. When the Nazis came to
power in 1933 he moved to Paris where he
continued to write journalism and began an
epic (and never to be finished) socio-symbolic
study of the city, known as the *Passagenwerk*.
The thirties proved to be a chaotic decade for
Benjamin, both personally and as a writer. He
talked regularly of emigration to Palestine but
was still in Paris in 1940. As the Germans
approached Benjamin, like so many others,
fled south towards Marseille where he
succeeded in getting an entry visa to the States.
He needed to escape France to use it and
joined a group of refugees crossing the
Pyrenees. They were stopped in the small
village of Portbou where the local authorities
refused to accept their papers and prepared to

return them to the Gestapo. Succumbing to
despair, Benjamin killed himself with an
overdose of morphine. The next day the local
authorities changed their minds and allowed
the other refugees to pass through.

How is Benjamin best categorised? He was a
literary critic of subtle perception and insight,
who wrote major essays on Proust and Kafka,
but he was much more than just a critic. He
was a Marxist, who was interested in the
material conditions that governed the
production of literary and artistic texts, yet he
was very far from being a dogmatic ideologue
and his *Moscow Diary*, posthumously published,
shows how his visit to Soviet Russia was, in
many ways, a disillusioning experience. He was
one of the earliest and most perceptive analysts
of the ephemeral, fragmented culture of the
twentieth century city. His landmark essay,
'The Work of Art in the Age of Mechanical
Reproduction', was one of the first to examine
the changing status of the once unique work of
art in a technological society which allowed
mass reproduction. In truth Benjamin was too
protean and wide-ranging a thinker to be
categorised at all. Rooted in the traditions of
German philosophy yet alert to the swirling
currents of modernity he was, at once, critic,
cultural historian and social analyst. He was, in
many ways, the most representative European
intellectual of the first half of the century and
his allusive, subtle and fragmentary work, seen

'That which withers in the age of mechanical reproduction is the aura of the work of art.'

at its best in essay collections like *One-Way Street* and *Illuminations*, faces the challenge of responding to the culture and experience of the modern city.

WRITINGS BY BENJAMIN

Charles Baudelaire
Verso pbk £10.00
1859841929

Illuminations
Pimlico pbk £12.50
0712665757

Moscow Diary
Harvard UP pbk £8.50
0674587448

One Way Street and other Writings
Verso pbk £12.00
185984197X

The Origin of German Tragic Drama
Verso pbk £15.00
1859848990

Understanding Brecht
Verso pbk £13.00
1859848141

The Arcades Project
Harvard UP hbk £24.95
067404326x

Publication of the imposing fragments (hundreds of pages of them) of Benjamin's intended *magnum opus*.

WRITINGS ON BENJAMIN

Marcus & Nead (eds)
The Actuality of Walter Benjamin
Lawrence & Wishart pbk £10.99
0853158630

A recently published collection of essays on Benjamin's ideas.

Benjamin for Beginners
Icon pbk £8.99
1874166870

Parini, Jay
Benjamin's Crossing
Anchor Books pbk £6.99
1862300399

An imaginative reconstruction of the last days of Walter Benjamin's life.

Brodersen, Momme
Walter Benjamin: A Biography
Verso pbk £14.99
1859840825

Kurt
GÖDEL | 1931

On Formally Undeterminable Propositions

Gödel was born a citizen of the Austro-Hungarian empire in what is now the Czech Republic town of Brno. He was a brilliantly precocious student of mathematics and entered the University of Vienna in 1923. He completed his doctoral dissertation in 1929 and joined the faculty staff at the university the following year. He worked in Vienna until 1940 when the opportunity arose to emigrate to the States. Gödel, who had been shocked out of an essentially apolitical stance by the murder of a Jewish colleague some years earlier, took his chance to escape an increasingly Nazi-dominated Europe. He settled at the Institute for Advanced Studies in Princeton where he was to remain for the rest of his life. In later years Gödel became increasingly eccentric and increasingly obsessed by his diet and his health. He became convinced that attempts were being made to poison him and, eventually, refused food altogether. He starved himself to death.

Like many of the greatest mathematicians Gödel made his most original and influential contributions to his subject when he was young. *Über Formal Unentscheidbare Sätze..*(On Formally Undeterminable Propositions . . .) was published when he was in his mid-twenties. This has some claim to being the single most important paper in logic and mathematics this century. Earlier mathematicians and philosophers like Frege and Bertrand Russell had assumed that it would be possible to provide a set of logical axioms from which the rest of pure maths would necessarily follow and had devoted much time and intellectual energy to the project of stating what these might be. Gödel showed that mathematics was essentially and unavoidably an incomplete subject. Frege and Russell had tried to make a closed system of something that was necessarily open-ended and their project could not succeed. With enormous intellectual ingenuity he showed that, in any axiomatic mathematical system, there are propositions that remain unprovable and undisprovable within the axioms of that system. Gödel's work initiated a new chapter in the history of mathematical logic and has contributed much to the development of the idea of a 'computable function' and to knowledge of the potential and the limits of computability.

'To every φ – consistent recursive class κ of formulae there correspond recursive r, such that neither ν Gen r nor Neg (ν Gen r) belongs to Flg – (κ) (where ν is the variable of r)'

WRITINGS BY GODEL

On Formally Undeterminable Propositions
Dover pbk £5.95
0486669807

WRITINGS ON GODEL

Smullyan, Raymond
Forever Undecided
Oxford UP pbk £7.99
0192821962

A collection of logical puzzles which provides an introduction to Gödel's theorems.

Hofstadter, Douglas
Gödel, Escher, Bach
Penguin pbk £17.99
0140179976

Karl

POPPER | 1935

The Logic of Scientific Discovery

Popper was one of the most influential philosophers of the century who has had a direct impact on those outside the world of academic philosophy in a way that few others have. Working scientists have appreciated and found useful his ideas on the nature of the scientific endeavour; politicians and social scientists have drawn upon his views of politics and history. Popper was born in Vienna into a cultured, middle-class family of Jewish origin and was educated at the University there. As a young man he was associated with the so-called *Wiener Kreis*, 'the group from whose ideas logical positivism developed', while remaining sceptical of many of the group's central tenets. His first book *Logik der Forschung* (The Logic of Scientific Discovery) appeared in 1935 and, two years later, with Austria increasingly overshadowed by Hitler's Nazism and anti-semitism, he took up a position at the University of Canterbury in New Zealand. He stayed there throughout the war and then moved to London to teach at the London School of Economics. In 1949 he was appointed professor of logic and scientific method at the University of London, a position he held until his retirement in 1969. His many other publications, in a working life that extended well beyond his official retirement, include *The Open Society and Its Enemies* (1945), *The Poverty of Historicism* (1957) and *Conjectures and Refutations* (1969).

Popper's work in the philosophy of science has some claims to being the most important in the field this century. From the publication of *The Logic of Scientific Discovery* onwards, he argued that the scientific method did not proceed from a range of observable facts towards generalisations and theories. Rather, scientists begin with imaginative hypotheses which they then test against experience. Experience and facts can work to falsify their theories but never completely to confirm them. Successful scientific theories are those which have, for the time being, survived attempts to falsify them.

Popper's philosophy of science proposed, indeed extolled, open-ended enquiry. In social and political theory he was driven also by a dislike of all-encompassing systems which attempted to stifle debate and denied the essential 'falsifiability' of the hypotheses on which they were founded. The two great intellectual pseudosciences of the age, because they refused to submit their tenets to the great, falsifying tribunal of fact and experience, were psychoanalysis and Marxism, both of which Popper had been drawn towards as a student. *The Poverty of Historicism* is a sustained attack on the idea, fundamental to Marxism, that there are inevitable laws of history with which certain political views are, equally inevitably, in tune.

'Our knowledge can only be finite, while our ignorance must necessarily be infinite.'

WRITINGS BY POPPER

Conjectures and Refutations
Routledge pbk £19.99
0415043182

In Search of a Better World
Routledge pbk £14.99
0415135486

Knowledge and the Body-Mind Problem
Routledge pbk £12.99
0415135567

The Logic of Scientific Discovery
Routledge pbk £19.99
041507892X

The Myth of the Framework
Routledge pbk £14.99
0415135559

The Open Society and Its Enemies Volume 1
Routledge pbk £15.99
0415040310

The Open Society and Its Enemies Volume 2
Routledge pbk £15.99
0415051347

The Poverty of Historicism
Routledge pbk £11.99
0415065690

The Self and Its Brain
Routledge pbk £12.99
0710095848

Unended Quest: An Intellectual Biography
Routledge pbk £12.99
0415086930

WRITINGS ON POPPER

Corvi, Roberta
An Introduction to the Thought of Karl Popper
Routledge pbk £14.99
0415129575

Stokes
Popper
Polity Press pbk £12.95
074560322X

Raphael, Frederic
Popper
Phoenix pbk £2.00
0753801892

Magee, Bryan
Popper
Fontana pbk £6.99
0006860087

John Maynard

KEYNES | 1936

A General Theory of Employment, Interest and Money

Born in Cambridge, where his father was a don, John Maynard Keynes was educated at Eton and King's College, Cambridge. As an undergraduate and a young don he met many of the people who formed the nucleus of what became known as the Bloomsbury Group and he was to become a leading member of the group. During the First World War he was an adviser to the Treasury and he was present at the Versailles Peace Conference but resigned his position to protest against the punitive economic terms being imposed on Germany. *The Economic Consequences of the Peace*, published in 1919, was a humanitarian polemic against the vindictiveness of the victors in the war. It went largely unheeded but was strikingly prescient about what those consequences might be. The depression in the thirties was the background for his enormously influential 1936 book *A General Theory of Employment, Interest and Money*. Appalled by the way a self-regulating market treated jobs and families as no more than 'a by-product of the activities of a casino,' Keynes proposed a new and more interventionist role for governments in overseeing their economies. During the Second World War he was Britain's representative at the Bretton Woods Conference from which the ideas for the IMF and the World Bank emerged. By the time he attended the conference, Keynes was a sick man and he died in 1946.

Keynes is, beyond question, the most important economist of the twentieth century. Others, such as Paul Samuelson, may have had more impact on the academic community or, like Milton Friedman, had their periods of direct political influence but the whole history of economic policy in the second half of the century can be seen as the history of reactions, favourable or unfavourable, to Keynes's ideas. In the twenties, in works like *A Tract on Monetary Reform* and *A Treatise on Money*, he was the first to break away from obsession with a return to the pre- Great War gold standard and to argue that monetary policy should concern itself instead with stability of employment and the internal price level. His great work, *A General Theory of Employment, Interest and Money*, was an ambitious attempt to re-interpret economic theory in the light of the reality of what had happened to the British and world economies in the late twenties and thirties. Previously economic theory had suggested that the self-regulated market could not suffer almost permanent under-employment of resources. Yes, there would be periodic fluctuations in trade and employment but there was nothing that government could, or indeed should, do in response to these. The economy would correct itself. If demand was directed away from one sector of the economy to another there would be unemployment in the first sector but increased demand in the second sector would necessarily mean a corresponding

> *'I think that capitalism, wisely managed, can probably be made more efficient for attaining economic ends than any alternative system yet in sight, but that in itself it is in many ways extremely objectionable.'*

increase in the demand for labour in that sector. Labour would transfer itself naturally from the sector experiencing lower demand from consumers to that experiencing higher demand. The process might take time but interference in the operation of the market would only hinder rather than help it.

The experience of the depression revealed the limitations of this kind of thinking and it was Keynes who expounded the alternative to the 'do-nothing' policies advocated by previous economists. He recognised that it was possible that an unregulated economy could deny employment to those seeking it. There was no effective self-regulation within the system and, far from re-adjusting itself to new patterns of demand, an economy might sink into stagnation. It was vital, in this situation, that the government, far from sitting back, should take measures to inject demand into the economy. A depression was a time when a government should be spending more money in order to achieve this. The result of the 'Keynesian Revolution', the legacy of which is still with us, was a transformation of the role of government in the management of the economy. As Keynes's ideas were more and more accepted by policy-makers (and the Second World War increased the need for a managed economy) government budgeting came to have a major role in determining the state of the economy.

The need for a national balance sheet and the need for government to respond to falls in demand and increases in unemployment came to seem truisms. Even in the last twenty years, in which there has been a significant reaction against the political consensus that Keynes's ideas produced, only the severest of monetarists has advocated a return to a completely 'hands-off' policy. In the West we continue to live in societies, and in economies, profoundly altered by the ideas of Keynes.

WRITINGS BY KEYNES

Essays in Biography
Macmillan pbk £19.99
0333402146

Essays in Persuasion
Macmillan pbk £17.99
0333376021

The General Theory of Employment, Interest and Money
Cambridge UP pbk £16.95
0521293820

Macmillan publish the collected works of Keynes in 30 hardback volumes.

WRITINGS ON KEYNES

Keynes, Milo (ed)
Essays on Keynes
Cambridge UP pbk £17.95
052129696X

Stewart, Michael
Keynes and After
Penguin pbk £7.99
0140136517

Pugh and Garratt
Keynes for Beginners
Icon pbk £8.99
1874166137

Harrod, Roy
The Life of John Maynard Keynes
Norton pbk £8.99
0393300242

The standard biography of Keynes is by Robert Skidelsky and is published by Macmillan. Only two volumes are available - John Maynard Keynes: Hopes Betrayed 1883-1920 (033357379X £12.99) and John Maynard Keynes: The Economist as Saviour 1920-1937 (0333584996 £14.99). D.E. Moggridge's book Maynard Keynes: An Economist's Biography (Routledge pbk £19.99 0415127114) is a good one-volume survey of Keynes's life by a renowned authority on the man and his work.

Alan
TURING | 1936

On Computable Numbers

Alan Mathison Turing was born in a London nursing home in 1912. Excelling at mathematics whilst at Sherborne school, he went on to study the subject at Cambridge, where his unconventional brilliance assured him a fellowship. Quite apart from his vital code-breaking work during the Second World War, few peers could have guessed what momentous impact Turing's academic work would have. In 1931 the Austrian logician Kurt Gödel had dealt a shattering blow to the efforts of mathematicians attempting to create a perfect formalisation of all mathematical reasoning. His incompleteness theorem showed that in any consistent axiomatic system there must exist propositions whose truth can never be determined. An example in logic of such an undecidable proposition is the famous 'I am lying' paradox.

Turing sought to establish whether or not such undecidable propositions could be identified from within their system i.e. by mechanically applying a set of rules derived from the basic axioms on which the system was based. He posited a simple machine able to print or delete symbols on any one square on an infinite length of tape at any one time. Any algorithm can be written as a set of instructions, and so for every algorithm there can be a machine set up to compute it. Turing then crucially reasoned that the work of a machine in interpreting and carrying out the instruc-

tions is itself a mechanical process, and so must be coded for another machine to perform. This other machine, styled the Universal Turing Machine, can effectively receive the code of any other machine and thus behave like it. If a machine capable of recognizing undecidable propositions existed, it would have to resemble the Universal Turing Machine. In examining all possible propositions coded as machines it would also have to examine itself, thereby receiving its own code with the implicit instruction to behave as itself behaving as itself. This contradiction forced Turing to conclude that decidability was impossible, and his discovery was published in his 1936 paper, 'On Computable numbers, with an Application to the Entscheidungsproblem.' With hindsight it is hard not to imagine the Universal Turing Machine as a modern computer, able to perform any coded task if supplied with the appropriate software. Yet it was ten years before such a computer, even in its most primitive form, existed, that Turing developed the ideas that provided the cornerstone of computer science, and thus changed the world.

ANDY WALKER,
Waterstone's Charing Cross Road

'I believe that at the end of the century the use of words and general educated opinion will have altered so much one will be able to speak of machines thinking without expecting to be contradicted.'

WRITINGS BY TURING

Turing's papers are not readily available to a non-academic readership. They are published in the Netherlands in hardback volumes produced by the North-Holland Press.

WRITINGS ON TURING

Hodges, Andrew
Alan Turing: The Enigma
Vintage pbk £8.99
0099116413

The standard biography.

Strathern, Paul
Turing and the Computer
Arrow UP pbk £3.99
0099237822

A brief introduction to Turing's ideas on computing.

Jean-Paul

SARTRE | 1943

Being and Nothingness

Jean-Paul Sartre was born in Paris, educated at the Ecole Normale Superieure and later studied in Germany, under Heidegger and other teachers. His first novel *Nausea* was published in 1938 and his major philosophical work, *Being and Nothingness,* appeared during the Second World War. After the war Sartre began to emerge as the leading figure in the new intellectual life of the Left Bank. With Simone de Beauvoir and others he founded the journal *Les Temps Modernes* as a vehicle for avant-garde and left-wing debate. He was soon recognised as the major philosopher of French existentialism and continued to play a central role in his country's intellectual life until shortly before his death. A Marxist, of an unorthodox kind, Sartre had links with the Communist Party through the 1950s and, in the following decade, he was a prominent opponent of American involvement in Vietnam and a high-profile sympathiser with the *évenements* of 1968.

Sartre was the central figure in atheistic existentialism and the idea at the heart of existentialism is that of choice. Existence precedes essence. Man is nothing at birth and what makes him what he becomes, are the choices and commitments he makes in his life. There is no God and no other crutches on which man can lean. He is alone in the universe, armed only with his will and capacity for choice.

Whether one thinks of Sartre primarily as a 'writer' (novelist, dramatist) or as a major philosopher, it is clear that he has had a significant impact on twentieth century intellectual life. His image of man as adrift in a godless world, hostage to his own freedom, and incapable of sustaining coincidence between his own consciousness and external reality, was a compelling one, particularly in the years of the war and in the ensuing austerity of the fifties. Sartre's moves to the left, from an alienated individualism to a revolutionary Marxism which was prepared to condone violence, also make him a symbolic figure for a generation of intellectuals. Today Sartre is an unfashionable figure but his influences on many of the thinkers who has now turned their backs on him have been considerable.

'So there is no human nature, since there is no God to conceive it.'

PHILOSOPHICAL WRITINGS BY SARTRE

Being and Nothingness
Routledge pbk £12.99
0415040299

Existentialism and Humanism
Methuen   pbk £6.99
041331300X

The Psychology of the Imagination
Routledge pbk £12.99
0415119545

Selected Writings on Literature and Politics
Penguin pbk £10.99
0140189211

Sketch for a Theory of the Emotions
Routledge pbk £8.99
0415119138

What is Literature?
Routledge pbk £12.99
0415104378

FICTION AND DRAMA BY SARTRE

The Age of Reason
Penguin pbk £7.99
0140181776

The Reprieve
Penguin pbk £7.99
0140181784

Iron in the Soul
Penguin pbk £7.99
0140181792

Nausea
Penguin pbk £6.99
0140181806

In Camera and Other Plays
Penguin pbk £8.99
0140181814

Words
Penguin pbk £6.99
0140182772

Sartre's account of his childhood in a French provincial town before the First World War.

WRITINGS ON SARTRE AND EXISTENTIALISM

The Cambridge Companion to Sartre
Cambridge UP pbk £17.95
0521388120

Thody & Read
Introducing Sartre
Icon pbk £8.99
1840460660

Thody, Philip
Jean-Paul Sartre
Macmillan pbk £12.99
0333537556

One of a series called Macmillan Modern Novelists, this book looks at Sartre's fiction and the ideas which permeate it.

McCulloch, Gregory
Using Sartre
Routledge pbk £14.99
041510954X

Cooper, David E.
Existentialism
Blackwell pbk £15.99
0631161929

Susan Sontag's book of essays *Against Interpretation* (Vintage pbk £6.99 009938731X) includes her discussions of Sartre and a number of other contemporary European figures, including Levi-Strauss, Genet and Simone Weil.

Friedrich

HAYEK | 1944

The Road to Serfdom

Friedrich von Hayek was an Austrian economist who became one of the country's leading champions of capitalism. Hayek's pioneering liberal economics were highly influential in Britain during the Thatcher regime of 1979 to 1991. Born and educated in Vienna, Hayek spent thirty years teaching at the London School of Economics and the University of Chicago before returning to his native city in 1962. He was the leading figure in the Austrian school of economists centred on Vienna.

Hayek cut his intellectual teeth during the ideological ferment of 1920s and 1930s Europe. The twenty years prior to the publication of his best known work, *The Road to Serfdom*, published in 1944, saw the continent increasingly dominated by totalitarian regimes. In Austria the state bureaucracy extended to most areas of life. In *The Road to Serfdom* Hayek expressed extreme scepticism towards any form of collective action, which he believed to be necessarily undermining of individual liberty. Instead politicians should 'roll back the frontiers of the state' and create the conditions for perfectly laissez-faire economic individualism.

Unsurprisingly, Hayek was extremely critical of state economic intervention. His views contrasted strongly with those of the interventionist Keynes whose ideas formed the orthodoxy of the immediate post-war period. Hayek insisted that even well-intentioned intervention in the economy was likely to do more harm than good, because it upset the balance of an inherently efficient system.

He argued that the free market operated more efficiently in several ways. It permitted the free flow of information and technology necessary for economic growth; it provided personal incentives necessary for a dynamic workforce; it met consumer demands; it forced down the costs of production; it encouraged entrepreneurial and scientific innovation; and it stimulated investment, since large profits provided the means to invest in new technologies.

Hayek's faith in the free market was profound. Whilst he conceded that companies would inevitably tend to compete for a monopoly position in the economy, he argued that even this led to benevolent results for the consumer. Even if the market failed, in recession or high unemployment, it was better for the state not to interfere. Nor was the state justified in applying redistributive taxation. Any redistribution should be based on voluntary contributions by the wealthy to the poor.

Hayek's most celebrated influence on the Thatcher regime was his monetarist doctrine which argued for strict control on the growth of the money supply in order to

'Most planners who have seriously considered the practical aspects of their task have little doubt that a directed economy must be run on more or less dictatorial lines.'

control inflation, even if the result was higher unemployment.

Hayek's faith in the free market was influenced by the work of Adam Smith. Hayek in turn influenced Milton Friedman and the Chicago School, the so-called neo-classicist economists who shared his advocacy of returning to the free market. Friedman and his allies, however, took a slightly less rigid line on the issue of state intervention.

Hayek was a virulent anti-communist who regarded the collapse of the communist regimes of eastern Europe and their planned economies, which he lived just long enough to see, as vindication of his lifetime's work and of his ideas.

JOE PONTIN, *Waterstone's Bristol Galleries*

WRITINGS BY HAYEK

The Fatal Conceit
Routledge pbk £15.99
0415041872

The Road to Serfdom
Routledge pbk £10.99
0415065607

Erwin
SCHRÖDINGER | 1944

What is Life?

Erwin Schrödinger was a leading figure in the group of scientists who developed quantum theory in the 1920s. His name is most familiar from its attachment to the thought experiment he devised in 1935, known as Schrödinger's Cat. (In the experiment a cat enclosed in a box either lives or dies according to the outcome of a quantum event. The paradox that Schrödinger highlighted was that, until the box was opened and an observation made, quantum theory stated that a universe in which the cat was dead and a universe in which it was alive both existed in parallel.) However his major achievement was the work he published in 1926 relating to wave mechanics which, together with Heisenberg's ideas on matrix mechanics, formed the basis of quantum theory. Einstein wrote to him that 'the idea of your work springs from true genius' and it was for this work that Schrödinger was awarded (together with the Cambridge professor Paul Dirac) the 1933 Nobel Prize for Physics.

Schrödinger was born in Vienna, where his father ran a family business, and he was educated there before beginning a peripatetic career as an academic. At various times he taught in Stuttgart, Breslau and Zurich and Berlin, where he was professor of theoretical physics at the time Hitler came to power. Although not himself Jewish, Schrödinger felt unable to remain in a country where anti-semitism had become official state policy and he moved to Oxford. Later in the thirties he returned briefly to his home country but was dismissed in 1938 from his position at Graz University because of his continued opposition to Nazism. Most of the forties and fifties he spent in Ireland where Eamon De Valera had invited him to join a newly founded Institute for Advanced Studies. He returned once again to Austria on his retirement and died in Vienna in January 1961.

As well as the highly complex work he published for his scientific peers, Schrödinger also wrote a number of works for a general audience which, like Heisenberg's *Physics and Philosophy*, aimed to elaborate the wider meanings of developments in the sciences. The best known of these is *What Is Life?* which he wrote when he was in Dublin and published in 1944. *What Is Life?* is a fascinating attempt to reconcile the findings of quantum physics, to which Schrödinger contributed so much, with the biology of living cells. How is it that the world described by quantum physicists, the world of subatomic particles in which random events are governed only by probability, is also, at a different level of organisation, the world of genetics and of living creatures?

'Thus the task is, not so much to see what no one has yet seen; but to think what nobody has yet thought, about that which everybody sees.'

WRITINGS BY SCHRÖDINGER

What Is Life?
Cambridge UP pbk £7.95
0521427088

Nature And the Greeks/
Science and Humanism
Cambridge UP pbk £7.95
0521575508

WRITINGS ON SCHRÖDINGER

Moore, Walter
Schrödinger: Life and Thought
Cambridge UP pbk £15.95
0521437679

Gribbin, John
In Search of Schrödinger's Cat
Transworld pbk £7.99
0552125555

Simone de

BEAUVOIR 1949

The Second Sex

In the late forties, France was alive with post-war euphoria. After the years of Nazi occupation, Parisians were riding high on a new tide of freedom and in search of new beliefs. Haunts of the new bohemians, like the Café de Flore and the Café Dôme, were buzzing with original thoughts and revolutionary ideas. Left Bank intellectuals like Jean-Paul Sartre, Albert Camus and Simone de Beauvoir were publishing essays, novels, plays infused with the new philosophy of existentialism, with its emphasis on a life of freedom of choice and individual moral responsibility. De Beauvoir and Sartre founded the journal *Les Temps Modernes* and, with the press returned to freedom of expression, their political and philosophical ideas began to exert a powerful influence.

At this time most leftist writers considered the emancipation of women as secondary to the cause of socialism, but in 1949, de Beauvoir published a ground-breaking and lengthy essay in two volumes which was to challenge this assumption. That essay was *The Second Sex*. 'One is not born a woman, one becomes one,' De Beauvoir wrote, reflecting existentialist ideas. Yet words like these have resulted in her being misunderstood by many modern feminists who believe she degraded the feminine by implying that the human condition is essentially masculine. However it is important to remember that she was writing in a France where contraception was still illegal and some

forms of abortion were still punishable (in theory) by the guillotine. Surely it is little wonder that she believed adopting 'masculine' values and sacrificing 'feminine' ones was a favourable option for modern women wanting to take a new place in society. Whatever the criticisms now levelled at de Beauvoir, *The Second Sex* became one of the most comprehensive and thorough studies of women ever written. De Beauvoir misses very little as she discusses and argues vehemently the role of 'the Other' in mythology, biology, sexuality, history, literature, psychoanalysis (of both adult and child life) and sociology. She presents a sweeping portrait of the past, present and future of the independent woman.

De Beauvoir was born in Paris and in 1929 was one of the few women studying philosophy at the Sorbonne. In the final examination, she was placed second, just a fifth of a point behind Sartre. It was at this time that they began an association that was to last their lifetimes, first as lovers, then as political and literary allies. It would continue for more than half a century. De Beauvoir always insisted that Sartre was the 'creative thinker' and his work of paramount importance. Yet, although the influence of each one upon the other's work is hotly debated, it is interesting to note that members of the Sorbonne examination jury, in later years, commented that 'of the two, she was the real philosopher.'

'One is not born a woman; one becomes one.'

They were a couple who never lived together, never married and never had children. Both, especially Sartre, indulged in 'contingent affairs.' De Beauvoir always claimed the partnership was a success but it is clear that there were several occasions when their relationship was under threat. It is interesting that *The Second Sex* appeared at one such crisis. While France experienced political liberation, de Beauvoir was contemplating a liberation of her own. She was becoming profoundly aware of her own ageing, Sartre was greatly attached to another woman and she herself was in the midst of a passionate love affair with the American novelist Nelson Algren. Algren's traditionalist view of the relationship between the sexes put a strain on this affair and her trips to America, where the absence of freedom for women, especially black women, was only too apparent, led her to question the imbalance between men and women. By her own admission, it was Sartre who proposed she write 'a book about women.' It is ironic that she produced a book that has, arguably, had more impact and effcted more change in people's lives, than anything Sartre himself published.

SHARON ROWE, *Waterstone's Cardiff*

NON-FICTION BY DE BEAUVOIR

America Day by Day
Indigo pbk £7.99
0575401605

Memoirs of a Dutiful Daughter
Penguin pbk £9.99
0140183310

The Prime of Life
Penguin pbk £12.99
0140183345

The Second Sex
Vintage pbk £9.99
009974421X

FICTION BY DE BEAUVOIR

All Men Are Mortal
Virago pbk £6.99
1860490026

The Blood of Others
Penguin pbk £7.99
0140183337

She Came to Stay
Flamingo pbk £7.99
0006540805

WRITINGS ON DE BEAUVOIR

Evans, Mary
Simone de Beauvoir
Sage pbk £15.99
0803988672

Evans, Ruth (ed)
The Second Sex:
New Interdisciplinary Essays
Manchester UP £13.99
0719043034

Fallaize (ed)
Simone De Beauvoir:
A Critical Reader
Routledge pbk £15.99
0415147034

Fullbrook, Kate
Simone de Beauvoir
Polity pbk £11.95
0745612032

Keefe, Terry
Simone de Beauvoir
Macmillan pbk £12.99
033363974X

Joseph

CAMPBELL — 1949

The Hero With a Thousand Faces

A key thinker in the realm of comparative mythology, Joseph Campbell achieved a lasting influence in many areas of thought, from anthropology to literature, psychology to cinema. His books on the origins and nature of mythology have a wide academic and popular readership, reflecting his broad, humanist approach to the subject.

Born in Connecticut in 1904, Campbell developed an early fascination for mythology and folk tales under the influence of Elmer Gregor, a writer of children's books about American Indian life and the frontier. Campbell was soon devouring ethnographic reports issued by the Smithsonian Institute and collecting as many examples of Indian legends as he could find. This early interest in ancient myths and folk traditions was revived at Columbia University where he abandoned biology to study English and Comparative Literatures, specialising in Arthurian and Grail stories. In 1927 he travelled to Europe on a scholarship where he encountered modern psychoanalysis in the writings of Freud and Jung and was introduced into the avant-garde circles of Paris. Here he formed significant friendships with Picasso, Georges Braque and the spiritual leader Jiddu Krishnamurti amongst others. This was a highly formative experience for Campbell and the modernist tradition that reached its zenith in France at this time influenced much of his early

thinking. He was particularly fascinated by the works of James Joyce whose restless experimentation with language and mythology had started to reflect his own interests in the creative capacities of the unconscious. After returning to America he accepted a position at Sarah Lawrence College, where he remained writing and teaching for 38 years.

Campbell's first mature book and perhaps his most influential, *The Hero With a Thousand Faces*, was published in 1949 and immediately established his reputation as an authority on world myth. It introduced several themes that endure throughout his work, most significantly the idea that all primitive narratives are spun out of simple, archetypal schemes that are common to all societies, and still serve to underpin the structures of modern literature. Campbell goes to great lengths to identify the unity of structure that lies beneath all myths and sees it as evidence that stories function in a society as mechanisms of social and psychological regulation. Hence the familiar patterns of life, birth, marriage, death etc, with all the attendant experiences, are reflected in folk stories that, far from being distractions, serve to transform the consciousness of the individual into the world of the society as a whole.

To illustrate this process Campbell introduces the scheme of the 'Hero's Journey' or 'monomyth', a universal structure that can be altered, extended and recombined into more complex forms of storytelling, and functions as a template or base that is responsible for all narratives from Homer to contemporary fictions. The monomyth is conceived as a microcosmic cycle in which the trials of life are represented and overcome by a central protagonist, who is usually obliged to embark on a journey, which will restore balance and continuity to the society from which he/she comes.

Campbell examines the journey in great depth, drawing from an impressive range of folktales from all over the world. Each myth selected confirms the underlying structure of the cycle in which the protagonist is subject to several key stages that inform the progress of the journey. The process is set in motion by a 'guide', often of supernatural origins. For example, Athena constantly directs and advises Odysseus, Jason is put on the right course by Hera and, in Celtic myth, Arthur is initiated into his fate by Merlin. (Campbell's range of erudition means that he can use not only these familiar examples but more recondite ones from Chinese, Arabic and Native American legends, amongst others.) The guide represents the great threshold between the familiar world of the Hero's past and the possibilities of his Heroic fate. To ignore the advice of the guide, or to let the call go unheeded, leads to tragedy. We see this in the tale of Orpheus whose impatience causes him to gaze upon his wife too quickly as she follows him from Hades, thus losing her forever.

Once the progress has begun the Hero is then tested in the face of adversity. This can take the form of riddles, labyrinths, monsters or armies. Or the Hero is charged with the task of bringing back some sacred object – a Golden Fleece, the Holy Grail, a Gorgon's head. Sometimes (as in the case of Heracles) several trials have to be completed. Campbell admits that, in individual cultures, fragments of half-remembered histories intrude to flesh out the shape of the monomyth. The symbolism, however, is arbitrary to the individual culture. Once the artefact has been returned or the task completed, a balance is re-established within that society. The Hero has become symbolic of the mediation of cosmic forces.

This is a very basic outline of what Campbell sees as an intensely complex psychological process. There is a palpable sense of fate in all mythology and he argues that this reflects the inevitable cycle of life, bound as it is by time and the rhythms of nature. Mythology, he observes, often frames rituals and festivities within a culture, especially initiatory, marriage and funeral rites. It often encourages the initiates to identify with the central protagonists of the journey and hence become not only themselves as individuals but also exemplars of their whole society and its values, past, present and future.

Campbell has been criticised for the lack of rigour in his work and it is true that he seldom pauses to examine the conceptual frameworks which underlie his theories of mythology. He often borrows from very different schools of psychoanalysis, taking what he needs to buttress his own ideas but ignoring any contradictions that arise. His laments about the lack of effective myth or ritual in modern, indus-

'The labyrinth is thoroughly known; we have only to follow the thread of the hero's path.'

trial societies can encourage a bogus mysticism that obscures the anthropological significance of his ideas and has, in part, been responsible for his influence on new age thinking and popular psychology. Yet, to his many admirers, these failings are inextricably linked with his strengths as a thinker. Throughout his work he maintains an eclectic, humanist approach and lets himself be guided by the material he works with, rather than by the constraints of theory. His books are highly accessible to anyone interested in mythology and are packed with rare examples of story-telling from all over the world. Above all else many of his works are simply a delight to read. His four-volume *The Masks of God* is a detailed examination of how the cycles of ancient mythologies inform the thinking of world religions. It also gives a remarkable appraisal of the ways mythology has influenced the differing metaphysical traditions that have arisen in the East and the West.

Campbell's work has had an impact on a wide variety of writers and filmmakers. In Hollywood, script writers have long used *The Hero With a Thousand Faces*, and the archetypal narratives it describes, as a screenwriter's handbook. George Lucas has claimed that the Star Wars films took their structure from Campbell's ideas. His writing also fuelled some of the structuralist debates of the sixties and is an important precursor to such works as Northrop Frye's influential *Anatomy of Criticism.* Despite the larger cultural ramifications of his work, Campbell saw his task as a simple one. He wanted to restore the functional nature of myths back to a society that, without this, was becoming more and more spiritually barren.

JAMES WYKES, *Waterstone's Charing Cross Road*

WRITINGS BY CAMPBELL

The Hero With a Thousand Faces
Fontana pbk £9.99
0586085718

**The Masks of God:
Primitive Mythology**
Arkana pbk £11.00
0140194436

**The Masks of God:
Oriental Mythology**
Arkana pbk £11.00
0140194428

**The Masks of God:
Occidental Mythology**
Arkana pbk £11.00
014019441X

**The Masks of God:
Creative Mythology**
Arkana pbk £11.00
0140194401

WRITINGS ON CAMPBELL

**Sartore (ed)
Joseph Campbell on
Myth and Mythology**
University Press of America pbk
£13.95
0819190810

A collection of readings from Campbell accompanied by editorial comment and analysis.

Roland

BARTHES | 1957

Mythologies

Roland Barthes was born in Cherbourg in 1915 and his father was killed in a naval action in the First World War the following year, leaving his son to be brought up by his mother and grandparents. His education took place in Bayonne in the South West and in Paris. His twenties were overshadowed by several spells of tuberculosis but the enforced idleness of convalescence allowed him opportunity for wide reading and to publish his first pieces of literary criticism. His life as an academic began abroad, in Rumania and Egypt, but he returned to France to teach at the *Ecole Pratique des Hautes Etudes*. In 1962 he became director of studies with responsibility for a seminar devoted to the 'sociology of signs, symbols and representations.' Three years before his death he was appointed to the Collége de France.

In *Mythologies* Barthes moved from the literary analysis of his first book, *Writing Degree Zero*, to an examination of the broader culture and the insidious way in which seemingly neutral images, practices etc carried a disguised ideological content. Indeed the modern myths Barthes identifies as present in the images and messages of advertising, entertainment and popular culture are, at their most successful, even more subtle. They present themselves as entirely natural, devoid of any need to be analysed or deciphered. Like Poe's Purloined Letter the message of the successful modern myth is hidden in full view. In the essays that make up *Mythologies* the example Barthes uses most tellingly is a front-cover photo from Paris-Match which shows a black soldier saluting the French flag. There is an ideological content to this – a set of assumptions about French imperialism. Yet the myth works to assure us that the signifier, in semiotic terms, (the black soldier saluting the flag) and the signified (French imperialism) are not distinct. There are no hidden messages.

Barthes's other writings have been enormously wide-ranging and his influence has been felt in many of the humanities and social sciences. *Camera Lucida* is a subtle investigation of what photographs say to us about presence and absence, life and death, which moves, via Barthes's thoughts on a photograph of his mother as a child, into delicate and poignant autobiographical memories. *Image-Music-Text* is a collection of writings on cinema, photography and literature including two of his most important essays, 'Introduction to the Structural Analysis of Narrative' and 'The Death of the Author'. *A Lover's Discourse* is a fragmentary, aphoristic analysis of the kinds of language used by a lover and the imagined figure of his beloved. In all of these books, and others, Barthes moves beyond the merely critical and into the realm of what he once described as 'the novelistic without the novel.'

'Myth is not defined by the object of the message, but by the way in which it utters that message.'

WRITINGS BY BARTHES

Camera Lucida
Vintage pbk £5.99
0099225417

Image-Music-Text
Fontana pbk £8.95
0006861350

A Lover's Discourse
Penguin pbk £8.99
0140125035

Mythologies
Vintage pbk £5.99
0099972204

Sontag, Susan (ed)
A Roland Barthes Reader
Vintage pbk
0099224917

S/Z
Blackwell pbk £14.99
0631176071

WRITINGS ON BARTHES

Moriarty, Michael
Roland Barthes
Polity P. pbk £13.95
0745604560

Noam

CHOMSKY | 1957

Syntactic Structures

Chomsky has been an important figure in American intellectual life for two reasons. Firstly he has been a prominent and courageously radical critic of American domestic and foreign policy. Secondly, in his own academic field of linguistics, he has produced ground-breaking theories of the relationship between language and the human mind. Born in Philadelphia, he was the son of a leading expert on medieval Hebrew and began his academic career as an undergraduate at the University of Pennsylvania. Since 1955 he has taught at the Massachusetts Institute of Technology. In his linguistic writing Chomsky has argued that the speed and efficiency with which children master language indicate that the mind is not a *tabula rasa* on which the rules of grammar and language are inscribed through experience. Rather these rules are encoded within the mind; we possess an innate faculty for language.

Throughout his career Chomsky has been a very individual socialist thinker, deeply critical of the US and its policies. In the sixties he was a leading opponent of involvement in South East Asia and he has been assiduous in gathering evidence of American interference of all kinds, from diplomatic to military, in the internal affairs of Latin America. His polemical writing on the relationship between the developed world, specifically America, and the Third World is both passionate in its moral condemnation and intellectually incisive in its close argumentation. He has also been scornful of the role played by the American media and the American intelligentsia in 'manufacturing consent' to policies which should be open to full scrutiny and criticism. In books like *Deterring Democracy* and *Manufacturing Consent* he has presented trenchant and tightly argued analyses of the history of American policy since the Cold War and the collusion of the media in the production of propaganda rather than information. In his political life Chomsky has occasionally acted with a surprising naivety (notoriously, he once wrote a preface to a Holocaust-denying text, not because he believed its thesis but because he believed in the author's right to express it) but he has been the most intellectually impressive voice of dissent in America over the last thirty years.

'Turning to the human mind, we also find structures of marvelous intricacy developing in a uniform way with limited and unstructured experience.'

CHOMSKY ON LINGUISTICS

Aspects of the Theory of Syntax
MIT Press pbk £12.95
0262530074

The Minimalist Program
MIT Press pbk £20.50
0262531283

The Sound Pattern of English
MIT Press pbk £20.95
026253097X

Syntactic Structures
De Gruyter pbk £14.95
3110154129

CHOMSKY ON POLITICS

The Chomsky Reader
Serpent's Tail pbk £15.99
1852421177

Class Warfare
Pluto P. pbk £12.99
0745311377

The Culture of Terrorism
Pluto P. pbk £14.99
074530270X

Deterring Democracy
Vintage pbk £9.99
0099135019

Manufacturing Consent
Vintage pbk £8.99
0099533111

Necessary Illusions
Pluto P. pbk £14.99
0745303803

Powers and Prospects
Pluto P. pbk £13.99
0745311067

Re-Thinking Camelot
Verso pbk £9.95
0860916855

World Orders Old and New
Pluto P. pbk £14.99
0745313205

Year 501
Verso pbk £12.00
0860916804

WRITINGS ON CHOMSKY

McGillvray
Chomsky
Polity P. pbk £14.99
074561888X

Lyons, John
Chomsky
Fontana pbk £6.99
0006862292

Maher & Groves
Introducing Chomsky
Icon pbk £8.99
1840461128

Barsky, Robert
Noam Chomsky: A Life of Dissent
MIT Press pbk £12.95
0262522551

Botha, Rudolf
Challenging Chomsky
Blackwell pbk £15.99
0631180273

Werner

HEISENBERG

1958

Physics and Philosophy

Werner Heisenberg was one of the founding fathers of quantum mechanics who gave his name to the 'uncertainty principle', one of the more startling concepts of that branch of physics. Born in Bavaria, Heisenberg studied at Munich and Göttingen before taking professorial positions at Leipzig and Berlin. It was, however, as a young man working with Max Born at Göttingen that he made his most lasting contribution to the understanding of quantum phenomena and formulated the uncertainty principle. It was for this work that he received the Nobel Prize in 1933. Heisenberg stayed in Germany throughout the Nazi period and directed their unsuccessful project to construct an atomic bomb. After the war he was one of the leading figures in the reconstruction of German science and became director of the Max-Planck Institute in Göttingen.

The uncertainty principle with which Heisenberg's name is linked embodies one of the most puzzling elements of quantum theory and one of the most baffling qualities of the behaviour of particles in the sub-atomic world. At its simplest the principle states that one cannot exactly measure essential properties of these sub-atomic particles. Or rather, by exactly measuring one property (momentum) you reduce the capacity to exactly measure another property (position). In other words, if you know the exact position of a particle you cannot exactly know its momentum and vice versa. And this is not the result of shortcomings in our technology and in the instruments we use to undertake the measurements. It is an intrinsic element in the nature of the universe at this microscopic level. The necessary consequences of the inherent uncertainty of the sub-atomic world are immense and many books have been devoted to rehearsing them. One of the earliest attempts to explain quantum theory and its philosophical consequences to a lay audience was Heisenberg's own book *Physics and Philosophy*. This begins by explaining how quantum theory has overturned the certainty and predictability of the Newtonian model of the universe and replaced it with a more mysterious universe, one governed by probability and relativity. Heisenberg then outlines what he believes will be the consequences, philosophically and socially, as the implications of advanced theories filter down to the bulk of the population.

'The atoms or the elementary particles . . . form a world of potentialities or possibilities rather than one of things or facts.'

WRITINGS BY HEISENBERG

Physics and Philosophy
Penguin pbk £7.99
0141182156

WRITINGS ON HEISENBERG

McEvoy
Quantum Physics for Beginners
Icon Books pbk £8.99
1874166374
(Due summer 2000)

Cassidy, David
Uncertainty: The Life and Science of Werner Heisenberg
W.H.Freeman pbk £16.95
0716725037

Claude

LEVI-STRAUSS | 1958

Structural Anthropology

Levi-Strauss was born in Belgium and took his first degree in Paris before moving to South America where he taught at the University of Sao Paulo. He spent most of the Second World War in the States and then returned to France in 1948. He was, for many years, Professor of Social Anthropology at the Collége de France. In contrast with many of the other great anthropologists of the century, his experience of fieldwork was limited but his importance as a theorist and as one of the leading figures in the wider intellectual movement known as structuralism can scarcely be exaggerated. Levi-Strauss's ideas have had an influence far beyond the boundaries of his particular academic discipline.

The basic principle behind structuralism, originating in the linguistic work of Saussure, is that an array of cultural phenomena (myths, works of art, rituals) can not be understood in isolation but only through their interrelations. Just as Saussure argued that a word in a language is only defined by its relationship to, and difference from, other words, so the structuralists argued that other cultural systems were analogous to language. In Levi-Strauss's case, he applied Saussure's ideas to the data he gathered as an anthropologist – to myths, rituals, kinship systems etc. He was not interested so much in the individual instances as in what they revealed about underlying structures which were common to widely differing societies. For example, myths from different parts of the world, which were very different in their surface details (necessarily since the cultures they came from were so different) might reflect the same basic structure beneath.

A book like *The Raw and the Cooked*, which examines more than 200 South American Indian myths in order to reveal their interrelations and basic structures, shows Levi-Strauss's methodology in practice. The two volumes of *Structural Anthropology*, which include essays on a variety of themes, also state most clearly what that methodology is. Other books by Levi-Strauss include *The Savage Mind* and *Myth and Meaning*. One of his most interesting works, *Tristes Tropiques*, once published by Penguin, is sadly unavailable. On one level this is an account of Levi-Strauss's time in Brazil but the book is punctuated by long passages about his ideas and amounts to an intellectual autobiography.

'Language is a form of human reason, which has its internal logic of which man knows nothing.'

WRITINGS BY LEVI-STRAUSS

The Jealous Potter
University of Chicago P. pbk £12.75
0226474828

Myth and Meaning
Routledge pbk £9.99
0415045118

The Raw and the Cooked
Pimlico pbk £12.50
0712660496

The Savage Mind
Weidenfeld pbk £14.99
0297995235

Structural Anthropology Volume I
Penguin pbk £15.00
0140138218

Structural Anthropology Volume II
Penguin pbk £12.00
0140138226

Although there are plenty of books on structuralism in its widest sense there is surprisingly little readily available on Levi-Strauss in particular. *Claude Levi-Strauss and the Making of Structural Anthropology* (University of Minnesota P. pbk £14.95 0816627614) is the best academic introduction to Levi-Strauss's thought available although there is also a title in the Icon-published 'Beginners' Guides (*Levi-Strauss for Beginners* pbk £8.99 1874166625) which uses a mixture of text and graphics to explain his ideas.

Frantz

FANON | 1961

The Wretched of the Earth

Born in French Martinique, Fanon served in World War II and then trained as a psychiatrist in France. His first book *Black Skin, White Masks*, published in 1952, was a striking combination of political and psychiatric speculations about the nature of colonialism and its demoralising impact on both colonised and colonisers. In the same year Fanon took up a position as a psychiatrist in an Algerian hospital. It was the period of the bloody and terrible struggle for Algerian independence from an imperialist France and, in the last years of his life, Fanon moved to a more and more revolutionary position. Fanon worked briefly as an ambassador for the provisional Algerian government. He died of leukemia at the age of thirty six.

Les Damnes de la Terre (The Wretched of the Earth) was published in the year of Fanon's death and rapidly became one of the key texts both for black radicals in the United States and those struggling throughout the world with the political and cultural fallout from a declining imperialism. In this book Fanon's message, born of the revolution in Algeria and of his own experiences of racism and colonialism, was a revolutionary one. He faces up unflinchingly to the role, and inevitability, of violence in the process of decolonisation. Indeed he goes further than that. He argues for the necessity of violence as a form of psychological purgative. Following on from his argument in

Black Skin, White Masks Fanon points out that colonisation had what might be seen as the most damning of its effects on the minds of the colonised. Through the 'collective catharsis' of violence, could come not only physical but also psychic liberation for them. The despair induced by the oppressive forces of imperialism could be exorcised by violence against the oppressor. The colonised would, in the revolutionary upheavals, discover a sense of identity and humanity to replace those imposed by the colonisers. Fanon's ideas have been condemned as advocating violence for its own sake but his books remain the most clear-sighted and passionate responses to the dying years of European imperialism.

*'For the black man there is only one destiny.
And it is white.'*

WRITINGS BY FANON

Black Skin, White Masks
Pluto P pbk £13.99
0745300359

The Wretched of the Earth
Penguin pbk £7.99
0140184147

WRITINGS ON FANON

Fanon: A Critical Reader
Blackwell pbk £17.99
1557868964

Fanon for Beginners
Writers & Readers pbk £7.99
086316255X

Thomas

KUHN   1962

The Structure of Scientific Revolutions

Kuhn was born in Ohio and studied physics at Harvard, receiving his Ph.D in 1949 and remaining at the University as an assistant professor in the history of science. His career was that of a highly successful American academic, who held professorial positions at many of the most prestigious universities, including Berkeley, Princeton and MIT. He was the author of many papers on the history of science and books such as *The Copernican Revolution* (1957), a study of how that revolution affected the development of Western thought, and *The Essential Tension* (1977), a series of studies of the interplay of tradition and innovation in the history of science. His was a distinguished career but it would not be one to be marked in a guide like this, had he not published *The Structure of Scientific Revolutions*, which began life as a series of lectures at the Lowell Institute, Boston in 1951 and was eventually published, much revised and expanded, by the University of Chicago Press eleven years later. Since publication it has sold more than a million copies and is recommended reading on a wide diversity of university courses. It is, arguably, the single most important and influential work in the philosophy of science published in the twentieth century.

In *The Structure of Scientific Revolutions* Kuhn argued that it was wrong to look at the history of science as an unbroken progression in

which knowledge was steadily and relentlessly accumulated. The history of science consisted of long periods of relative stagnation punctuated by exceptional intellectual revolutions and upheavals. After these revolutions, in Kuhn's words, 'one conceptual world view is replaced by another.' The word which Kuhn used to describe these conceptual world-views, and a word which his usage has made popular, is 'paradigm.' A paradigm is that flexible framework of assumptions within which science continues to be conducted until a revolution bursts its bounds and, after a period of confusion and competing theories, a new paradigm is instituted. During the period when a paradigm is operating most successfully, scientists are working to bring fact and accepted theories into as close an agreement as possible. Therefore facts which inconveniently challenge the existing paradigm tend to be ignored. Only when a paradigm is in the process of being destroyed – in those moments of revolution – can some of these inconvenient facts be acknowledged and incorporated into a newly created paradigm. Kuhn's view of the scientific enterprise is opposed to both traditional views of the scientific method and to the theory of 'falsification' put forward by Popper but it has been a remarkably influential one in the decades since it was first published. Kuhn himself has explicitly compared his ideas on the evolution of scientific ideas to the Darwinian theory of the evolution of living organisms.

> *'Novelty emerges only with difficulty, manifested by resistance, against a background provided by expectation.'*

WRITINGS BY KUHN

The Copernican Revolution
Harvard UP pbk £8.50
0674171039

The Essential Tension
University of Chicago P. pbk £12.75
0226458067

The Structure of Scientific Revolutions
University of Chicago P. pbk £8.75
0226458083

WRITINGS ON KUHN

Losee, John
A Historical Introduction to the Philosophy of Science
Oxford UP pbk £10.99
0192892479

This guide to the philosophy of science examines the subject as far back as the Ancient Greeks but includes a lengthy discussion of more recent developments in the subject.

Newton-Smith, W.H.
The Rationality of Science
Routledge pbk £13.99
0415058775

A book which examines the theories of Kuhn, Feyerabend and others from a critical perspective

Martin Luther

KING

1963

I Have a Dream

The civil rights movement began in 1955, triggered by a commonplace act of racism on a bus in Montgomery, Alabama. On 1 December a black seamstress, Rosa Parks, refused to relinquish her seat to a white passenger, as required by Alabama law. She was prosecuted, and black leaders decided to dispute the case. They formed the Montgomery Improvement Association and appointed a young Baptist minister from a local church, Martin Luther King Jr., as the president.

King had little political experience when he was thrust into the limelight. He had been born in Alabama in 1929. Despite the abolition of slavery in 1863, and the subsequent defeat of the southern states in the US civil war, Alabama at the time, like other southern states, was openly racist. The black population was poor, disenfranchised, terrorised and demoralised. Segregation laws required blacks to use separate public facilities. King, the son of a Baptist pastor, was well educated (he received a theological doctorate in June 1955), articulate and good looking. His oratory, influenced by the charismatic evangelist, the Reverend Billy Graham, quickly won attention and rallied support. As the civil rights movement gathered pace, King became its unofficial leader. *I Have a Dream* covers the period from King's first emergence as a public figure to his assassination.

King's unique contribution was the idea of racial equality and harmony; his method was to confront racism through non-violent protest or passive resistance. Two of his most influential works were written in 1963 and are reproduced in this anthology: the essay, 'Letter from a Birmingham Jail', and the speech, 'I Have a Dream'.

Seven years into his campaign, in spring 1963, King joined protesters demanding the desegregation of restaurant seating in Birmingham, Alabama. Many of King's fellow protesters were badly beaten by police and King himself was arrested and jailed. When a group of local clergymen criticised the protests and urged blacks to show patience, King responded with his 'Letter'. Confrontation, he insisted, was the only way to achieve change: 'We know through painful experience that freedom is never voluntarily given by the oppressor; it must be demanded by the oppressed.' Not only were protesters justified in disobeying unjust laws; they had shown 'amazing discipline in the midst of inhuman provocation'.

King's tactics were strongly influenced both by Christian tolerance and by Gandhi's non-violent movement for Indian independence. King had studied Gandhi as a student, and in 1959 he visited India as a guest of the Prime Minister Jawaharlal Nehru, Gandhi's former close ally.

King's 'I Have a Dream' speech was the culmination of the March on Washington, a rally in August 1963 demanding desegregation and

> '*I have a dream that one day on the red hills of Georgia the sons of former slaves and the sons of former slave owners will be able to sit down together at the table of brotherhood.*'

voting rights legislation. Before 200,000 assembled protesters, and a world-wide television audience of millions, King hailed 'the greatest demonstration for freedom in the history of our nation'. The bulk of the short speech was an eloquent demand for equal rights; for the immediate concession of the protesters' demands ('it would be fatal to overlook the urgency of the moment'); and a restatement of the case for non-violence. The last third of the speech was a stirring evocation of a world of racial harmony, involving the passionate repetition of the refrain, 'I have a dream'. This dream was 'deeply rooted in the American dream that one day this nation [would] rise up and live out the true meaning of its creed—we hold these truths to be self-evident, that all men are created equal.'

The brilliance of the 'I Have a Dream' speech helped seal King's reputation as a visionary leader, and in 1964 he was awarded the Nobel Peace Prize. In the remaining part of the decade, Congress passed a series of civil rights laws which outlawed segregation and upheld blacks' voting rights. King himself was assassinated in 1968 while on a civil rights mission to Memphis, Tennessee

Throughout his career King was under contrary pressures from the radical and pragmatic wings of the civil rights movement. His skill was in helping a divided organisation coalesce at key moments into a powerful and united protest movement. Just as Gandhi was not simply a nationalist leader, so King's aims were broader than racial harmony. He sought equality for all, and more than thirty years after his death, he remains one of the most potent icons of non-violent protest the century has produced.

JOE PONTIN, *Waterstone's Bristol Galleries*

WRITINGS BY KING

I Have A Dream:
Writings and Speeches
HarperCollins pbk £7.99
0062505521

Autobiography
Little Brown hbk £18.99
0316848220
(Due in paperback April 2000)

Compiled from King's papers
and edited by Clayborne Carson

A Testament of Hope
HarperCollins pbk £9.99
0060646918

The University of California Press
have undertaken the task of
publishing a multi-volume
academic edition of the papers of
Martin Luther King.

WRITINGS ON KING

Garrow, David J.
Bearing the Cross
Vintage pbk £9.99
0099302608

Pulitzer-Prize winning biography
of King and the civil rights
movement.

Harmer, Harry
Martin Luther King
Sutton pbk £4.99
0750919329

One of a series of Pocket
Biographies.

Oates, Stephen B.
Let the Trumpet Sound
Canongate pbk £12.99
0862418372

A new edition of a prize-winning
biography.

Posner, Gerald
Killing the Dream
Little Brown pbk £11.99
0316848387

A book about King's assassination.

Marshall

McLUHAN   1964

Understanding Media

For a number of years after his death, until relatively recently, McLuhan would probably have been dismissed by most commentators as the product of a particular period, a sixties guru with a gift for coining catchphrases, who had no long-term intellectual influence. In the age of the Internet and the World Wide Web, it is his critics who appear period pieces and McLuhan whose words seem increasingly prophetic. At the height of McLuhan's fame, the novelist and commentator Tom Wolfe asked the question : 'Suppose he is what he sounds like: the most important thinker since Newton, Darwin, Freud, Einstein and Pavlov? What if he is right?' It is not necessary to share Wolfe's hyperbole to recognise that McLuhan may well be the most significant and most far-seeing theorist of mass communications of the last half-century.

McLuhan was born in Edmonton, Canada and educated first at the University of Manitoba and then at Cambridge. In his twenties he converted to Catholicism and his academic career was spent teaching in Catholic institutions, most notably St. Michael's College at the University of Toronto where he was a member of the English department for more than thirty years. In the sixties he became director of a new Center for Culture and Technology at the University and it was there that he formulated most of the ideas for which he became famous. His many books include *The Gutenberg Galaxy*

(1962), *Understanding Media* (1964) and *War and Peace in the Global Village* (1968).

McLuhan was eager to explore the social and cultural consequences of the rise of the mass media and the resulting changes in the status of the written text in a society now dominated by largely visual media. He argued that just as the introduction of print by Gutenberg in the 15th century had produced a fragmented society of private individuals, reading texts in privacy and isolation from others, so the new electronic media offered opportunities to return to collective forms of cultural activity. In the 'global village' (a phrase he invented) there was the possibility of a return to communality. Indeed McLuhan went much further than that. The new technologies, by altering the ways in which we perceived and experienced the world, would, in effect, make of us new human beings, with a quite different sense of personal identity. These ideas, so recently considered shallow and obsolete, may yet receive a new significance in a new millennium.

'The new electronic interdependence recreates the world in the image of a global village.'

Theodor

ADORNO 1966

Negative Dialectics

In the twenties and thirties a neo-Marxist school of thought emerged in Germany, centred on the Institute of Social Research at Frankfurt. Usually known as 'critical theory', this has proved an enormous influence on twentieth century philosophy and social thinking and, in the work of Jurgen Habermas, this influence looks set to continue into a new century and a new millennium. Members of the 'Frankfurt School' have included Max Horkheimer, Herbert Marcuse, Erich Fromm and, for a period, Walter Benjamin. One of the most wide-ranging thinkers whose name has been attached to the school was Theodor Adorno. Adorno studied both philosophy and music at the University of Frankfurt and then spent time in Vienna where he was a student of the composer Alban Berg. In the early thirties he was an associate of the Institute of Social Research and, when the Nazi accession to power drove the Institute into exile in America, Adorno, after a period in England, also travelled to the States. He taught there until the Institute was able to return to Germany when he, too, returned.

Of all the thinkers of the Frankfurt School Adorno was the one whose work has had an impact on the broadest spectrum of philo-sophical, social and cultural subjects. As a musicologist and music critic he wrote books on his old teacher Berg, on Mahler and on the aesthetics of film music. He also produced densely argued texts, such as *Quasi Una Fantasia* and *The Philosophy of Modern Music*, in which he examined the nature of music and outlined his own ideas about the connections between music and morality. Like his friend and intellectual associate Walter Benjamin, Adorno was one of the earliest major thinkers to turn his attention to popular culture and his essays on the subject range from examinations of television to dissections of Nazi propaganda. *The Authoritarian Personality*, an influential work now sadly out of print, was a scathing analysis of the kind of conformist personality which combined deferment to higher authority with a bullying attitude to those lower in any given hierarchy. His most important work of philosophy was *Negative Dialectics*, a sweeping denunciation of virtually all other philosophers for distorting the true nature of reality by trying to force it into conceptual straitjackets. For Adorno this led necessarily to oppression and to systems, both philosophical and political, in which the individual is turned into some kind of object, to be manipulated and misled. Only by means of a consistently critical 'negative dialectics' through which all systems and theories are revealed as lacking what they claim, can this be resisted.

'In illusion, there is a promise of freedom from illusion.'

WRITINGS BY ADORNO

Alban Berg
Cambridge UP pbk £14.99
0521338840

The Culture Industry
Routledge pbk £14.99
0415058317

Dialectic of Enlightenment
Verso pbk £12.00
1859841546

Hegel
MIT Press pbk £9.95
0262510804

Minima Moralia
Verso pbk £12.00
0860917045

Negative Dialectics
Routledge pbk £16.99
0415052211

Quasi Una Fantasia
Verso pbk £15.00
1859841597

WRITINGS ON ADORNO

Witkin, Robert
Adorno on Music
Routledge pbk £14.99
0415162920

Held, David
Introduction to Critical Theory
Polity Press pbk £14.95
0745607691

Fredric Jameson
Late Marxism: Adorno, or the
persistence of the dialectic
Verso pbk £12.00
1859841562

Jarvis, Simon
Theodor Adorno:
A Critical Introduction
Polity Press pbk £13.95
0745611796

Jacques

LACAN | 1966

Ecrits

The most controversial and influential psycho-analyst of the second half of the twentieth century has been Jacques Lacan. Despite the arguments that raged over his methods and ideas Lacan always claimed to be carrying forward the project of Freudian psycho-analysis. Even in the last year of his life, having (not for the first time) distanced himself from many of his peers and supporters, Lacan was telling them, 'It is up to you to be Lacanians if you wish; I am Freudian.' Thirty years earlier he had defended his use of short sessions of analysis, as opposed to the standard analytical hour, against charges of heresy and unorthodoxy. Freud, he said, had argued that the unconscious is timeless, so it made no sense to insist upon standard sessions.

Born in Paris, Lacan took a medical degree at the Sorbonne and then trained as a psychia-trist. By 1934 he was undergoing analysis himself (a required part of the initiation as a Freudian psychoanalyst) and had become a member of the *Société Psychoanalytique de Paris*. He had also begun his lifelong project to reinterpret Freud. He remained a practising psychoanalyst rather than an academic. In 1963 he founded the *Ecole Freudienne de Paris* and was director until 1980 when he announced its dissolution and the formation of a new campaign to 'return to Freud', *La Cause Freudienne*. Lacan's reputation rests largely on *Ecrits*, a collection of essays and lectures dating from 1936 to 1966, and on the weekly seminars which he ran at the University of Paris from 1953 and which were an influence on an entire generation of French intellectuals.

Lacan is notoriously difficult and his prose opaque even by the standards of French academia. However, in the simplest possible terms, his achievement was to revolutionise attitudes to Freud by applying the linguistic analyses of thinkers such as Saussure and the Russian linguist Roman Jakobson to the unconscious. By describing the structure of the unconscious as a 'language', Lacan was to provide fertile theoretical bases for the analysis of the relationship between the individual and society, and between language, patriarchal Law and social repression. In specifically psychoan-alytic terms he encouraged the study of language as an essential factor in the exami-nation of the development of consciousness. Most famously he introduced the notion of the 'mirror' phase into the study of childhood development, that point at which a child first recognises himself in a mirror and acquires an identity which separates him from the mother. Lacan's work, and the flamboyance of his personality, made a deep impact on psychoan-alytic theory and the wider discourses which have drawn upon it.

'For the function of language is not to inform but to invoke.'

Ecrits: A Selection
Routledge pbk £17.99
0415043239

The Ethics of Psychoanalysis
Routledge pbk £17.99
0415090547

Feminine Sexuality
Macmillan pbk £17.99
0333341554

The Four Fundamental Concepts of Psychoanalysis
Vintage pbk £8.99
0099225514

WRITINGS ON LACAN

Zizek, Slavoj
Enjoy Your Symptom: Lacan in Hollywood and Out
Routledge pbk £12.99
041590482X

Grosz, Elizabeth
Jacques Lacan:
A Feminist Introduction
Routledge pbk £14.99
041501400X

Bowie, Malcolm
Lacan
Fontana pbk £6.99
0006860761

Leader, Darian
Lacan for Beginners
Icon Books pbk £8.99
1874166315

Zizek, Slavoj
Looking Awry
MIT Press pbk £13.95
026274015X

Subtitled 'An Introduction to Jacques Lacan through Popular Culture'.

Jacques

DERRIDA | 1967

Of Grammatology

Jacques Derrida was born in what was then French Algeria and studied at the Ecole Normale Superieure in Paris, where he was later to teach for more than twenty years. His work draws upon previous thinkers, from Nietzsche and Heidegger to Freud and Saussure, to create the sceptical approach to language and meaning which is called deconstruction. Derrida has written widely on philosophical, cultural, literary and art historical questions and, particularly in the last twenty years, has become something of an international academic superstar. However it can be argued that his most characteristic work is still his 1967 book Of *Grammatology*.

Of Grammatology remains a work that is an act of violence for some; for others it is a statement of philosophical, social, even political liberation. It is a critique of structuralist thought. Structuralism examines all aspects of our lives, language, social institutions, literature and so forth. Structuralism states that we are only able to view these and their constituent parts as a structure, i.e. meaning is derived from context. Outside context there is no meaning. Once we examine something (for example a word in isolation) outside its frame of reference, all meaning and significance is lost. *Of Grammatology* denies any absolute truth of meaning, even within structure. For Derrida, context does not lead to meaning or signification. Derrida's critique shows how texts can

be deconstructed or unravelled, because at the very heart of language is a fundamental ambiguousness of meaning.

Derrida attacks the canon of western philosophy by attacking the supremacy of spoken over written language, and the convention by which the written form of language is subservient to the spoken form of language. Nobody is immune from Derrida's witty criticism. He undermines the philosophical primacy of the spoken word, by way of the greats of classical and modern philosophy, and concludes that the weakness in the philosophical reliance on the spoken is that it requires the written form to clarify what they actually want to say. Why is this so controversial and important? Derrida, by undermining one aspect of language undermines any universal truth in philosophy. Derrida himself tries not to fall into the same philosophical trap, by using the written form in a way that is impossible in spoken language, with puns and plays on words which depend on their written existence.

Yet Deconstruction does not exist to reverse the primacy of spoken and written language. That would merely be the continuation of dominance and thus propagate the concept that there is a universal belief that is true in all circumstances. Derrida does not wish Deconstruction to be seen as a method or strategy, displacing other ideas and becoming the way to approach philosophical questions. This again would perpetuate the belief in universal truth.

Derrida's influence on academia, and not just in the field of humanities has been huge. In the emerging fields of Post-Colonial Theory and Queer Theory, deconstruction is often employed to subvert dominant views on race and sexuality. Gayatri Chakravorty Spivak, the translator of *Of Grammatology*, is an influential critic in her own right in the area of Post-Colonial Studies. Her use of deconstruction is an exercise in challenging the dominance of western thought. Spivak's writing has used deconstruction to undermine the supremacy of the west in all forms, intellectually, politically and economically. Spivak seeks to demolish the divide between developed and developing countries, to show that the divide between the two can be seen as a construction of the dominant west.

In the field of Gender Studies and Queer Theory, deconstruction finds a home. Derrida's ideas of deconstruction are applied to certainties of the gender of the subject, male and female and to the dominance of hetero-sexuality in societies. For critics such as Judith Butler, the body becomes a site of deconstruction; the male/female division is seen as meaningless, a construction of modes of thought that seek to impose femaleness and maleness as a 'natural' construct.

Often the question is asked 'why are deconstructionist texts so difficult to read?' For Derrida and others the difficulty is a by-product of the nature of writing and debate. Deconstructionist critics are aware that ideas and writing are fundamentally open to the same techniques of analysis as they themselves use. Their own deconstructionist texts are open to deconstruction. The difficulty in writing and reading these texts are a conscious reminder of their own flaws.

One attack levelled against Derrida and his acolytes is that the subject and the political becomes merely a system of shifting meaningless, flawed signifiers, without meaning and certainty. Others argue that that reflects life. Read the works and decide for yourself.

DAVE CUMMINGS, *Waterstone's*

'The thesis of the arbitrariness of the sign . . . must forbid a radical distinction between the liguistic and the graphic sign.'

WRITINGS BY DERRIDA

Acts of Literature
Routledge pbk £15.99
0415900573

Archive Fever
University of Chicago P. pbk £9.50
0226143678

The Derrida Reader
Edinburgh UP pbk £14.95
0748609644

The Gift of Death
University of Chicago P. pbk £8.75
0226143066

Of Grammatology
Johns Hopkins UP pbk £16.50
0801858305

The Politics of Friendship
Verso pbk £15.00
1859840337

The Secret Art of Antonin Artaud
The MIT Press pbk £17.50
0262041650

Specters of Marx
Routledge pbk £12.99
0415910455

Writing and Difference
Routledge pbk £11.99
0415039797

WRITINGS ON DERRIDA

Norris, Christopher
Derrida
Fontana pbk £6.99
0006860575

Wood, David
Derrida: A Critical Reader
Blackwell pbk £17.99
063116121X

Howells, Christina
Derrida
Polity P. pbk £12.95
0745611680

Johnson, Christopher
Derrida
Phoenix pbk £2.00
0753801841

Collins, Jeff
Introducing Derrida
Icon pbk £8.99
1840461187

Germaine
GREER   1970
The Female Eunuch

The feminist movement of the sixties and seventies produced a number of significant texts. Betty Friedan's *The Feminist Mystique*, published in 1963, was a groundbreaking study of the expectations Western society placed on women and the self-hatred that often followed women's attempts to meet definitions imposed upon them. In *Sexual Politics*, a collection of related pieces published in 1969, Kate Millett revealed the ways in which patriarchal bias operated in history and in culture and how male assumptions about women were reflected in mythology, religion, literature and social customs. The book that most represents that period in feminist thought and history remains, however, Germaine Greer's *The Female Eunuch*, which appeared in 1970. In retrospect other books may seem more thorough in their scholarship and more rigorously argued, but no book had the rage, the wit and the passion of Greer's work and none reached and effected so profoundly so many women.

Germaine Greer was born in Melbourne in Australia and educated at the University there. She came to the UK in 1964 and took a Ph.D at Cambridge, studying Shakespearean comedy. In the late sixties she was teaching English Literature at the University of Warwick, was a well-known figure in the counter-culture of the period and a regular contributor to the underground press. *The Female Eunuch* reflected the anarchic energy of its author and its refusal to fit any of the categories expected of it angered many people, including other feminists. It was bought, however, by the million. Greer's argument was directed against the assumptions so often made about women's inferiority. These assumptions were made easier because the roles society offered women effectively 'castrated' them and produced varying levels of self-contempt. This, in turn, produced a hatred of women in men. As Greer famously wrote, 'Women have very little idea of how much men hate them.' Her thesis about how the institutions of society created the oppression of women and prevented so many from fulfilling their potential was supported by an eclectic range of reference and quotation from history, literature and popular culture. For thirty years *The Female Eunuch* has remained in print as a clarion call to women to take responsibility for their own lives and to refuse the attempts of men, supported by the institutions of a patriarchal society, to stifle their creativity and energy.

'The stereotype is the Eternal Feminine. She is the Sexual Object sought by all men, and by all women. She is of neither sex, for she has herself no sex at all. Her value is solely attested by the demand she excites in others.'

WRITINGS BY GREER

The Female Eunuch
Flamingo pbk £8.99
0586080554

The Whole Woman
Doubleday hbk £16.99
0385600151

Nearly thirty years after the publication of *The Female Eunuch*, Greer returns to re-examine the fundamental issues of feminism.

James D.
WATSON | 1970

The Double Helix

Although first published in 1970, James D. Watson's book describes events in the early 1950s surrounding the discovery of the structure of DNA, one of the greatest scientific achievements of the century. Watson was born in Chicago in 1928 and was only in his mid-twenties when he joined Francis Crick at the Cavendish Laboratory in Cambridge. Crick, more than a decade older, had graduated in physics from University College, London and only begun research as a biologist after service as an Admiralty scientist in the war. Working together from late 1951, Watson and Crick began to investigate the structure of DNA. At the time it was realised that DNA carried genetic information but no proposed structure had revealed why and how this was so. Watson and Crick looked at molecular models which would fit the results of the crystallographic study of DNA which Rosalind Franklin was conducting at King's College, London under the direction of Maurice Wilkins. Their great insight, their 'eureka' moment, was when they realised that the DNA molecule had the shape of a double helix. Each molecule consists of two strands twisted in such a way that the nitrogen-containing base adenine is linked with that of thymine and that of guanine with cytosine. Each of these nitrogen-containing bases defines a particular nucleotide in the DNA. As was to become clearer in the years following Crick and Watson's dramatic scientific paper of 1953, each of these is an element in the genetic code which transmits genetic information. Watson, Crick and Wilkins shared the Nobel Prize for Medicine in 1962. Rosalind Franklin, who died of cancer in 1958 and whose role in the discovery is played down by Watson in a series of varyingly patronising dismissals in *The Double Helix*, was not so lucky. *The Double Helix* remains an exceptionally satisfying read for non-scientists because it tells the story of what was indisputably one of the great intellectual leaps forward this century but tells it from the perspective of a far from disinterested or dispassionate protagonist. Watson is clear not only about his and Crick's youthful impatience with their Cambridge elders but also their intense and anxious rivalry with the great American chemist Linus Pauling who was also working on the problem. The book is a revelation of the way real scientists, with the usual set of human foibles and follies, work in the real world.

'I felt slightly queasy when at lunch Francis winged into the Eagle to tell everyone within hearing distance that we had found the secret of life.'

WRITINGS BY WATSON

Watson, James D.
The Double Helix
Penguin pbk £7.99
0140268774

WRITINGS RELATED TO DNA

Gribbin, John
In Search of the Double Helix
Penguin pbk £9.99
0140248137

Bodmer & McKie
The Book of Man
Abacus pbk £8.99
0349106207

Ridley, Matt
Genome: The Autobiography of a Species in 23 Chapters
Fourth Estate pbk £8.99
185702835x
(Due April 2000)

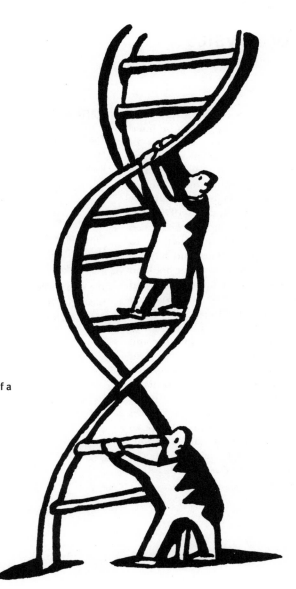

Fritjof

CAPRA | 1975

The Tao of Physics

In the seventies a number of books appeared, aimed at a general readership, which outlined the correspondences between the ideas of Eastern religions and those of the most advanced theories of Western physics. (The earliest proponents of quantum theory such as Heisenberg and Schrödinger had already noted some of the similarities.) In 1979 Gary Zukav published *The Dancing Wu Li Masters* which was an accessible introduction to quantum theory, particle physics and Eastern mysticism. However the most popular book on the subject, and one which has remained almost permanently in print since its first publication in 1975, is Fritjof Capra's *The Tao of Physics*. Capra had undertaken research in physics in many universities in America and Europe, including Stanford, Vienna and Imperial College, London and had spent time as a lecturer at the University of California at Berkeley. He also had a long-standing interest in Taoism, Zen Buddhism and other Eastern religions. *The Tao of Physics* was his attempt to marry together his scientific and religious interests and to show that, far from being mutually incompatible, they were both reflections of the same reality.

WRITINGS BY CAPRA

The Tao of Physics
Flamingo pbk £8.99
0006544894

The Turning Point
Flamingo pbk £9.99
0006540171

Uncommon Wisdom
Flamingo pbk £8.99
0006543413

The Web of Life
Flamingo pbk £8.99
0006547516

'We shall often encounter statements where it is almost impossible to say whether they have been made by physicists or by Eastern mystics.'

1975 **Fritjof Capra** The Tao of Physics

Paul

FEYERABEND | 1975

Against Method

Paul Feyerabend was born into a middle-class Viennese family and, as a very young man, served in the German Army and was awarded the Iron Cross. After the war he studied science at the University of Vienna and then turned to philosophy for his doctoral thesis which he produced in 1951. The following year he came to England to study under Karl Popper at the London School of Economics. Ironically Feyerabend was to become Popper's severest critic. At this stage, however, he was a dedicated supporter of Popper whose book *The Open Society and Its Enemies* he translated into German. In 1959, offered a permanent position at the University of California, Berkeley, Feyerabend moved to the US, becoming a naturalised US citizen. Over the next decade he moved gradually towards the position he articulated in *Against Method*, which appeared in an essay form in 1970 and, much expanded, as a book in 1975. This is the position he described as 'epistemological anarchism.'

As a philosopher of science Feyerabend had begun as an adherent of Popperian ideas about the need for a proliferation of theories, from which, by a process of 'falsifiability', the most successful and rational theory would emerge. He moved towards a disbelief in the rationality of science. The main thesis of *Against Method*, and his arguments draw upon his extensive knowledge of the history of science, is that there is no such thing as a single scientific method, which should be privileged above all other methods of achieving knowledge about the external world. Scientists achieve success for their theories by strategies of politics and rhetoric rather than through their advancement of objective knowledge. Rather than following a 'scientific method' they are methodological opportunists.

The rest of Feyerabend's career was spent in refining (and defending) these relativistic views. *Science in a Free Society* was published in 1978 and included both responses to hostile reviews of *Against Method* and further clarification of what he meant by epistemological anarchism. Many of his finest philosophical papers, including 'Science as an Art' in which he argued against the notion that the history of science was a history of 'progress', were collected in *Farewell to Reason* (1987). Paul Feyerabend died in Zurich, to which he had moved, in February 1994. His work, together with that of Thomas Kuhn, can be seen as the most revolutionary work in the philosophy of science this century and a profound challenge to the epistemological supremacy of the scientific method.

'Knowledge so conceived is . . . an ever-increasing ocean of mutually incompatible (and perhaps even incommensurable) alternatives, each single theory, each fairy tale, each myth that is part of the collection forcing the other into greater articulation and all of them contributing, via this process of competition, to the development of our consciousness.'

WRITINGS BY FEYERABEND

Against Method
Verso pbk £14.00
0860916464

Farewell to Reason
Verso pbk £13.00
0860918963

Killing Time
University of Chicago P pbk £11.25
0226245322

Feyerabend's autobiography

Three Dialogues on Knowledge
Blackwell pbk £14.99
0631179186

WRITINGS ON FEYERABEND

Preston, John
Feyerabend
Polity Press pbk £13.99
0745616763

Peter

SINGER | 1975

Animal Liberation

Peter Singer, born in 1946, graduated from the University of Melbourne in 1967 and worked at a number of universities around the world before his appointment as Professor of Bioethics at Princeton University in July 1999. He is the author of numerous papers and more than two dozen books, including *Practical Ethics* (1979) and *Rethinking Life and Death* (1995), both essentials on any philosophy undergraduate's reading list. However, it is *Animal Liberation*, first published in 1975 and widely regarded as the bible of the animal liberation movement that will surely be seen as his most important and influential work. Indeed, it is hard to envisage the cause of equal consideration for non-humans without its philosophical framework.

Although Singer is never sensationalist or hysterical in his tone, a first reading of *Animal Liberation* is a harrowing experience and one that inevitably angers the reader. The power of the work is its simplicity. We are, and have for centuries been, guilty of what Singer , who is credited with coining the term, calls speciesism. That is the disregard of the interests of other animals in favour of our own human needs, wants and desires. Singer equates the struggle against speciesism with the fight against racism and sexism. If we accept that all humans are worthy of equal consideration regardless of race or sex, and

beyond these attributes, of intelligence, physical ability and any other characteristic, we are left with the right to equal treatment on the grounds of the ability to feel, to be sentient. Therefore, says Singer, how can we not apply this rule to other species equally capable of feeling and, vitally, of suffering. For Singer, the idea is encapsulated in the words of the utilitarian philosopher Jeremy Bentham, 'The question is not, Can they reason? nor, Can they talk? but, Can they suffer?'

Having established the capacity to suffer as the only logical basis on which we should measure our treatment of other species, Singer proceeds with an unsentimental analysis of two areas in which we routinely abuse animals: experimentation and factory farming. He allows those practices he terms abusive to speak for themselves through scientific papers, government reports and articles published in trade journals. They do not make pleasant reading. Nevertheless, it is the very lack of sentimentality which leaves the reader horrified and gives Singer's criticism of these practices its authority. One is repeatedly struck by the lack of worth placed on the lives of those animals involved in, for example, scientific experiments. More importantly one is struck by the apparent pointlessness of so many of the experiments. Singer presents the findings of one experiment,

'All the arguments to prove man's superiority cannot shatter this hard fact. In suffering, the animals are our equals.'

designed to produce psychopathological tendencies in monkeys, which involved the routine electrocution, social isolation and maternal deprivation of thousands of new-born monkeys over a ten-year period. The reader is left to wonder, as does Singer, what the purpose of this was and what results, beyond the obvious, were achieved. Even when the human benefits of particular medical experiments are more apparent, Singer's position remains essentially the same; if suffering to another sentient being, regardless of species, is the result, the means is morally unacceptable.

Singer extends the same principle to the use of animals for human consumption and, specifically, to the issue of factory farming. He gives an objective presentation of the relevant facts about a practice that results in the deaths and mistreatment of millions of animals every year. The suffering caused is immense and stems directly from our dietary preference for protein provided by animal flesh. Singer's arguments for vegetarianism are familiar but compelling. He makes it clear that we can eat a perfectly healthy diet that avoids animal products. Why, he then asks, must the satisfaction of human taste be at the cost of the suffering of another sentient being. The issue again is a moral one and Singer sees it as a question for the individual. 'Will we rise to the challenge and prove our capacity for genuine altruism by ending our ruthless exploitation of the species in our power, because we recognise that our position is morally indefensible?'

Singer's arguments for consideration of the 'rights' of animals are all the more radical when seen in the context of past religious and philosophical thought on the subject. Pre-Christian Old Testament ideas were clear. Animals were put on earth to serve man and this is the view that has dominated western thought for millennia. From Aristotle through Renaissance humanism to the mechanistic outlook of Cartesian thinking, the emphasis has been on the value of the human and the interests of non-humans have been consistently regarded as subordinate to those of mankind. However there have also been strands of thought in the western tradition, tracing their origins back to Greek thinkers such as Pythagoras, which have advocated a moral regard for animals. In the eighteenth century Enlightenment writers' increased concern for the treatment of animals indicated that man's dominion had, at least, shifted towards the paternalistic and, in the following century, arguments emerged that focussed on the animal and its right to consideration.

Animal Liberation was, therefore, not the first work to demand a moral code in our dealings with other species but it remains unique in that it sets out to empower the reader. In that lies its strength. Not only does Singer base his arguments on a new set of ethics but he provides concrete examples of how individual humans can contribute to a shift in attitude. As he makes clear, economic leverage is the key to change.

At the close of the twentieth century, man's treatment of animals was, arguably, worse than it has ever been. The importance of Singer's work is that it provides the ethical groundwork for many of the demands for a consideration of animal interests which have arisen since its publication. Without doubt, Singer's will continue to be one of the most authoritative and influential voices as the debate continues into this new century.

GAVIN PILGRIM,
Waterstone's Charing Cross Road

WRITINGS BY SINGER

Animal Liberation
Pimlico pbk £12.50
0712674446

OTHER BOOKS ON THE SUBJECT

Clark, Stephen J.
Animals and their Moral Standing
Routledge pbk £13.99
0415135605

Benton, Ted
Natural Relations
Verso pbk £13.00
0860915905

Penman, Danny
The Price of Meat
Gollancz pbk £9.99
0575063440

Edward O.

WILSON

1975

Sociobiology

Edward O. Wilson published *Sociobiology: The New Synthesis* in the summer of 1975. As Professor of Zoology at Harvard he already enjoyed a reputation as the world's leading entomologist, having discovered the existence of pheromones and written the definitive work *The Insect Societies*. It was when studying rhesus monkeys that Wilson began to speculate on the genetic influence on social behaviour and of creating a multi-disciplinary, unified theory of sociobiology. His new book was intended to provide an encyclopedic summary of all the available evidence for the biological basis of social behaviour in animals. By his own admission he was astonished by the controversy he was about to cause.

On publication Wilson's closely argued chapters on the behaviour of social animals earned great praise, but the final chapter entitled 'Man: From Sociobiology to Sociology' provoked a furore. Whilst conceding the influence of environment, culture, and free will on human behaviour, he argued that phenomena such as aggression, altruism and the division of labour between the sexes have a genetic predisposition underlying them. Wilson's Harvard colleagues, Richard Lewontin and Stephen Jay Gould, publicly attacked his theories on the basis that there was little evidence to support them. Moreover, they claimed, his arguments were open to political abuse by those seeking to justify existing inequalities in society. Reviled as a genetic determinist, Wilson was even subject to physical assault. Rising to speak to the American Association for the Advancement of Science in 1977, he had a jug of water poured over his head by demonstrators, chanting, 'Wilson, you're all wet!'

In the ensuing decades new generations of researchers have contributed to the corpus of sociobiology. Whilst the complex motivations underlying human behaviour may never be entirely explained away by them, Neo-Darwinian interpretations of sexual behaviour and morality by Matt Ridley sit alongside those of language and mind by Steven Pinker. However such are the memories of Wilson's experience, that few scientists seeking a popular readership explicitly refer to sociobiology. It is hard not to agree with Richard Dawkins's last word on Wilson's seminal book: 'I wish people would read it more and write about it less'.

ANDY WALKER,
Waterstone's, Charing Cross Road

'Let us now consider men in the free spirit of natural history, as though we were zoologists from another planet completing a catalogue of social species on Earth. In this macroscopic view the humanities and social sciences shrink to specialised branches of biology.'

WRITINGS BY WILSON

Sociobiology (abridged edn)
Harvard UP pbk £15.95
0674816242

The Diversity of Life
Penguin pbk £8.99
0140169776

In Search of Nature
Penguin pbk £7.99
0140265880

On Human Nature
Penguin pbk £8.99
0140245359

Michael
FOUCAULT | 1976–84
The History of Sexuality

That Michel Foucault has been one of the most influential intellectuals of the twentieth century is now a commonplace. What is remarkable is the scope of that influence. It has not been largely confined, like that of, say, Heidegger, to a single discipline. Foucault's work has affected philosophy, history, sociology, political theory and psychiatry; in the process it has worked precisely to undercut and question such disciplinary boundaries.

Foucault's life was spent mainly inside academia, although his relationship to it was often rather oblique. He was born in Poitiers into a middle-class family and, after attending a Catholic school, went on to study philosophy at the Ecole Normale Superieure and the Sorbonne (where he worked under the Marxist Louis Althusser). After receiving his diploma, Foucault spent time as an observer of psychiatric practice in mental hospitals. A concern with carceral institutions was to remain a focus of Foucault's writings and his political interventions. In the 60s he began to publish a series of highly original and now classic texts such as *Histoire de la Folie* (Madness and Civilization) and *L'Ordre du Discours* (The Order of Things) which inaugurated Foucault's 'archaeology' of modern knowledge. Elected to the College de France in 1970, he named his chair 'Professor of the History of Systems of Thought'. In the 70s Foucault became increasingly involved in

politics and, while teaching at Berkeley, California, in an emerging gay counter-culture. It was at this time that he began what is, perhaps, his most influential text, the three volume *History of Sexuality*.

The History of Sexuality appears a straight-forward title. Perhaps we imagine we can predict the story it has to tell: how sexual desire in its true and natural form emerges, finally, from centuries of silence, superstition and censorship, to speak in its own voice, to affirm its rights and pleasures. What we get is something altogether different. Yet, if Foucault rejects this received narrative of repression and eventual liberation, it isn't because he insists that, on the contrary, we were formerly liberated and are now repressed. It is rather that the whole liberation/repression model is itself misconceived and unduly delimits the kind of thoughts and 'truths' available to us. Typically he insists that we invent different categories and questions, not just answers.

Our notion of 'sexuality', suggests Foucault, is a peculiarly modern category of self-under-standing. It would have been incomprehensible to the Greeks. In contrast with Christianity, the Greeks did not have a single moral code which applied equally to everyone. Sexual conduct was always tailored to the individual's way of life and social position. No universal imperative could erase social distinctions. The individual ought to maintain, in the act of sex, a position analogous to his or her place in society. The ethics of sex, for the Greeks, was the question of the moderation of sexual acts. A sexual act was not bad *per se*, but only if performed in excess, a question of degree rather than essence. Desire was taken for granted; it was not itself an ethical issue or problem.

Christianity replaced this immoderate/moderate opposition with that of good/bad. It introduced a universal moral code by which acts themselves were to be judged. Moreover Christianity now made desire itself the substance of ethics. The goal became purity, conceived of as the eradication of desire, not, as with the Greeks, self-mastery, conceived of as the moderation and correct management of desires and pleasures. These developments produced a radical mutation in subjectivity. The self now 'turned inward'; its every impulse and silent craving were now to be examined and, if necessary, expurgated. 'Conscience' is nothing less than the universal code transformed into a reflex of the soul, a visceral mechanism of censorship. The institution which both reflects and reproduces this Christian form of subjectivity is the Confession.

With the advent of modern society, however, this Christian 'regime of truth', its organising categories and habits of thought, began to be overturned. Up until, roughly, the nineteenth century, sexual acts were perceived and codified according to a scheme of the permissible and the illicit, good and bad. But henceforth sex was made visible through notions of the Normal and the Pathological. These notions defined not simply acts but individuals.

'Sodomy was a category of forbidden acts, the nineteenth century homosexual was a personage.' Sex was now annexed to the field of medicine and mental illness. 'Sexuality' is born as a way of defining identity.

What happened through the nineteenth century was that the whole realm of sexual pleasure, was codified, particularised, divided up and made the object of 'scientific' knowledge. Every gesture or way of speaking became readable as a 'symptom'. The minutiae of somatic life were particularised and made legible to the pornographically 'neutral' medical gaze. By creating and taxonomising 'abnormalities', 'perversions', 'aberrations', this medical discourse left implicit the 'norm', the norm which need not be mentioned but, like a clearing in a wood, was defined by what encircled it.

To make something an object of knowledge is by no means a neutral act, a transparent web of concepts and categories laid over a reality which is left intact by that action. The will to knowledge is, inevitably, expressive of a desire to objectify, distance, master and control. 'Sex was driven out of hiding and compelled to lead a discursive existence.' Knowledge, and especially knowledge of what is 'normal', of what constitutes 'true' sexuality, function as regulatory and policing concepts. They are inseparable from power.

The continued talk today of 'healthy' and 'unhealthy' sexualities, the recourse to 'sexuality' as the key to our identity, the now commonplace notion of 'getting in touch with one's sexuality', the sheer volume of discourse given over to the 'problem' of sex can all be seen as local shifts within a more basic transformation in the discourse about 'sexuality' begun in the nineteenth century. Indeed the idea of 'sexual identity' , historically specific and bound up with certain forms of power subtends the line of demarcation which, we like to think, separates us from the 'repressed' Victorians. Take the example of psychoanalysis. Much psychoanalytical discourse is predicated on the idea of an inner sexual nature. Its questions and answers are delimited by the idea that we have such a 'nature' and that this lies at the root of our person. Our 'sexuality' has been repressed and we must only rediscover it to be 'ourselves.' We deliver ourselves into the hands of experts – psychoanalysts – who are qualified to uncover and define this object of knowledge. In fact, the therapist-patient relation seems like an uncanny repetition of the scene of Confession. 'With its deciphering of hidden thoughts {Christianity} implies that there is something hidden in ourselves and that we are forever in a state of self-delusion which hides that secret.'

It is for such reasons that Foucault treats the notion of sexual liberation and sexual 'identity' with extreme suspicion. Such notions assume as self-evident what is, in reality, the product of certain discourses and historically specific habits of thought and structures of subjectivity. It is a power relation all the more insidious because it has been rendered invisible, because it 'disguises' itself as talk about freedom and liberation. It is, indeed, experienced by the subject as a process of liberation.

We can see, in this brief description of *The History of Sexuality*, something of the central themes of Foucault's thinking. Firstly, the radical reappraisal of power, the critique of 'repression' and 'prohibition' as being the best ways of characterising the operation of power in modern societies, and a concern instead with those forms of power which are actually internalised by the subject. Secondly, the notion that discourses, such as those around and about sexuality, do not simply reflect the contours of a reality already present but systematically produce the realities of which they speak. Thirdly, the recognition that subjectivity, the self's relationship to itself, is not simply a given, the starting point of all experience and knowledge, but is itself historically variable and produced by structures which precede and determine it.

Finally, and in Foucault's own words, his work has been concerned 'to show how things have been historically contingent, for such and such reason intelligible but not necessary. We must make the intelligible appear against a background of emptiness and deny its necessity.' Foucault's motto might be: where nature was, culture and history shall be. In other words what is taken for granted as natural and normal is to be unmasked, dismantled and shown to be both culturally created and complicit with forms of power which are all the more effective and insidious for passing themselves off as Truth.

MARK BOWLES
Waterstone's Charing Cross Road

'We must make the intelligible appear against a background of emptiness and deny its necessity.'

WRITINGS BY FOUCAULT

Archaeology of Knowledge
Routledge pbk £14.99
0415045371

The Birth of the Clinic
Routledge pbk £13.99
0415039576

Discipline and Punish
Penguin pbk £10.99
014013722X

Foucault Live:
Interviews 1961-1984
Semiotext(e) pbk £11.99
157027018X

The Foucault Reader
Penguin pbk £10.99
0140124861

The History of Sexuality:
Volume I
Penguin   pbk £7.99
0140268685

The History of Sexuality:
Volume II
Penguin pbk £9.99
0140137343

The History of Sexuality:
Volume III
Penguin pbk £8.99
0140137351

Madness and Civilization
Penguin pbk £13.99
0415040183

The Order of Things
Routledge pbk £13.99
0415040191

WRITINGS ON FOUCAULT

Deleuze, Gilles
Foucault
Athlone P. pbk £12.99
0485121549

Hoy, David
Foucault: A Critical Reader
Blackwell pbk £17.99
0631140433

McNay, Lois
Foucault: A Critical Introduction
Polity P. pbk £11.95
0745609910

Merquior, J.G.
Foucault
Fontana pbk £6.99
0006862268

Horrocks & Jevtic
Introducing Foucault
Icon pbk £8.99
1840460865

Macey, David
The Lives of Michel Foucault
Vintage pbk £8.99
0099334011

Eribon, Didier
Michel Foucault
Faber pbk £9.99
0571169732

Edward

SAID   1978

Orientalism

During the 19th century, many European painters and travellers became fascinated with the lands and peoples that had been captured, tamed and subsumed as the European empire expanded. Due to its relative accessibility, by both land and sea, the Levant and the Near East became the subject of many painters and writers. As a result, the 'Orient' became defined as the desert lands surrounding the Mediterranean Sea from Turkey at the Northeast end to Algeria at the Southwest.

Seeking to represent the people and landscape as 'accurately' as they could, the new pictorial representations of this part of the Empire have much in common. They are nearly photographic in their clarity, depicting typical street and domestic scenes. Common images, using lush colours, depict Arabs with horses, tigers, selling fruit, charming snakes, and represent a life that was totally alien to the people of 19th century Europe.

The French artist Eugene Delacroix (1798-1867) travelled to North Africa in 1832 and from the pencil and ink sketches he brought home, he fashioned a series of rich, Rubenesque oil paintings, which fulfilled his original imaginings about the Orient. In the same way the 19th Century photographer Erme Desire produced a series of beautifully symmetrical images of artisans at works between 1864- 1867. These images, although correctly defining the North African workplace (tailors/potters) as a space locally conducive to social interaction, were unrepresentative of the larger society that they were trying so hard to document.

The start of the 20th century led also to an era of popular photographic prints and postcards of Algerian women in traditional (and often revealing) dress became a common delivery through the letter boxes of the French bourgeoisie. These images represented the European idea of the harem full of beautiful and scantily clad oriental women. The banality of the messages written on the reverse side highlights the discrepancy in morality which allowed the 'civilised' fully clad French middle and upper classes to accept the nakedness of the socially (and supposedly racially) inferior Algerian women. This has been paralleled in more recent times with the images of rural African people in the glossy and stylish pages of *National Geographic*.

But it was not just the pictorial arts that represented this area. Books such as the record of Napoleon's campaigns and explorer Sir Richard Burton's translation of *The Thousand and One Nights* also represented the Oriental peoples to the European world in a way that defined them as the antithesis of all that was civilised and European.

It was only in the mid-1970s that a serious critique of this practice of oriental representation was published. Edward W. Said, a Palestinian living and teaching in North America, published his definitive and now seminal *Orientalism: Western Conceptions of the Orient.* Defining Orientalism as 'a Western style for dominating, restructuring, and having authority over the Orient', he expanded his theory of the power structure imposed by colonial forces on native peoples and heavily criticised the stereotypical representation of the people of the Near East. Said combines the modern theories of the great French thinker and political activist Michel Foucault, the very learned and older philological style of the scholar Eric Auerbach and his own experiences as a marginalised Palestinian living and working in the United States, to produce a well thought out, erudite cultural study of the 19th century painters, writers and scholars of the Orient. His book has gone on to influence a whole generation of colonial critics like Barbara Harlow, Michael Young and Homi Bhabha. Said traces the sources of Orientalist thought from the expansion of the British and French empires and through the writings of Ernest Renan and the speeches of Lord Arthur Balfour. He examines the writings of (amongst others) Gustave Flaubert, Sir Richard Burton, Gerard de Nérval, as well as the rise in biblical scholarship and of course current western attitudes towards Islam which he believes were latent in 19th century artistic and cultural discourse. As he says himself in his introduction, his book 'tries to show that European culture gained in strength and identity by setting itself off against the Orient as a sort of surrogate and even underground self'.

The above quotation has also become the cornerstone of Said's own thought and in expanded form is the first principle behind his more recent large-scale study *Culture and Imperialism.* While *Orientalism* managed to encapsulate his thought up to the 1970s, his more recent book is effectively the summation of a career spent thinking writing and teaching about the huge effect that European Imperialism had on European Culture. Discussing authors like Jane Austen, W.B. Yeats, Joseph Conrad as well as the work of Verdi, Said traces the often denied influences that Imperial expansion had on these writers. For example, he points out that the eponymous estate of *Mansfield Park* is financed by colonial business; thus these activities form the premise for the novel's existence.

As a Palestinian exile working in North America, Said was well used to the negative use of stereotypes that can be used to alienate and indeed indoctrinate the ill informed. (He has been called 'The Professor of Terror ' due to his rejection of the way Palestinians are portrayed in the media) His most personal book (before his recently published autobiography) was *After the Last Sky: Palestinian Lives*, which records a visit to Palestine, with photographs by Jean Mohr. This is a moving reflection of the plight of the dispossessed in Israel and Lebanon and examines the current image of the Palestinian as terrorist. The examination of ideas Edward W. Said started in *Orientalism* has informed, fuelled and sustained his life's work both in and out of the academy and has enlightened his readers about representation in the visual, literary and journalistic media.

CORMAC KINSELLA
Waterstone's Dublin Dawson Street

'European culture gained strength and identity by setting itself off against the Orient as a sort of surrogate or even underground self.'

WRITINGS BY SAID

Beginnings
Granta pbk £12.99
1862071608

Covering Islam
Vintage pbk £7.99
009959501X

Culture and Imperialism
Vintage pbk £8.99
0099967502

Musical Elaborations
Vintage pbk £6.99
0099967405

Orientalism
Penguin pbk £9.99
0140238670

The Politics of Dispossession
Vintage pbk £9.99
0099223015

The World, The Text and the Critic
Vintage pbk £8.99
0099916207

Jürgen

HABERMAS 1981

The Theory of Communicative Action

Some of the most influential ideas in twentieth century philosophy, politics and sociology have emerged from what is usually known as the 'Frankfurt School', which developed in the 1920s and 1930s in the Institute for Social Research in that city. The director of the Institute for many years was Max Horkheimer and other leading figures included Adorno, who was director for the last decade of his life, and Herbert Marcuse. From the 1950s onwards a second generation of German intellectuals was drawn to the Institute, which had spent the Nazi years in exile in the US, and the most significant thinker in this second generation has been Jürgen Habermas. The Frankfurt School's most notable achievement was to create a 'critical theory' which married Marxism with a wider awareness of other social and cultural ideas. This project has been carried on by Habermas.

Habermas was born in Dusseldorf and educated at the Universities of Bonn and Marburg before becoming an assistant to Adorno at the Frankfurt Institute in 1956. He has spent some time as a professor of philosophy at Heidelberg but most of his academic life has passed at Frankfurt. Habermas's interest has always centred, not on the economic determinants of society in the tradition of Marx, but on the nature of human communication and consciousness and the ways in which these interact with social facts to produce social action. He shares Marx's ambition to elaborate a complete social theory but he strives to incorporate a greater sense of the importance of knowledge and ideas in shaping history and a larger acknowledgement that cultures and their historical development cannot be reduced to economic processes alone. In a sequence of books published over the last thirty years and more Habermas has made major contributions to arguments about the nature of knowledge and rationality and about the kinds of knowledge provided by the social sciences. Perhaps his most important work, published in Britain in two volumes, is the massive *Theory of Communicative Action*. As the length of the work suggests Habermas's definition of communicative action is a complicated one. Marx's ideas about class struggle and revolution have been overtaken by historical developments. In their place Habermas introduces the idea of 'crisis', the moment when individuals within a society recognise that their needs are not being met and that the institutions of that society exist to exploit them. In response to this crisis individuals interact socially and culturally and (at its simplest) it is this interaction to which Habermas refers when he uses the term Communicative Action. It is through communicative action that change occurs within a society, not through the opposition of economically determined classes. In an intellectual climate increasingly influenced by relativism and post-modern ironies, Habermas remains an influential voice calling for the application of reason and rationality to the human sciences.

'The communicative model of action does not equate action with communication. Language is a means of communication which serves mutual understanding whereas actors, in coming to an understanding with one another so as to co-ordinate their actions, pursue their particular aims.'

WRITINGS BY HABERMAS

Autonomy and Solidarity
Verso pbk £12.00
0860915794

A Berlin Republic
Polity pbk £12.99
0745620450

Between Facts and Norms
Polity pbk £16.95
0745620116

**Communication and
the Evolution of Society**
Polity pbk £13.95
0745608469

The Habermas Reader
Polity pbk £14.95
0745613942

Justification and Application
Polity pbk £13.95
0745616399

Knowledge and Human Interests
Polity pbk £14.95
0745604595

The Legitimation Crisis
Polity pbk £13.95
0745606091

**Moral Consciousness and
Communicative Action**
Polity pbk £13.95
0745611044

The New Conservatism
Polity pbk £14.99
0745614116

**On the Logic of the
Social Sciences**
Polity pbk £13.95
0745608620

The Past As Future
Polity pbk £13.95
074561454X

**The Philosophical Discourse
of Modernity**
Polity pbk £13.95
0745608302

Post-Metaphysical Thinking
Polity pbk £13.95
0745614124

**The Structural Transformation
of the Public Sphere**
Polity pbk £14.99
0745610773

**The Theory of Communicative
Action Vol 1**
Polity pbk £15.95
0745603866

**The Theory of Communicative
Action Vol 2**
Polity pbk £15.95
0745607705

WRITINGS ON HABERMAS

White, Stephen
Cambridge Companion to
Habermas
Cambridge UP pbk £15.95
052144666X

Outhwaite, William
Habermas: A Critical Introduction
Polity pbk £11.95
0745602053

Dews, Peter
Habermas: A Critical Reader
Blackwell pbk £15.99
0631201351

Jean Francois
LYOTARD | 1984
The Post Modern Condition

Born in Versailles, Lyotard spent his early career as a teacher of philosophy at a French secondary school (he also spent two years at a school in what was then French Algeria) before entering higher education. At the time of his retirement in 1989 he was a professor of philosophy in the University of Paris. In the last decade of his life, when he was at the height of his intellectual fame and reputation, he held a number of posts in American universities. During the 50s and 60s Lyotard was a Marxist, a member of the editorial board of the newspaper *Pouvoir Ouvrier*, a firm opponent of French imperialism and an active participant in the *évenements* of 1968. In the 70s and 80s he moved away from his Marxist position and became one of the best-known exponents of post-modernism, with its ironic distrust of the grand narratives of history (such as Marxism) and its refusal to privilege one narrative over another.

Postmodernism has, in the nineties, become a buzz-word and the adjective 'post-modern' has been applied to everything from literature to fashion. To be post-modern in the arts can seem to be nothing more than to adopt a style that revels in irony, playfulness, pastiche and self-referentiality. Returning to a defining text of postmodernism such as Lyotard's *The Post-Modern Condition* reminds us that the questions of postmodernism begin as philosophical ones, essentially epistemological ones. Lyotard's book is subtitled 'A Report on Knowledge' and aims to ask questions about what kinds of knowledge, if any, science and philosophy and the arts can provide. As Lyotard himself writes, 'The typically modern questions are, among others : What is there to be known? Who knows it? How do they know it and with what degree of certainty? The typically postmodern questions do not reach that far. Instead of locating the task for the knower, they attempt to locate the knower himself. What is the world? What kinds of worlds are there? How are they constituted and how do they differ?' The postmodernist mistrusts the large-scale narratives of modernity (Marxism, Freudianism etc) with their claims to an exclusive knowledge and instead celebrates a multiplicity of discourses, each with their own internal rules and logic, each resistant to value judgements from outside the discourse.

'Postmodern knowledge is not simply a tool of the authorities; it refines our sensitivity to differences and reinforces our ability to tolerate the incommensurable.'

WRITINGS BY LYOTARD

Collected Writings on Art
Academy Editions pbk £17.95
1854904485

The Differend
University of Minnesota P pbk
£11.95
0816616116

The Inhuman
Polity Press pbk £13.95
0745612385

The Libidinal Economy
Athlone Press pbk £14.95
0485120836

The Post-Modern Condition
Manchester UP pbk £13.99
0719014506

WRITINGS ON LYOTARD

Readings, Bill
Introducing Lyotard
Routledge pbk £13.99
0415055369

Benjamin, Andrew (ed)
Judging Lyotard
Routledge pbk £14.99
0415052572

Williams, James
Lyotard
Polity Press pbk £12.95
0745611001

Jean

BAUDRILLARD 1987

Cool Memories

Although he discourages biographical detail, which he distrusts, a few facts about Baudrillard can be noted. He was born in Rheims in 1929 and before he emerged, in the eighties and nineties, as the guru of the virtual and its absorption of the real, he had led a relatively conventional academic career. He began this career as a student of German literature (indeed his first publication was a translation of a work by Brecht) and it was only later that he turned to sociology, gaining a doctorate in the subject. In 1966 he was appointed to a position at the University of Paris and subsequently he joined the *Institut de Recherche sur l'Innovation Sociale*. Beginning with the publication in 1970 of The Consumer Society, Baudrillard has turned his attention to the myths and structures of contemporary Western, capitalist societies and its distraction from reality. Particularly in the last decade he has become, like Foucault and Derrida before him, an international intellectual 'star'. Baudrillard began by analysing the nature of consumption in the West and its capacity to deny satisfaction to the consumer but has, more and more, come to be known for his views on reality and virtuality. Reality, in Baudrillard's opinion, is being progressively eroded and our attention distracted from it by the relentless expansion of television and other modes of communication. These have, increasingly, become not referents to a reality beyond them but worlds of their own. Society has lost its old sustaining myths and is now dominated by an ideology founded on what Baudrillard calls 'the ecstasy of communication'. In books like America and the volumes of *Cool Memories*, Baudrillard has pioneered a mode of writing which mingles excursions through the hyper-realities of contemporary society with philosophical and cultural speculation to produce an original form of postmodern writing.

> *'Since the world is on a delusional course, we must adopt a delusional standpoint to the world.'*

WRITINGS BY BAUDRILLARD

America
Verso pbk £12.00
0860919781

The Consumer Society
Sage pbk £14.95
0761956921

Cool Memories II
Polity pbk £12.95
0745612539

Cool Memories III
Verso pbk£12.00
1859841236

The Cool Provocateur
Verso pbk £11.00
1859842410

Fatal Strategies
Pluto Press pbk £12.99
0745314538

The Illusion of the End
Polity pbk £12.95
0745612229

The Perfect Crime
Verso pbk £12.00
1859840442

The Revenge of the Crystal
Pluto pbk £12.99
0745314430

The Transparency of Evil
Verso pbk £12.00
0860915883

WRITINGS ON BAUDRILLARD

Gane, Mike
Baudrillard:
Critical and Fatal Theory
Routledge pbk £14.99
0415037751

Gane, Mike (ed)
Baudrillard Live
Routledge pbk £14.99
0415070384

Selection of interviews
with Baudrillard.

Kellner (ed)
Baudrillard: A Critical Reader
Blackwell pbk £16.99
1557864667

Horrocks, Chris
Introducing Baudrillard
Icon Books pbk £8.99
1840460873

Genosko, Gary
McLuhan and Baudrillard
Routledge pbk £12.99
0415190622

Stephen

HAWKING | 1988

A Brief History of Time

Over the last ten years Stephen Hawking, like Einstein before him, has become an iconic figure, representative of the furthest flung speculations of the human mind. That the mind which makes these speculations is trapped within a body wasted by motor neurone disease, and now confined to a wheelchair, has added to the potency of Hawking as symbol. Born in 1942, Hawking grew up in St. Albans and was educated first at Oxford, where he gained his BA in 1962, and then at Cambridge where he did his doctorate. Since 1979 he has held the Lucasian chair in mathematics at Cambridge, a position once held by Sir Isaac Newton. The first symptoms of the progressive and incurable illness, which today prevents him from reading, writing, calculating and speaking without technological assistance, appeared in the 60s. Hawking, with characteristic courage and determination, has claimed that the illness has been a help rather than a hindrance to his career insofar as it has freed him to think about the most abstract problems in physics and cosmology. In addition to his position within the academic world, Hawking came to the attention of a wider audience with the publication of *A Brief History of Time* in 1988 which has sold millions of copies and spent more than four years on the Sunday Times bestseller lists.

Hawking's work has been fruitful in a number of areas but has concentrated on attempts to combine quantum theory and relativity into a more general theory that would satisfactorily explain everything in the physical world from the tiniest of subatomic particles to the birth and destiny of the Universe itself. He has been particularly concerned with the application of quantum theory and relativity to the phenomena known as black holes. In 1974 he made the startling discovery that black holes, from which it was assumed nothing could escape, can, in fact, radiate energy as particles are created in their vicinity. *A Brief History of Time* is a historical survey of man's attempts to understand the universe from the time of the Ancient Greeks to the most recent speculations of cosmologists. It reveals to non-scientists the kind of advanced answers provided by scientists to questions about the origin, nature and eventual destiny of the universe.

'God not only plays dice, He also sometimes throws the dice where they cannot be seen.'

WRITINGS BY HAWKING

A Brief History of Time
Bantam pbk £7.99
0553175211

Black Holes and Baby Universes
Bantam pbk £6.99
0553406639

WRITINGS ON HAWKING

White & Gribbin
Stephen Hawking:
A Life in Science
Penguin pbk £7.99
0140271686

INDEX BY AUTHOR

WHERE TO FIND US

ABERDEEN
236 Union St
Tel: 01224 571655

269-271 Union St
Tel: 01224 210161

ABERYSTWYTH
University of Wales
Tel: 01970 623251

ALTRINCHAM
24 George St
Tel: 0161 941 4040

AMSTERDAM
Kalverstraat 152,
Amsterdam,
The Netherlands
Tel: 00 312 0 638 3821

ASTON UNIVERSITY
12 Gosta Green,
Aston Triangle
Tel: 0121 359 3242

AYLESBURY
31-32 Friars Square
Tel: 01296 423153

BASINGSTOKE
2 Castle Square
Tel: 01256 333030

BATH
4–5 Milsom St
Tel: 01225 448515

University of Bath
Claverton Down
Tel: 01225 465565

BEDFORD
11-13 Silver St
Tel: 01234 272432

Cranfield University Bookshop,
College Rd,
Wharley End
Tel: 01234 754280

BELFAST
Queen's Building,
8 Royal Avenue
Tel: (028) 9024 7355

44-46 Fountain St
Tel: (028) 9024 0159

BIRKENHEAD
188/192 Grange Rd
Tel: 0151 650 2400

BIRMINGHAM
128 New St
Tel: 0121 631 4333

24–26 High St
Tel: 0121 633 4353

Birmingham University,
Ring Rd North, Edgbaston
Tel: 0121 472 3034

BLACKPOOL
4 The Tower Shopping Centre,
Bank Hey St
Tel: 01253 296136

BLUEWATER
West Village, Greenhithe
Tel: 01322 624831

Upper Thames Walk, Greenhithe
Tel: 01322 624829

BOLTON
32–36 Deansgate
Tel: 01204 522588

BOURNEMOUTH
14/16 The Arcade
Tel: 01202 299449

71-73 Old Christchurch Rd
Tel: 01202 297142

Bournemouth University
Talbot Campus,
Fern Barrow, Poole
Tel: 01202 595528

BRADFORD
The Wool Exchange
Tel: 01274 723127

26 Market St
Tel: 01274 741211

University of Bradford,
Great Horton Rd
Tel: 01274 727885

Management Centre Bookshop,
Emm Lane
Tel: 01274 481404

BRAEHEAD
King's Inch Rd, Renfrew
Tel: 0141 885 9333

BRIGHTON
55–56 North St
Tel: 01273 327867

71–74 North St
Tel: 01273 206017

BRISTOL
27–29 College Green
Tel: 0117 925 0511

Cribbs Causeway,
33 Lower Level,
The Mall
Tel: 0117 950 9813

The Galleries, Broadmead
Tel: 0117 925 2274

University of Bristol,
Tyndall Avenue
Tel: 0117 925 4297

BROMLEY
20–22 Market Sq
Tel: (020) 8464 6562

BRUNEL UNIVERSITY
Cleveland Rd, Uxbridge
Tel: 01895 257991

BRUSSELS
Boulevard Adolphe Max 71-75,
B1000 Brussels, Belgium
Tel: 00 322 219 2708

BURY
4 Union Arcade
Tel: 0161 764 2642

CAMBRIDGE
6 Bridge St
Tel: 01223 300123

22 Sidney St
Tel: 01223 351688

CANTERBURY
20 St Margaret's St
Tel: 01227 456343

CARDIFF
2a The Hayes
Tel: (029) 2066 5606

1-2 St. David's Link,
The Hayes
Tel: (029) 2022 2723

CARMARTHEN
Trinity College
Tel: 01267 238100

CHELMSFORD
The Meadows Centre,
High St
Tel: 01245 493300

CHELTENHAM
88–90 The Promenade
Tel: 01242 512722

CHESTER
43–45 Bridge St Row
Tel: 01244 328040

The Row, 14 Eastgate
Tel: 01244 345066

CHICHESTER
The Dolphin and Anchor,
West St
Tel: 01243 773030

COLCHESTER
16 Culver Precinct
Tel: 01206 767623

12-13 High St
Tel: 01206 561307

University of Essex,
Wivenhoe Park
Tel: 01206 864773

CORK
69 Patrick St
Tel: 00 353 21 276522

University College
Boole Library Basement
Tel: 00 353 21 276575

COVENTRY
22 Cathedral Lanes,
Broadgate
Tel: (024) 7622 7151

Coventry University,
26 Earl St
Tel: (024) 7622 9092

Coventry University Bookshop,
Earl St
Tel: (024) 7623 0880

CRAWLEY
83-84 County Mall
Tel: 01293 533471

CROYDON
1063 Whitgift Centre
Tel: (020) 8686 7032

DERBY
78–80 St Peter's St
Tel: 01332 296997

University of Derby,
Keddleston Rd
Tel: 01332 331719

Chevin Avenue,
Mickelover
Tel: 01332 511462

DORKING
54–60 South St
Tel: 01306 886884

DUBLIN
7 Dawson St
Tel: 00 353 1 679 1260

The Jervis Centre
Tel: 00 353 1 878 1311

DUNDEE
35 Commercial St
Tel: 01382 200322

DURHAM
69 Saddler St
Tel: 0191 383 1488

University Bookshop,
55-57 Saddler St
Tel: 0191 384 2095

EASTBOURNE
120 Terminus Rd
Tel: 01323 735676

EDINBURGH
128 Princes St
Tel: 0131 226 2666

13–14 Princes St
Tel: 0131 556 3034/5

83 George St
Tel: 0131 225 3436

EGHAM
Royal Holloway College,
Egham Hill
Tel: 01784 471272

EPSOM
113 High St
Tel: 01372 741713

EXETER
48–49 High St
Tel: 01392 218392

Roman Gate,
252 High St
Tel: 01392 423044

FOLKESTONE
1–2 Guildhall St
Tel: 01303 221 979

GATESHEAD
17 The Parade
Metro Centre
Tel: 0191 493 2715

GLASGOW
153–157
Sauchiehall St
Tel: 0141 332 9105

174-176 Argyle St
Tel: 0141 248 4814

GUILDFORD
35–39 North St
Tel: 01483 302919

50-54 High St
Tel: 01483 457545

HANLEY, STOKE-ON-TRENT
The Tontines Centre,
Parliament Row
Tel: 01782 204582

Lewis' Arcade,
Potteries Shopping Centre
Tel: 01782 219550

HARROGATE
40 James St
Tel: 01423 509435

HATFIELD
7-8 The Galleria, Comet Way
Tel: 01707 270 161

University of Hertfordshire,
College Lane
Tel: 01707 284940

HEREFORD
18–20 Commercial St
Tel: 01432 275100

University of Hertfordshire,
Mangrove Rd
Tel: 01707 285505

Wall Hall Campus,
Aldenham
Tel: 01707 285745

HUDDERSFIELD UNIVERSITY
Queensgate
Tel: 01484 472200

HULL
The Grand Buildings,
Jameson St
Tel: 01482 580234

University of Hull
Tel: 01482 444190

ILFORD
158-160 High Rd
Tel: (020) 8478 8428

INVERNESS
50–52 High St
Tel: 01463 717474

IPSWICH
15–19 Buttermarket
Tel: 01473 289044

KEELE
University of Keele
Tel: 01782 627001

KETTERING
72–76 High St
Tel: 01536 481575

KING'S LYNN
76–77 High St
Tel: 01553 769934

KINGSTON-UPON-THAMES
23–25 Thames St
Tel: (020) 8547 1221

Wood St,
The Bentall Centre
Tel: (020) 8974 6811

Kingston University,
2 Brook St
Tel: (020) 8546 7592

LANCASTER
2–8 King St
Tel: 01524 61477

Lancaster University,
Bailrigg
Tel: 01524 32581

LEAMINGTON SPA
1 Priorsgate,
Warwick St
Tel: 01926 883804

LEEDS
36–38 Albion St
Tel: 0113 242 0839

93–97 Albion St
Tel: 0113 244 4588

6 Gledhow Wing,
St. James Hospital,
Beckett St
Tel: 0113 243 3144

LEICESTER
21/23 High St
Tel: 0116 251 6838

26 Market St
Tel: 0116 254 5858

LIVERPOOL
14-16 Bold St
Tel: 0151 708 6861

52 Bold St
Tel: 0151 709 0866

LONDON
BUSINESS BOOKSHOP, NW1
72 Park Rd
Tel: (020) 7723 3902

CAMDEN, NW1
128 Camden High St
Tel: (020) 7284 4948

CHARING CROSS RD, WC2
121 Charing Cross Rd
Tel: (020) 7434 4291

CHEAPSIDE, EC2
145–147 Cheapside
Tel: (020) 7726 6077

CHISWICK, W4
220-226 Chiswick
High Rd
Tel: (020) 8995 3559

THE CITY, EC2
Waterstone's Business,
9 Moorfields
Tel: (020) 7628 7479

THE CITY, EC3
1 Whittington Ave,
Leadenhall Market
Tel: (020) 7220 7882

CITY UNIVERSITY, EC1
Northampton Square
Tel: (020) 7608 0706

COVENT GARDEN, WC2
9 Garrick St
Tel: (020) 7836 6757

EALING, W5
64 Ealing Broadway Centre
Tel: (020) 8840 5905

EARL'S COURT, SW5
266 Earl's Court Rd
Tel: (020) 7370 1616

ECONOMIST BOOKSTORE, WC2
Clare Market,
Portugal St
Tel: (020) 7405 5531

FINCHLEY, N12
782 High St
Tel: (020) 8446 9669

GOLDSMITHS' COLLEGE, SE14
New Cross
Tel: (020) 8469 0262

GOWER ST, WC1
82 Gower St
Tel: (020) 7636 1577

HAMPSTEAD, NW3
68 Hampstead
High St
Tel: (020) 7794 1098

HARRODS, SW1
87 Brompton Rd
Tel: (020) 7730 1234

IMPERIAL COLLEGE, SW7
Imperial College Rd
Tel: (020) 7589 3563

IMPERIAL COLLEGE SCHOOL OF MEDICINE
Charing Cross Campus,
Reynolds Building,
St Dunstan's Rd
Tel: (020) 8748 9768

Hammersmith Campus,
Commonwealth Building,
Du Cane Rd
Tel: (020) 8742 9600

ISLINGTON, N1
11 Islington Green
Tel: (020) 7704 2280

JAMES STREET, W1
10–12 James St
Tel: (020) 7629 8206

KENSINGTON, W8
193 Kensington High St
Tel: (020) 7937 8432

KING'S COLLEGE, WC2
Macadam House, Surrey St
Tel: (020) 7836 0205

KING'S ROAD, SW3
150-152 King's Rd
Tel: (020) 7351 2023

LONDON GUILDHALL UNIVERSITY, E1
Calcutta House,
Old Castle St
Tel: (020) 7247 0727

LONG ACRE, WC2
8 Long Acre
Tel: (020) 7836 1359

LUDGATE CIRCUS, EC4
Procession House
Tel: (020) 7236 5858
opening January 2000

MARGARET ST, W1
28 Margaret St,
Oxford Circus
Tel: (020) 7580 2812

NOTTING HILL, W11
39 Notting Hill Gate
Tel: (020) 7229 9444

OLD BROMPTON RD, SW7
99 Old Brompton Rd
Tel: (020) 7581 8522

OXFORD STREET, W1
19-23 Oxford St
Tel: (020) 7434 9759

PICCADILLY, W1
203/206 Piccadilly
Tel: (020) 78512400

QUEEN MARY & WESTFIELD, E1
329 Mile End Rd
Tel: (020) 8980 2554

THAMES VALLEY UNIVERSITY, W5
St. Mary's Rd & Westel House,
Ealing
Tel: (020) 8840 6205

TRAFALGAR SQUARE, WC2
The Grand Building
Tel: (020) 7839 4411

WIMBLEDON, SW19
12 Wimbledon Bridge
Tel: (020) 8543 9899

LUTON UNIVERSITY
Park Square
Tel: 01582 402704

MACCLESFIELD
47 Mill St
Tel: 01625 424212

MAIDSTONE
19 Earl St
Tel: 01622 681112

234 Chequers Centre
Tel: 01622 752831

MANCHESTER
91 Deansgate
Tel: 0161 837 3000

2-4 St Ann's Square
Tel: 0161 832 0424

MANCHESTER AIRPORT
Terminal 1 Airside
Tel: 0161 489 3405

MERRY HILL
95/96 Merry Hill Shopping
Centre, Brierley Hill
Tel: 01384 751551

MIDDLESBROUGH
Captain Cook Centre
Tel: 01642 242682

University of Teesside
Southfield Road
Middlesbrough
Tel: 01642 242017

MILTON KEYNES
51-53 Silbury Arcade
Tel: 01908 696260

570 Silbury Boulevard
Tel: 01908 607454

NEWBURY
64 Northbrook St
Tel: 01635 569998

NEWCASTLE
104 Grey St
Tel: 0191 261 6140

Emerson Chambers,
Blackett St
Tel: 0191 261 7757

NORTHAMPTON
19 Abington St
Tel: 01604 634854

NORWICH
21–24 Royal Arcade
Tel: 01603 632426

University of
East Anglia
Tel: 01603 453625

NOTTINGHAM
1–5 Bridlesmith Gate
Tel: 0115 948 4499

25 Wheeler Gate
Tel: 0115 947 3531

NUNEATON
1–3 Queen's Road

OXFORD
William Baker House,
Broad St
Tel: 01865 790212

PERTH
St John's Centre
Tel: 01738 630013

PETERBOROUGH
6 Queensgate
Tel: 01733 313476

40 Bridge St
Tel: 01733 555323

PLYMOUTH
65/69 New George St
Tel: 01752 256699

PRESTON
3–5 Fishergate
Tel: 01772 555766

READING
89a Broad St
Tel: 0189 581270

The Oracle Centre
12 Holybrook Mall
Tel: 0189 503400

Reading University,
Whiteknights
Tel: 0189 874858

Bulmershe Court,
Woodland Court, Earley
Tel: 0189 318699

RICHMOND-UPON-THAMES
2–6 Hill St
Tel: (020) 8332 1600

SALISBURY
7/9 High St
Tel: 01722 415596

SCARBOROUGH
97-98 Westborough
Tel: 01723 500414

SHEFFIELD
24 Orchard Sq
Tel: 0114 272 8971

Meadowhall Centre,
26 The Arcade
Tel: 0114 256 8495

SHREWSBURY
18–19 High St
Tel: 01743 248112

SOLIHULL
67-71 High St
Tel: 0121 711 2454

SOUTHAMPTON
69 Above Bar
Tel: 01703 633130

7–9 Hanover Building,
Vincent Walk
Tel: 01703 232118

University of Southampton,
Gower Centre
Tel: 01703 558267

Southampton Medical School,
Southampton General Hospital
Tel: 01703 780602

SOUTHEND-ON-SEA
49–55 High St
Tel: 01702 437480

SOUTHPORT
367 Lord St
Tel: 01704 501088

STAFFORDSHIRE UNIVERSITY
Station Rd
Tel: 01782 746318

Beaconside
Tel: 01785 254201

STIRLING
Thistle Marches
Tel: 01786 478756

20-22 Murray Place
Tel: 01786 451141

STOCKPORT
103 Princes St
Tel: 0161 477 3755

86 Merseyway
Tel: 0161 474 1455

STRATFORD-UPON-AVON
18 The High St
Tel: 01789 414418

SUTTON
71-81 High St
Tel: (020) 8770 0404

SWANSEA
17 Oxford St
Tel: 01792 463567

University of Wales
Taliesin Arts Centre,
Singleton Park
Tel: 01792 281460

SWINDON
27 Regent St
Tel: 01793 488838

25/26 Brunel Plaza,
Brunel Shopping Centre
Tel: 01793 436465

TAUNTON
County Hotel, East St
Tel: 01823 333113

TELFORD
219–223 Dean Street
Telford Shopping Centre
opening February 2000

TUNBRIDGE WELLS
32/40 Calverley Rd
Tel: 01892 535446

ULSTER UNIVERSITY
Central Buildings,
Cromore Rd, Coleraine
Tel: (028) 7032 4735

WARRINGTON
21–23 The Mall,
Golden Square Shopping Centre

WATFORD
174–176 The Harlequin Centre,
High St
Tel: 01923 218197

WINCHESTER
The Brooks,
Middle Brook St
Tel: 01962 866206

97 High St
Tel: 01962 840379

WOLVERHAMPTON
13-15 Victoria St
Tel: 01902 427219

University of Wolverhampton,
Wulfruna St
Tel: 01902 322435

Dudley Campus, Castle View
Tel: 01902 323374

Shropshire Campus, Priors Lee,
Telford
Tel: 01902 323815

WORCESTER
95 High St
Tel: 01905 723397

WREXHAM
9/11 Regent St
Tel: 01978 357444

YORK
9-10 High Ousegate
Tel: 01904 610044

28–29 High Ousegate
Tel: 01904 628740

WATERSTONE'S ONLINE
www.waterstones.co.uk
Hawarden Terrace,
Larkhall, Bath
Tel: 01225 448595
Fax: 01225 444732
enquiries@waterstones
online.co.uk